# Praise for *Gamification Made Simple*

"The gamification component significantly enriched our learning experience by transforming theoretical content into practical, engaging scenarios. Working as a team fostered a collaborative environment where diverse perspectives were not only welcomed but essential for success. This approach helped solidify complex concepts while also improving our communication and teamwork abilities. It made learning feel more applicable and meaningful. I felt more connected to both the material and my classmates."
—*Braelyn Hoskyns, MSE, elementary self-contained teacher, Oakland Elementary (Clarksville, Tennessee)*

"The Game stands at the highest level of Bloom's taxonomy. It challenges your problem-solving, creativity, and ability to work as a team while applying research-based strategies. This is not a drill or recall activity—this is a real-world situation simulation that sharpens your thinking while offering a safe space to grow. It was an incredible experience."
—*Claudia Molina, elementary teacher, Foreign Language Academy, Kansas City Public Schools (Kansas City, Missouri)*

"The Game brought learning to life in a way I hadn't experienced before. Working in a team, solving real-world challenges, and having to think strategically made the learning stick. It also helped me realize how important communication is when you're navigating group work. This experience made me feel more prepared for the field."
—*Zohaira Chaudhry, MSE, special education consultant (Lahore, Pakistan)*

This gamified case study created a rare space where students could apply their knowledge while building interpersonal skills. The competitive yet cooperative setting promoted peer interaction, problem-solving, and content mastery. The game helped me better understand course content by placing it in real-world contexts, which increased my confidence and motivation to participate."
—*Rohini Knudson, MSE, former software developer at Microsoft; currently transitioning careers (Woodinville, Washington)*

The game was truly invaluable to me. It created a safe space where I could collaborate openly, and it gave me a deeper understanding of my colleagues' roles—insights I wouldn't have gained otherwise. It not only reinforced course content but also strengthened my communication and teamwork skills. I truly wish all courses used this model of learning."
—*Tamara Hatch, MSE, coordinating teacher, Valleyview Ranch Colony School (Valleyview, Alberta, Canada)*

# Gamification Made Simple

# Gamification Made Simple

A Guide for Higher Education Professionals

Glennda McKeithan

Ann Marshall

BLOOMSBURY ACADEMIC
NEW YORK · LONDON · OXFORD · NEW DELHI · SYDNEY

BLOOMSBURY ACADEMIC

Bloomsbury Publishing Inc, 1359 Broadway, New York, NY 10018, USA
Bloomsbury Publishing Plc, 50 Bedford Square, London, WC1B 3DP, UK
Bloomsbury Publishing Ireland, 29 Earlsfort Terrace, Dublin 2, D02 AY28, Ireland

BLOOMSBURY, BLOOMSBURY ACADEMIC and the Diana logo are trademarks of
Bloomsbury Publishing Plc

First published in the United States of America 2026

Copyright © Bloomsbury Publishing, 2026

Cover design by Kathi Ha
Cover image © iStock.com/Macrovector

Title page image used with permission from Karla Thomas, Packhouse Creations

All rights reserved. No part of this publication may be: i) reproduced or transmitted in any form, electronic or mechanical, including photocopying, recording or by means of any information storage or retrieval system without prior permission in writing from the publishers; or ii) used or reproduced in any way for the training, development or operation of artificial intelligence (AI) technologies, including generative AI technologies. The rights holders expressly reserve this publication from the text and data mining exception as per Article 4(3) of the Digital Single Market Directive (EU) 2019/790.

Bloomsbury Publishing Inc does not have any control over, or responsibility for, any third-party websites referred to or in this book. All internet addresses given in this book were correct at the time of going to press. The author and publisher regret any inconvenience caused if addresses have changed or sites have ceased to exist, but can accept no responsibility for any such changes.

Library of Congress Cataloging-in-Publication Data is available

ISBN: HB: 979-8-8818-0284-4
PB: 979-8-8818-0285-1
ePDF: 979-8-8818-6215-2
eBook: 979-8-8818-0286-8

Typeset by Deanta Global Publishing Services, Chennai, India
Printed and bound in the United States of America

For product safety related questions contact productsafety@bloomsbury.com.

To find out more about our authors and books visit www.bloomsbury.com and sign up for our newsletters.

# Contents

\* = Level I - Novice Game Designers; \*\* = Level II - Experienced Game Designers

Foreword xi
Acknowledgments xiii

Introduction 1

**1** Introduction to Gamification in Higher Education 5
  Game Master's Prelude 5
  What Is Gamification? 8
  How Are GBL Experiences Linked to Human Development? 8
  How Has GBL Evolved in Education? 9
  How Has GBL Evolved? 11
  How Might GBL Address Higher Education Challenges? 12
  How Might GBL Address Digital Literacy Needs? 14
  How Can GBL Prepare Students for Real Challenges? 17
  How Can GBL Keep My Teaching Relevant? 18
  Can GBL Be Used in Any Program? 18
  What Is the Impact of GBL on Learning Success? 20
  How Can RPGs Support Skill Development? 21
  Game Log 22

**2** Team Engagement and Role Theory 25
  Game Master's Prelude 25
  Why Is Building an Effective Team So Important? 26
  How Does Game Theory Shape Team Interactions? 30
  Can Belbin's Team Roles Enhance Collaborations? 31
  How Can Shapers Help Teams Overcome Challenges? 32
  How Can Completer-Finishers Impact Quality Control? 33

How Do Implementers Help Teams Task Analyze Plans? 33
How Do People-Oriented Roles Strengthen RPG Teams? 34
How Do Coordinators Help Teams Build Consensus? 34
How Do Team Workers Support Cohesion? 35
How Do Resource Investigators Help Teams? 35
How Do Monitor Evaluators Help Make Objective Decisions? 36
How Can Plants Help Teams with Creative Solutions? 36
How Do Specialists Help Teams with Specific Expertise? 37
What Team Structure Best Fits My RPG Goals? 37
How Do I Create Engaging Avatars for My RPG? 38
Game Log 43

**3 Planning, Designing, and Implementing RPG Games** 47

Game Master's Prelude 47
What Are My Next Steps? 48
How Do I Turn Course Objectives into Game Tasks? 50
How Can I Develop an Initial Game Frame? 51
How Can I Add an RPG into My Existing Course? 55
How Can I Keep Players Focused and Involved? 59
How Can I Assess Student Skills Effectively? 67
How Can My RPG Accommodate My Adult Learners? 70
What Factors Shape a Positive Player Experience? 71
How Is Planning Related to Engagement? 76
How Can I Ensure Tasks Are Challenging and Achievable? 76
What Role Do Incentives Play? 81
How Can I Plan an Effective First Game Round? 83
What Might Be Included in the Second Game Round? 85
What Might Be Included in the Third Game Round? 86
How Can a Reflection Round Enhance Learning? 86
Why Is Beta Testing Important? 90
Game Log 91

**4 Game Mechanics for Meaningful Learning** 93

Game Master's Prologue 93
Why Are Game Mechanics and Elements Important? 94
How Do Game Mechanics Influence Learning Outcomes? 98
How Can I Assess Individual Student Learning? 98
How Can I Use Badges, Levels, and Milestones to Improve My RPG? 100
What Are the Core Principles of Effective Game Design? 104

What Are Some Common Mistakes in Game Design? 105
How Can I Promote Skill Development and Knowledge Application? 111
What Framework Might Help Me Create My RPGs? 115
Which RPG Format Best Fits My Educational Goals and Classroom Environment? 117
How Can Player Feedback Help Me Improve and Refine My Game? 118
Game Log 120

**5 Maximizing Engagement and Minimizing Problems** 121
Game Masters Prologue 121
What Challenges Might I Encounter? 122
How Can Role Conflicts Impact Teams? 124
How Can Game Masters Guide Teams Without Taking Over? 130
How Can I Effectively Measure Learning? 134
How Do I Maintain Player Motivation? 141
Game Log 144

**6 AI, Social Media, and the Future of RPGs in Higher Education** 147
Game Master's Prelude 147
What Are the Potential Ethical Considerations of RPGs? 148
Can RPGs Make Online Courses More Relevant? 149
Can RPGs Help Students Adapt to Changing Policies and Workforce Demands? 152
How Can RPGs Build Content-Relevant Communication Skills? 154
How Can Social Media Integration Strengthen My Program? 156
What If I Design a Game for Others to Manage? 160
How Can Experience and Knowledge of Students Improve My RPG? 163
How Can AI Help with RPG Game Development? 165
What Are GPTs and How Can They Help Me Build an RPG? 169
What Is Overgamification and How Can I Avoid It? 172
Game Log 174

Glossary of Terms 177
References 185
Appendix A 203
Appendix B 206
Appendix C 211
Appendix D 214

Appendix E  218
Appendix F  220
Appendix G  223
Appendix H  225
Index  227
About the Authors  233

# Foreword

What is now known about learning has changed dramatically from what we thought we knew ten years ago. We understand more about how the brain processes and makes sense of the world. We can track how emotions, cultures, and experiences titrate what is taken in, processed, stored, and applied. We understand the mechanisms that underlie learning. We have schools where students, teachers, and researchers work together to invent games, tasks, and lessons that can be measured on the spot using brain imagery and tracking devices. The binary between teacher and learner has blurred as they engage together in developing and assessing new designs for learning. Learning no longer requires being present in the same space. It does require highly skilled learning experts designing new processes for learning that accelerate knowledge development, and exchange. Those experts include students who often intuit more about the digital world and its expression of knowledge than educators who have been working from ontological scripts in their knowledge arenas, crafting lesson designs that they have polished over years of experience with a variety of students.

From preschool through graduate school, teachers, and students are repositioning their identities, practices, and goals for learning. This journey is not for the faint of heart. It requires a belief that we can do better for all kinds of learners, with all kinds of capacities, in all kinds of settings. It requires adventuresome practitioners like Glennda and Ann who continue to challenge themselves to be curious, thoughtful, open, and questioning. It requires new scripts about what constitutes knowing and learning.

Gamifying academic content for educators builds on what we know about how people learn and develop expertise. In optimal gamified contexts, learning occurs between and among learners, optimizing assessment of the landscape, honing strategic knowledge, using dynamic evaluation to rachet approaches to performance, and assessing outcomes to improve in the next iterations of a game. What does the game space offer? Engagement with colleagues who bring a variety of social/emotional, cognitive, and cultural tools that can be shared across players. In response to the game space, learners develop powerful methods for communicating, shaping, and polishing their practices. This is high leverage learning for educators. Glennda and Ann learned to gamify by being convinced through their own gamification experiences that gamifying is worth the investment of time, resources, and ingenuity in translating content into immersive gamified experiences. And then, they systematized it so that their readers can develop their own practices in gamification. What's needed? Like Glennda and Ann, bring the joy of creation, learning, prototyping, and refining to your teaching. Your students will benefit as will their students. This book will set you on a journey guided by their wisdom and experience. Thank you ladies for putting these tools in the hands of educators everywhere.

Dr. Elizabeth B. Kozleski, Professor (Research)<br>of Education Stanford Graduate School of Education

# Acknowledgments

Writing *Gamification Made Simple* has been a challenging and rewarding experience, and we are thankful to everyone who supported us. We want to start by thanking our students for inspiring us to share the amazing power of game-based learning in higher education (first as a presentation) and later as a book. We appreciate your willingness to try something new, take risks, and give honest feedback about how game experiences impacted your learning in our courses.

We are thankful to Lisa Mann and Dr. Deborah Griswold at the University of Kansas who helped us brainstorm early ideas for the game and its original characters. We also thank Dr. Elizabeth Bailey Kozleski for introducing Glennda to gamification and challenging her to find ways to make learning more innovative. Her introduction opened the door to a whole new way of thinking about teaching and learning.

We're grateful to the artists who brought creativity to this book. Karla Thomas (Glennda's sister) is an accomplished artist and award-winning photographer whose amazing cover artwork gave this book its beautiful first impression. Karla, your talent and love made this even more special. Thank you. And to Ryan Krantz (Glennda's grandson), thank you for your creative and thoughtful artwork on our author bio page. Your contribution added a personal touch that means the world to us.

We thank our families for their love, patience, and support. Glennda would like to thank her husband Michael and her kids Mike Jr, Cindy, and Ryan for sharing their gaming knowledge and experiences. A special thank you to her dad, Glenn Kashner, for the years of unwavering support. And in loving memory of her mom, Candy Kashner—your belief in Glennda and your excitement about books still guides and inspires her. We know you would have been overjoyed to see this book come to life.

Ann would like to thank her husband Larry and their children Konrad, Adam, and Kelli for always cheering her on, reminding her of the value of this work, and always believing in her. Your support helped make this possible.

This book was built through curiosity, laughter, and shared commitment. We are proud of what we created together and grateful for what we hope is a lifelong friendship that has evolved through this journey. We hope this book inspires you, encourages you, and gives you ideas to make learning more engaging and joyful.

—Glennda and Ann

# Introduction

We're so glad you're here—and we're excited to share *Gamification Made Simple: A Guide for Higher Education Professionals* with you. If you're reading this, chances are you're looking for ways to re-engage your students, reinvigorate your teaching, or try something new in your courses. You might have heard the term "gamification" before but not sure what it actually means, or maybe you've never heard the term until now (but think it sounds pretty cool). Either way, we've been in your shoes. As you will learn about in Chapter 1, initially, we did not know what it meant or how it might be implemented into our courses. We assumed it involved a lot of technology, programming, or specialized training in graphic design, and it honestly felt a little out of our reach. As educational professionals with experience in higher education and K-12 settings (one of us in special education and the other in speech-language pathology), we spent most of our careers focusing on how people learn, communicate, and grow. We did not know how to design games. But our curiosity got the better of us. We started small. The first step was to create a role-playing activity for a graduate course, build teams, assign characters, and add light elements of choice, challenge, and collaboration. Something shifted. Our students showed up more prepared. They talked more. They problem-solved more. And they told us—many times—that the game made them nervous, but helped them learn more deeply and enjoy the process. That first version of the game was simple (and very imperfect), but it worked. The final round of our game always involves reflection. During one of those reflections, a student said, "I was thinking about Bloom's Taxonomy and how we are supposed to teach our children." She continued, "This activity is at the very top of Blooms because we are creating. I have to be my avatar, even though I don't agree with my avatar. My job on the team is to create and engage, but not as myself, as my avatar." She went on to say that this experience and the ability to apply what they learned in class in a simulated environment is "important for us college students." We were genuinely surprised that the game was more powerful than we initially intended, and made such a significant impact on my students! We were hooked on game based learning after that first game! Together, we added features, refined the storyline, incorporated feedback, and further developed the in a communications class we were co-teaching. We learned that gamification doesn't have to be complicated to be effective. You do not need to be technology experts with a background in-game design. You do need to be open to thinking about new ways to potentially engage with and motivate your learners. The book is the resource we wish we'd had. The goal was to create a practical guide to gamification designed to meet you where you are. Whether you're brand new to the concept or already experimenting with game-based elements, we've organized this book so you can easily jump in, try things out, and revisit the more advanced concepts as your confidence grows.

To make the book approachable, we've included:

- Concrete examples of game activities and course designs across different disciplines.
- Step-by-step guidance for integrating game elements into your class—online or in person.
- Clear labeling of suggested experience levels for each section.

So, the sections of our chapter may look strange because they are question-based headers, inspired by peer feedback. The questions are intended to help you engage with the content, reflect on your own teaching, and understand exactly how each section will help you create or refine your game. If you're new, we recommend focusing on the Level I: Novice sections. These walk through foundational concepts and basic steps for building a simple but effective game. Level II: Intermediate/Experienced sections provide additional ideas for refining and expanding your game. You can always come back to them when you're ready to level up. One of the most helpful pieces of feedback we received during peer review was that readers wanted to connect with the material more—especially those who were new to gamification. That's why we've added a "Game Master's Prologue" at the beginning of each chapter. The short reflections are written in a conversational tone and help explain why the chapter matters, how it connects to real-world teaching challenges, and what inspired us to include it. We also end each chapter with a "Game Log"—a personalized summary and a plan for what's coming next. Think of it as your checkpoint or save screen. It gives you a moment to reflect, regroup, and get ready for the next part of your game design journey. Another important piece of feedback we received was that some readers felt overwhelmed by the vocabulary and structure of traditional game design.

We hear you. So there is a glossary at the end of the book so you do not need to try to remember what the terms mean as you work through the relevant chapters. In our enthusiasm for learning about this approach, we may have (okay, definitely) gotten carried away with the jargon at times. We made a conscious effort in this edition to break things down, simplify explanations, and make sure each term is introduced with examples that are easy to understand and visualize. The examples and practical suggestions are what make this book different from others on the same topic. While some gamification texts focus heavily on the history or theory, ours is grounded in real examples and suggested steps to make decisions about your own courses and how you might implement this amazing resource into your program. Whether you teach undergraduate students, graduate students, or adult learners; whether you teach marketing, speech pathology, social work, nursing, or educational leadership—you can gamify your course. And we're here to show you how. You don't have to start big. You just have to start. We hope this book inspires you to experiment, reflect, and maybe even play a little. Most of all, we hope it helps you reconnect with the parts of teaching that brought you here in the first place—curiosity, creativity, and connection.

Let's play!

—Glennda McKeithan and Ann Marshall

# 1 Introduction to Gamification in Higher Education

## Game Master's Prelude

*After 30+ years in education—20+ years in K-12 classrooms as a special education and English teacher, and a decade as a teacher educator—I have progressed through the stages of teacher effectiveness. Early in my teaching career, I developed survival skills and strategies to address the needs of my students in relation to the curricular demands and required state assessments. After about ten years as a public school teacher, I felt more confident about my practice, and I developed a predictable routine of lesson planning, extracurricular duty performance, and communication techniques with parents and colleagues (Huberman, 1989; Scherer et al., 2020). My focus was on maintaining my established routines, and strategies rather than making the time to explore new methods to more effectively enhance my practice. About that time I decided to become a teacher mentor, and I realized that my "if it isn't broke, don't fix it," attitude was becoming professional stagnation. I learned that I needed to truly embrace the idea of lifelong learning and make an effort to become a teacher who recognizes the need to continuously reflect on my own practices, consider student needs and be open to new ideas. The realization was important in my role as a middle and high school teacher as well as when I became a college professor, where I encountered similar challenges in figuring out what to teach, how to teach it, and how to assess student achievement. Almost ten years ago, I learned about gamification from my first department chair in higher education. She was very forward thinking and her research was grounded in system's change and leadership policy. The game she designed helped to teach and reinforce complex content to her students. While I was impressed when I heard about the game, I didn't really understand it, and I imagined that the process required huge amounts of time to develop, advanced technological skills and lots of research (who has time for that)? I dismissed it as another fad, lacking a clear understanding of its potential impact beyond making my program appear innovative. Reflecting on my progress through the stages of teacher effectiveness, I now understand how important it is to move beyond doing what we know how to do. In my earlier years, I was not interested in learning new methodologies. I recycled instructional strategies I was confident using and did not see the connection between what I was teaching and helping students achieve skills beyond content mastery. I was again, becoming stagnant in my teaching as my energies were focused on what I already knew how to do (design instruction for students to individually understand the important concepts of the course). Unfortunately, practitioners who rely solely on their existing knowledge of best practices and meaningful strategies are limited in what they can accomplish. My practice did not offer my students opportunities to meaningfully engage in collaborative problem-solving and application of newly learned content. I was not teaching and reinforcing the soft skills students need to communicate what they know to others in a way that others might listen to them and consider new ideas. About this time a colleague teaching one of the leadership classes that used the game agreed to present for a teacher education and demonstrate how it could be applied in higher education. I attended that presentation, and I realized that the idea was much simpler than I imagined. I started thinking of ways I might integrate this into my practice to create an environment where my students actively participate, collaborate, and apply what they have learned in practical settings. While game-based learning can be effective in many different settings, this book focuses on helping higher education instructors (aka new game designers) discover how easy it can be implemented into their practice. In my own practice, I found that once I designed the first game, the game shell or framework of the game was very easily copied and reused in different courses. Now that the game is developed, it is very easy to make adjustments as needed according to content updates and changing student needs. Our goal is to show new game designers how to develop a game shell/framework that is appropriate for their course that can be readily applied and adjusted as needed. In this first chapter I talk about the potential benefits for learners in both face-to-face and online settings. Given that this book is designed for higher education, the facts are presented as informed knowledge and supported with evidence from the literature. While many of the terms identified are defined in text, we have included a glossary of terms at the back of the book to minimize confusion for new game designers. Based on feedback from peer reviews of the first few chapters we have converted the section headers into questions to help readers know what is covered in each section and whether they need to read that section now or refer to it later. After each header the level of game designer experience is linked to help readers understand whether they should read that section now or come back to it later. We are assuming that new* game designers want to understand the basics (novice—level one). Novice game designers can focus on understanding the fundamentals of game-based learning and how it can be developed and used for their courses. Experienced game designers may have some understanding of how to develop a game, and they are open to learning more ways to improve or enhance the game experiences in their courses. As educators, we must commit to continually improving to remain relevant in our field and help our students prepare for real-life challenges in the contemporary world. By exploring new teaching methods and staying engaged with innovative practices, we serve as models to our students on the importance of reflection, open-mindedness, continuous learning, and improvement in our teaching, regardless of our tenure in the profession. I am excited to coauthor this book with my former graduate student, doctoral graduate assistant, and friend who brings invaluable experience as a speech-language pathologist in K-12 settings and game master for graduate students. Her insights and practical expertise as a game player, game master, and course designer, have been instrumental in helping us to develop game-based learning strategies that enhance student engagement and learning outcomes. Our goal is to share our combined knowledge and experiences to inspire educators and instructional designers to consider the benefits of gamification and to learn exactly how to apply it in their own programs.

## *Level I (Novice Game Designers)*

While there are numerous definitions of *gamification* noted in the literature, the term can be defined simply as the integration of game design elements and mechanics into non-game environments. The goal of *Game-Based Learning* (GBL) is to improve student engagement and promote student achievement (Majuri et al., 2018). Research on GBL in higher education supports its potential effectiveness in meeting the varied needs of adult learners. Integrating game elements such as points, badges, and challenges into educational activities (which we elaborate more on in Chapter 3) can increase motivation and participation (Costello, 2017). Game-Based Learning can motivate adult learners to actively explore content, collaborate with peers, and develop critical thinking skills in a supportive and safe environment (Featherstone, 2016). Game-Based Learning can naturally accommodate different learning styles and preferences and include adaptive feedback mechanisms to help adult learners interested in developing practical knowledge application skills (Ibisu, 2024). Game-Based Learning can help players to develop a better understanding of complex concepts. We will discuss how to do this more in later chapters, but you will learn how to develop GBL strategies directly aligned with your content learning objectives so that the game elements are purposeful and directly contribute to educational goals (Rivera & Garden, 2021). While GBL shows promise in enhancing short-term engagement and motivation, its long-term impact on learning retention and transfer of skills to real-world contexts requires ongoing research and refinement (Toda et al., 2023). Throughout this book, educators and instructional designers in higher education are encouraged to continually assess student needs and explore the integration of GBL strategies into instructional planning and delivery to enhance the educational experience and promote lifelong learning among adult learners (Toda et al., 2023). Throughout the text, we will explore how integrating GBL into your practice can promote collaboration, critical thinking, and problem-solving skills needed for success in academic and professional contexts (Bell, 2018).

In this book, the focus is on the integration of games into higher education settings, specifically through the concepts of Gamification, GBL, and Game Play. Each of these terms refers to using game elements or entire games to facilitate learning. While they have distinct definitions, they can often be used synonymously due to their overlapping goals and methods. Examples include earning points, badges, and rewards for completing tasks, setting challenges, and providing immediate feedback. Game-Based Learning involves integrating games into the curriculum where students learn through playing. Game-Based Learning can include digital games, board games, or role-playing scenarios designed to teach specific concepts or skills. *Game Play* refers to the act of playing games to engage players in games to facilitate learning (Plass et al., 2020). While Gamification, Game-Based Learning, and Game Play have distinct aspects, they are used synonymously throughout the text and refer to using games to enhance learning experiences. The research notes because the differences between the terms are somewhat vague, it is acceptable to use the terms interchangeably in educational contexts (Li & Tsai, 2013).

## What Is Gamification?

## How Are GBL Experiences Linked to Human Development?

### *Level II (Experienced—Intermediate Game Designers)*

Teachers, parents, and childcare providers know that GBL can play an important role in teaching basic skills and behaviors for human development across cultures. Games commonly integrated into childhood can play an important role in developing needed skills as children (Smith, 1982). In the United States, games like *Pat-a-Cake* and *Hide and Seek* can help children develop and refine social interaction, emotional expression, and language development skills. *Hopscotch* teaches balance and counting by hopping on numbered squares. Game-Based Learning can help children to engage with caregivers and peers, promoting learning through playful exploration and meaningful connections with others (Elkind, 2007). Childhood games from cultures around the world can teach and reinforce varied traditions and skills development (Dotson, 2020). In China, *Diabolo* challenges coordination with a spinning toy on a string (Caillois, 2006). India's *Kho Kho* emphasizes agility and strategy in a tag-style game. Japan's *Kendama* tests hand-eye coordination with ball-catching on cups and spikes. Brazil's *Capoeira* blends martial arts, music, and dance for fitness and cultural pride (Bhattacharya, 2023). South Africa's *Ampe* uses rhythmic movements and jumping to support physical fitness and coordination (Nabie, 2015). Childhood games can teach and reinforce verbal and nonverbal communication with others. Through verbal games like nursery rhymes or games involving storytelling, children learn to express themselves coherently and creatively (Miller & Kocurek, 2017). Nonverbal games, such as mimicking gestures or using facial expressions, help children understand and communicate their emotions and intentions. Building blocks or puzzles can help young children develop observation skills, strategize, and find solutions independently or collaboratively with others (Dotson, 2020).

## How Has GBL Evolved in Education?

### *Level II (Experienced—Intermediate Game Designers)*

Gamification has been utilized in education for more than a century. Early attempts at using games for education include Milton Bradley's (1860) *The Checkered Game of Life* which is also known as *The Game of Life*, and Elizabeth Magie's (1903) *The Landlord's Game* which is also known as the *Monopoly* game. Both games help players make their way through different stages of life in which they have to use critical thinking, reasoning, and problem-solving to make sound choices about common life experiences related to work, family, and money (Donovan, 2017). In the early 1900s, educators experimented with educational games to teach letters with building blocks, math manipulatives, and spelling or geography puzzles. The games engaged learners by utilizing elements of competition and skill development in an interactive learning experience. More familiar examples are the use of learner rewards and incentives in an educational setting. Teachers may reinforce and motivate learning math, spelling, or other content with stickers, certificates, or other tangibles to enhance the learning experience (Tobias & Fletcher, 2011). Early GBL experiences are often considered the foundation for GBL technologies of the twenty-first century. In the 1980s, when personal computers became more popular, digital games helped to make learning more interactive and enjoyable. In 1983, *Math Blaster!* helped players reinforce math skills in a space-theme learning environment. In 1985, players learned about history, geography, resource management, problem-solving, and decision-making by playing *The Oregon Trail* and *Hunting for Carmen Sandiego*, in *Where in the World is Carmen Sandiego?* (Frank, 2011; Squire, 2011; Utoyo, 2018).

More than 25 years ago, serious games with a purpose beyond entertainment gained popularity in education. *Serious games* were designed to teach specific skills or concepts and were used for training, simulation, and educational purposes (De Gloria et al., 2014). The term gamification was first used in 2002 by Nick Pelling to reference the integration of game-like elements into non-game contexts (Leaning, 2015). Around this time, integrating GBL elements became more popular as educators began to include badges, leaderboards, and rewards into learning experiences (Saleem et al., 2022). *Math Bingo* and *Word Bingo* were commonly used in elementary schools to teach and reinforce basic, developmentally appropriate academic concepts and critical thinking. In "Math Bingo," players develop foundational math skills in addition, subtraction, multiplication, and division by solving problems presented as bingo questions. The game also encourages strategic thinking as players must quickly choose and mark correct answers. Collaboratively, players communicate with each other to share strategies and learn from one another (Offenholley, 2012). *Word Bingo*, also helps with content, communication, and foundational skill building. Players develop vocabulary building, spelling, and word recognition skills as they match words with those on their bingo cards. Again, the GBL experience promotes critical thinking as well as content learning in word association and sight word recognition (Ulfa & Inayati, 2022). Game-Based Learning activities can help players of all ages build a foundation for communication, social interaction, and cognitive abilities to support growth and success across settings and content to help learners develop useful skills in the present and in the future (Manzano-León et al., 2021; Kapp, 2012).

Advances in technology over the years have expanded the possibilities of educational GBL experiences. The development of interactive computer games like *Reading Eggs* and *Prodigy* can offer personalized (even prescriptive and adaptive) learning experiences based on player needs. *Reading Eggs* is a GBL experience in which young learners develop and enhance thier literacy skills through interactive lessons, games, and e-books, adapting the difficulty level based on individual progress. Programs such as these can help players learn at their own pace, while simultaneously reinforcing comprehension and vocabulary skills (Rivera & Garden, 2021; Roberts, 2020). *Prodigy* is a GBL math program that adjusts difficulty levels in real-time as players work their way through the game. The adaptability of the GBL offers players a continuous challenge while supporting mastery of newly learned academic concepts (Ramic-Brkic & Balik, 2023). Game-Based Learning experiences can effectively engage players in targeted activities that influence behavior and achievement. Game-Based Learning experiences can help to prepare learners with essential skills and competencies for learning and success in today's complex world (Kapp, 2012).

## How Has GBL Evolved?

### *Level II (Experienced—Intermediate Game Designers)*

Over the past two decades, GBL has gained popularity due to its potential to promote engagement, comprehension, and collaboration across educational settings and content areas (Ramic-Brkic & Balik, 2023). In marketing, companies have successfully used GBL to improve customer interaction and brand loyalty (Dymek & Zackariasson, 2016). Starbucks' loyalty program uses gamified elements like earning stars for purchases, which motivates more frequent visits and increases customer retention. In healthcare, GBL has been used to promote healthy behaviors and patient engagement. Apps like *Pokemon Go* encourage physical activity by merging gameplay with real-world exercise, contributing to improved fitness levels among users. Health tracking apps use GBL features (e.g., goal setting, progress tracking) to motivate people to adopt healthier habits. Human resources often integrate GBL experiences into employee training and performance. Companies might develop interactive simulations where employees can practice real-life scenarios, earning points or badges as players progress through training modules. Game-Based Learning in human resources might integrate competition, rewards, and interactive challenges into workplace professional development training and performance management. The *My Marriott Hotel* platform simulates hotel management scenarios in a virtual environment. Players engage in realistic situations where they make decisions and handle challenges of hotel operations. Players actively participate and engage with the professional development content as they earn rewards or points for completing tasks, achieving goals, and reinforcing the natural, intrinsic motivation of GBL experiences as players are more likely to retain knowledge through hands-on, meaningful practice in a simulated setting (Ajisoko, 2020; Parshuram & Ramesh, 2020). *Recyclebank* is a GBL platform designed to promote environmental sustainability through recycling. Players earn points for recycling materials, which can then be redeemed for rewards from partnering businesses. The GBL encourages communities to recycle by making the process rewarding and engaging as players collect recyclables, register their recycling efforts, and track points (Park, 2017).

## How Might GBL Address Higher Education Challenges?

### Level I (Novice Game Designers)

The successful application of GBL across diverse fields supports its effectiveness in driving behavioral change, improving engagement, and player achievement (Manzano-León et al., 2021). Game-Based Learning can effectively address a range of student needs, including the development of positive attitudes, active participation, collaboration, self-guided study, assignment completion, and retention of learned material (Ninaus et al., 2019). Today, GBL is a recognized concept in education; however, the integration in *Institutions of Higher Education* (IHE) is not consistent. A primary challenge may be that many instructors (aka new game designers) lack the knowledge and skills to understand how to integrate GBL into their curriculum. The purpose of the book is to guide instructors in IHE to better understand what gamification is and how and its integration into their courses can reinforce learning objectives and industry standards, enhance engagement, and learning outcomes across diverse content areas (Zirawaga et al., 2017).

The landscape of higher education for adult learners has evolved significantly, catalyzed further by cultural shifts stemming from the 2020 pandemic. Adult learners, those pursuing education later in life while balancing work, family responsibilities, and other commitments, have increasingly been looking for accessible and engaging learning opportunities from IHEs. To ensure our programs are relevant and valued by contemporary adult learners (Fallahi, 2019; Knowles et al., 2020). IHEs must be willing to evolve and meet the changing needs of our students—especially at a time when the value of our nation's colleges and universities is being questioned by our political leaders. Today's learners are no longer satisfied with passive learning or one-size-fits-all instruction (Ambrose & Wankel, 2020; Anderson & Krathwohl, 2020; Merriam & Baumgartner, 2020). To remain relevant, educators must rethink how they design and deliver instruction, ensuring it aligns with the realities of modern adult students. Accelerated by the Covid-19 pandemic, these changes prompted a demand for online and hybrid learning models across academia. In response to the shifting landscape of adult education, characterized by diverse learner preferences and heightened competition among educational institutions, IHEs are actively integrating innovative strategies to attract and retain adult learners. Traditional colleges and universities are struggling with decreased enrollment rates which has triggered many IHEs to examine their programs to consider more student-friendly, pragmatic Masteratic approaches to retain and attract their adult learners according to the specific needs and preferences of their programs (Alexandar, 2020). One of the primary trends in IHE today is the emphasis on flexibility and accessibility. Contemporary adult learners often juggle multiple responsibilities such as work and family commitments, making flexibility in scheduling and course delivery formats an important consideration. IHEs are increasingly offering online courses and hybrid models combining online and in-person instruction, accelerated programs, and modular courses that allow learners to progress at their own pace. The more flexible formats can accommodate the busy schedules of adult learners according to their individual circumstances (Kim & Maloney, 2020). Practical, job-relevant skills are increasingly recognized as necessary by adult learners often seeking learning experiences and programs that directly translate into career advancement. As a result, IHEs are expanding their offerings of professional development courses, certificate programs, and degrees that align closely with industry needs to enhance the employability of graduates and attract learners interested in upgrading specific skills (Ambrose & Wankel, 2020). Table 1.1 shares some examples of how the expectations of adult learners have changed over the past twenty years for instructors to consider.

Another significant trend is the integration of technology in education. Digital advancements have significantly improved teaching and learning across content areas as there are now a variety of tools and platforms IHEs can use to enhance collaboration and learning experiences. IHEs are more commonly using *learning management systems* (LMS), *virtual reality* (VR), *augmented reality* (AR), and *artificial intelligence* (AI) to create interactive learning experiences that appeal to adult learners. Current trends in IHEs include meeting the varied needs of contemporary adult learners through flexible delivery formats, practical skill development, technology integration, and personalized learning to attract and retain adult learners and maximize the potential that educational experiences are relevant and responsive to the evolving demands of the contemporary workforce standards. The integration of GBL can enhance motivation and learning outcomes across programs and curriculum (Ginder et al., 2018). Addressing the varied needs of contemporary learners can strengthen an IHEs competitive edge as the program meets the needs of adult learners seeking needed real-world skills. Game-Based Learning can enhance traditional learning methods by integrating elements like quizzes, badges, and leaderboards into course curricula. Platforms such as *Kahoot!* and *Quizlet* can offer players an interactive learning experience as they compete, collaborate, and demonstrate mastery of academic content. Student motivation and participation improve as well as retention of course material (Ginder et al., 2018).

## How Might GBL Address Digital Literacy Needs?

### *Level I (Novice Game Designers)*

While we will talk about this more in Chapter 6, it is important to note the post-pandemic cultural changes which emphasize the importance of digital literacy and adaptability in IHEs. Adult learners are increasingly drawn to programs that offer practical skills aligned with evolving job market demands, such as data analytics, digital marketing, and remote collaboration tools. The integration of GBLs can help to address the evolving needs and preferences of adult learners seeking accessible, engaging, and relevant educational experiences (Soffer & Cohen, 2019). Understanding the evolving

Table 1.1 Shifting Expectations of Adult Learners

| Learner Characteristics | 2004 (Ambrose & Wankel, 2020; Knowles et al., 2020) | 2024 (Ambrose & Wankel, 2020; Anderson & Krathwohl, 2020; Fallahi, 2019; Merriam & Baumgartner, 2020) |
|---|---|---|
| Learning Preferences | Adult learners in the past were often passive learners, perhaps intimidated by instructors, unsure about the value of different perspectives, and may have been hesitant to actively participate in discussions. Many were interested in higher education as a way to earn credentials. | Contemporary adult learners expect to understand the relevance of what they are learning, desire collaboration and interaction with peers and prefer interactive learning over traditional lecture and testing. Willing to keep learning if the content feels relevant, not just for earning a credential. |
| Teacher-Student Relationships | Adult learners in the past tended to have respect and defer to authority figures and recognized the instructor as the content expert without question. Students were less likely to advocate for themselves. | Learners are more comfortable expressing themselves, less intimidated by authority and consider the teacher-student relationship from a consumer perspective. Expect meaningful instruction, open communication, rapid individualized feedback, and teacher consideration of their needs. |
| Personalized Learning Expectations | Adult learners in the past were often willing to do whatever the instructor asked for even if that included working longer hours (losing sleep, sacrificing time with family, etc.) to get things done on time. These students may have felt instructors had limited acknowledgment of, or consideration of, their personal needs. | Students may be less willing to commit extensive hours to coursework and are looking for adult learning experiences that consider other personal and professional responsibilities. Expect instructors to consider their needs when planning and delivering instruction and looking for a more personalized approach to learning. |

characteristics and expectations of these learners is vital when IHEs make decisions about what content to teach and how to effectively teach this content when designing effective educational programs and professional development opportunities (Fallahi, 2019). Online instruction is here to stay for contemporary adult learners, particularly those balancing work and other responsibilities during the day. The flexibility of online learning helps learners to manage their professional and personal obligations while pursuing professional development needs. Online learning allows learners to access course materials, participate in discussions, and complete assignments at their convenience, whether it's during evenings, weekends, or other available time slots.

Synchronous online classes, conducted via video conferencing tools like *Zoom* or *Microsoft Teams*, provide real-time interaction with instructors and peers. The options accommodate varying time zones and can promote more authentic interactions and collaboration among adult learners regardless of geographic location (Croxton, 2014). Adult learners appreciate the time they save by not having to commute to a physical campus as they study and complete assignments at their own pace (Fallahi, 2019). Online learning is particularly inviting for adult learners who are attending school part time and working during the day. Improvements in online learning with regard to the available digital resources and multimedia along with the ability to view content on mobile phones and tablets can be motivating for contemporary adult learners (Dyer et al., 2018).

Contemporary IHEs must be willing to offer adult learners programs and learning experiences that enhance tangible skills and provide opportunities for career advancement. Integrating GBL into educational practices can effectively address these needs (Kim & Maloney, 2020; McKeithan et al., 2021; Soffer & Cohen, 2019). Incorporating the motivational power of GBL into IHE programs can enhance student learning experiences and prepare learners for success in their chosen fields (Ginder et al., 2018). Adult learners today have a huge variety of choices in online education, necessitating instructional designers across all fields to prioritize practicality and employability in their course offerings. Integrating GBL in higher education can help IHEs as they shift from traditional lecture-based formats toward more student-centered, engaging learning environments (Bell, 2018; Jaramillo-Mediavilla et al., 2024; Kapp, 2012; Kim & Maloney, 2020). For example, in nursing or business courses, students might engage in virtual patient care simulations or business strategy games, respectively, to hone critical thinking and decision-making skills. Game-Based Learning can enhance comprehension and cultivate essential twenty-first-century skills like collaboration, communication, and leadership (Kuo et al., 2014). While we will learn more about this later in the text, to achieve these goals, IHEs must ensure that learning goals and content must be relevant and aligned with current workplace demands and standards in order to provide students with practical knowledge, skills, and competencies (Alismail & McGuire, 2015).

## How Can GBL Prepare Students for Real Challenges?

### *Level II (Experienced—Intermediate Game Designers)*

In response to shifting workforce demands shaped by technological advancements, globalization, economic recovery efforts, and the impacts of the Covid-19 pandemic, higher education is increasingly turning to GBL to prepare adult learners for the evolving job market (Ajmal et al., 2022; Manzano-León et al., 2021; Tharpe, 2022). Adult learners are looking for learning experiences that meaningfully connect the research and theory with practical skills applicable in today's work landscape. Game-Based Learning can be used to help students develop employability skills needed for the twenty-first-century workforce. Business simulations can be used in GBL experiences to help learners better understand complex market scenarios, teaching data analysis, strategic decision-making, and resource management (Dymek & Zackariasson, 2016). In healthcare, virtual patient simulations can prepare students for clinical practice through realistic scenarios (Ramic-Brkic & Balik, 2023). As AI continues to reshape industries GBL can be used to better provide learners with the adaptive skills needed in AI-integrated workplaces (Fallahi, 2019; Zhan et al., 2024) as students develop meaningfully (Halabieh et al., 2022). IHEs must acknowledge that modern learners prioritize programs offering opportunities to develop essential skills through practical, immersive learning experiences.

*Transferable skills* are competencies and abilities that individuals can apply across different roles, industries, and situations and can include critical thinking, problem-solving, communication, teamwork, adaptability, and leadership. The skills are particularly needed for contemporary learners as our students may transition between roles and industries throughout their careers (Hoque et al., 2023). Game-Based Learning can help to meet the demand for developing transferable skills by offering our learners opportunities to participate in simulations (role-playing scenarios) in which they are tasked with real-world collaborative challenges to actively apply new learning (Alismail & McGuire, 2015). Experiential learning activities can create an environment that challenges learners to apply what they know and experience consequences in a risk-free environment to enhance proficiency in transferable skills and build confidence in their application of key curriculum constructs (Halabieh et al., 2022).

## How Can GBL Keep My Teaching Relevant?

### Level II (Experienced—Intermediate Game Designers)

IHEs are increasingly challenged to adapt their teaching approaches to better equip graduates with the multifaceted skills needed to thrive in an increasingly competitive and fast-paced global economy (Halabeih et al., 2022). Recruiting and retaining contemporary adult learners has become a challenge for IHEs given the numerous alternative options available to our learners, including numerous online options, professional development through for-profit universities, workplace training, and shorter certificate programs (Kim & Maloney, 2020; Mamgain et al., 2014). We will look at this more in Chapter 6, but it is important to note that providing relevant, applicable, learning experiences can attract prospective students (Bledsoe & Simmerock, 2013; Costello, 2017).

## Can GBL Be Used in Any Program?

### Level II (Experienced—Intermediate Game Designers)

Adult learners, who often juggle multiple tasks like checking texts and emails, require instructional approaches that are immediately relevant and practical. Students prefer learner-centered and experiential learning methods that actively engage them and provide opportunities to apply their learning in practical settings and collaborate meaningfully with peers. Adult learners, coming from diverse backgrounds, have varied needs and appreciate instructors who create engaging learning experiences that leverage their unique knowledge and prior experiences (Fallahi, 2019; Manzano-León et al., 2021). IHEs must offer personalized support and guidance, understanding the complexities adult learners face in developing effective study skills, time management strategies, and navigating technology in higher education (Ninaus et al., 2019). Integrating GBL experiences across instructional formats (e.g., face-to-face, online, synchronous, and asynchronous) can offer our learners experiential learning opportunities that are valued by contemporary adult learners (Sammel et al., 2014). Adult learners come from a variety of backgrounds with multifaceted needs (Fallahi, 2019). Our students appreciate instructors who can provide meaningful learning experiences which allow them to engage with content while simultaneously using their unique knowledge and prior experiences (Manzano-León et al., 2021). Contemporary adult learners also expect more hands on and readily available assistance with developing effective study skills, time management strategies, and technology assistance. A well-designed GBL can assist players and the instructor in reinforcing these skills (often also the gamemaster) throughout the gaming experience (Ninaus et al., 2019).

Game-Based Learning can be implemented through interactive modules, gamified quizzes, or scenario-based learning exercises (Sammel et al., 2014).

Cognitive benefits relate to mental processes like thinking, learning, and memory, while affective benefits concern emotions, motivation, and attitudes. A well-designed GBL experience can support intellectual and emotional growth of our learners across disciplines. In medical programs, platforms like *BodyInteract* can offer learners patient simulations that enhance critical thinking and decision-making skills which can in turn deepen their understanding practices (Branch, 2022). In technology and computer science, GBLs like *CodeCombat* and *LightBot* can promote logical thinking and programming skills (Weymouth & Atuah, 2022). In biology and chemistry, games like *Foldit* can assist learners in scientific exploration to develop problem-solving abilities and understanding of complex concepts (Liu et al., 2020). In social sciences like criminal justice and international relations, games like *Papers, Please* encourage ethical reasoning and decision-making (Cabellos et al., 2022). Communication and marketing programs may use GBL storytelling and planning games like *The Sims* to promote innovating thinking and collaboration (Sabtu, 2023). Incorporating GBL into higher education programs supports cognitive development and emotional well-being. Game-Based Learning can meet the evolving needs of contemporary adult learners and equips them with the tools and competencies required for professional success in today's complex and ever-changing work environments.

## What Is the Impact of GBL on Learning Success?

### *Level II (Experienced—Intermediate Game Designers)*

Institutions of Higher Education are increasingly relying on online instruction, yet variability in quality and faculty expertise can hinder learning outcomes (Al Gamdi, 2017). Many instructors lack direct experience as online students and may resist learning or using unfamiliar technology or instructional strategies, which can negatively impact effective teaching practices. Integrating GBL into your program can improve student engagement in online and traditional settings (Tharpe, 2022). Student achievement increases when courses include active learning activities and assignments that allow students to apply new learning (Bryan et al., 2018). Embracing a culture of adaptability and innovation, IHEs can better support their faculty and students (Soffer & Cohen, 2019). Some distance education instructors lack experience as online learners and may not know how to create meaningful and engaging online learning experiences for their students (McKeithan et al., 2021). Our book emphasizes the importance of incorporating GBL techniques to promote more active and productive learning environments across content areas (Saleem et al., 2022).

Subsequent chapters will elaborate on and give examples of how gamification in higher education can help to make online instruction more effective. Teacher-student and peer interactions play an important role in creating an environment that fosters engagement, supports student motivation, and prepares learners for real-world applications (Kapp, 2012). We will share several examples of how games can be developed and played using a universal structure that can be readily applied to most learning formats and content areas. We will discuss the use of game mechanics, feedback mechanisms, and social interaction elements in our gamification approach, as well as the positive impact that gamification has had on student engagement, motivation, and learning outcomes. We will also share strategies for selecting appropriate game mechanics, setting goals and objectives, designing content, and assessing student achievement (Manzano-León et al., 2021).

# How Can RPGs Support Skill Development?

## *Level I (Novice Game Designers)*

Game-Based Learning experiences are more common than you realize, as educators in elementary, middle, high school, and college settings frequently use game elements to increase engagement and learning outcomes. Point systems are commonly used to motivate students and monitor their progress, earn points for correct quiz answers, earn rewards such as extra recess or small prizes, and so on. Similar to points, badges may be used in K-12 and IHEs to promote achievements and provide visual recognition of accomplishments. Displaying student rankings on bulletin boards or electronic leaderboards is often used to promote competition and encourage students to excel. Offering rewards or prizes for reaching educational milestones is a commonly used tool to reinforce behavior and effort. Role-play scenarios are often integrated into K-12 and higher education settings to promote problem-solving and critical thinking skills. An elementary health teacher may ask students to do role-playing exercises to explore healthy decision-making and practice conflict resolution techniques. Simulations can offer students practical applications of theoretical knowledge. In a college nursing program, students might use simulations to diagnose and treat patients. *Role-Playing Games* (RPGs) represent a specialized form of GBL where participants assume character roles and make decisions that intricately shape the game's narrative.

While various gamification examples, features, and attributes of GBL have been explored in this chapter, the focus of this book is on RPGs and their effective integration into any curriculum area. Role-Playing Games offer a unique opportunity to apply new learning in real-world contexts and to develop critical skills such as problem-solving, decision-making, and collaboration. Role-Playing Games were chosen as a focus because once the initial game design is complete, it is easier for instructors to reuse the game setup or framework and adapt it to meet specific and evolving curriculum objectives. Educational RPGs incorporate predetermined educational objectives and encourage players to learn and grow through gameplay (Daniau, 2016). Role-Playing Games can offer contemporary learners the chance to assume the role of a fictional character or avatar and work cooperatively within the constraints of a real-world team to solve challenges and make decisions related to real-world applications of their new content learning. Role-Playing Games can offer unique opportunities for players to engage with peers in an interactive storyline, consider different perspectives and apply new knowledge in practical contexts. For example, in business courses, players may work cooperatively as a member of a board of directors where they take on roles such as CEO, CFO, and department heads, navigating financial decisions and strategic planning collaboratively. The experience can sharpen a player's content knowledge and enhance skills in leadership, negotiation, and decision-making. Future chapters will further explore the specific and practical examples of how RPGs can provide players with a unique opportunity to practice and apply skills in simulated real-life scenarios with minimal consequences. Role-Playing Games require players to consider diverse viewpoints, essential for academic and professional environments. Role-Playing Games can effectively teach and reinforce collaboration and *soft skills* for teamwork. Players learn to actively listen, appreciate different experiences, and capitalize on individual strengths within a cooperative GBL experience.

## Game Log

*I consulted with my grandson and my son who are experienced RPG D&D players prior to developing my first RPG. I learned that in gaming, a "Game Log" serves as a record of key events, decisions, and milestones in a player's journey. The Game Log provides a quick recap of the essential moves made, insights gained, and strategies uncovered, so you can reflect on your progress and prepare for the next challenge. Moving forward, each chapter in this book is designed to address your own learning quest. Just like in a well-designed RPG game, reflecting on your progress and insights can help sharpen your skills. In this first chapter, I introduced an overview of gamification (I use the term synonymously with Game-Based Learning and game playing) as an innovative approach in higher education. I hope that I made a convincing argument that GBL experiences can potentially improve your student's learning and achievement. A well-designed GBL can offer students meaningful and practical learning experience. Reflecting on my own journey, I've learned how these methodologies can be integrated into my existing teaching methods to better meet the evolving needs of contemporary adult learners by making learning interactive, relevant, and enjoyable. In subsequent chapters you will learn more about the strategic use of game mechanics to effectively design GBL strategies aligned with educational goals from various academic disciplines. As we move forward, we will share easy to interpret practical strategies, challenges, and future directions for integrating GBL into higher education via text, tables, and specific examples. In Chapter 2, you will be introduced to Team Dynamics and Role Theory, where you will learn how to develop characters and strategically use team roles to enhance gameplay. Chapter 3 focuses on Planning, Designing, and Implementing educational RPGs, emphasizing the importance of setting clear objectives and creating structured game plans that engage your students effectively. In Chapter 4, you will learn more about structuring your game with game mechanics. You will learn to incorporate key elements like points and badges to boost student engagement. Chapter 5 will guide you on Optimizing Engagement in online courses, providing practical tips for creating interactive virtual environments and evaluating learning outcomes. Finally, in Chapter 6, you will learn more about the Challenges and Considerations of gamified learning, exploring strategies to balance competition and collaboration while fostering meaningful engagement. The goal is for the book to provide you with the tools to enhance your teaching practices to better meet the needs of your learners.*

# 2 Team Engagement and Role Theory

## Game Master's Prelude

*Okay, full disclosure, when I first developed an RPG for my courses, I didn't know very much about game theory or team theory. My initial approach was to review an RPG developed by a colleague set in futuristic worlds. The avatars were anime characters and tasks in a utopian society, and the reality seemed very loosely connected to real-world dilemmas. I decided to simplify the RPG experience using a more straightforward scenario set in a fictional high school, which was a context I knew well from my own experience as a teacher that also aligned with the higher education content in my teacher education assessment course. The team type that I chose to have my students demonstrate their knowledge of new learning was an Individualized Education Program (IEP) Team. The IEP team was selected because they are often tasked with the interpretation and application of existing data and to consider the assessment, the student's situation, and to work cooperatively with the team to make appropriate decisions for the featured learner. The avatar characters were based on personality types encountered over the years, and I worked closely with a colleague to develop a backstory that incorporated a variety of backgrounds and experiences relevant to team behaviors and relationships. My teaching partner shared her own knowledge of team theory and Belbin's roles which was eventually added to the avatar biographies and integrated into our evolving RPG game for our graduate student players. While the first attempts at the game were far from perfect, the RPG was a HUGE success for students. I will talk more about scenario/problem-solving game development in the next chapter. Our game was implemented in three rounds over an eight-week period, and the third round of the game required players to talk about what they learned from the game. I was genuinely surprised by the student feedback on how powerful the experience was for their learning. As you read this chapter, you will learn a bit about the principles of game theory that should be considered when developing RPGs. You will learn about Belbin's Team Roles and how to use them to build a balanced team in your game. Trust me, considering these aspects of the game now can save you lots of time later as you* will not need to make as many revisions. We strongly encourage game designers to be mindful of the need to include different experiences and perspectives that can impact what a character thinks, how they make decisions and how they interact with others when developing avatar personalities. It may be beneficial to consider integrating some of these aspects into your avatar development if you feel it is appropriate for your learners to consider them in conjunction with the tasks they are assigned. In the last chapter, the focus was on the theoretical and potential benefits of GBL. We hope by the end of this chapter, you will start putting these ideas into practice for your game!

## Why Is Building an Effective Team So Important?

### Level I (Novice Game Designers)

At this point, since you are reading Chapter 2, I hope Chapter 1 successfully convinces you that providing opportunities for your learners to apply newly learned content and develop relevant and meaningful skills in real-world scenarios can be beneficial. Role-Playing Games can be effective tools to help learners solve problems in simulated environments as players work collaboratively to complete given tasks in the assigned game rounds. The first step in game development for a *game designer* or person responsible for creating the game is to align the game objectives with course objectives. The next step is for the game designer to select the type of team the players will work on to apply new learning. Once the team has been identified and the tasks selected for the teams to complete, the game designer will begin to develop avatars (team characters assigned to players that represent varied experiences and perspectives). In this context, a *course instructor* in higher education is the educator responsible for delivering content, assessing student performance, and facilitating learning within the course. The *game master* sets up the game, facilitates the rounds, guides the team, and supports the players during the game to ensure the game runs smoothly. The game master (who you will learn more about in the next chapter) can play an important role in facilitating learning by offering hints, assessing progress, regulating play, and adjusting the game as needed to meet players' needs (Daniau, 2016). Throughout this text, the terms game designer, course instructor, and game master may be used interchangeably, reflecting their interconnected roles in the creation and management of educational gaming experiences. However, it is possible for the game designer to develop a game for a class that is taught by a course instructor who may or may not have the role of facilitating the game (e.g., if a graduate teaching assistant is serving as the game master). Table 2.1 shows examples of varied teams across selected programs in higher education that game designers may want to consider when developing the RPG (e.g., education, business, medical sciences, criminal justice, interdisciplinary studies, etc.). Departments related to education (e.g., Teacher Education, Educational Leadership, Policy Studies, Curriculum and Instruction, Counseling and Psychology, Instructional Technology, Adult and Continuing Education, etc.) may be focused on enhancing team competencies in which subject matter experts, teachers, administrators, service providers and educational specialists work collaboratively to make decisions related to curriculum development, student assessment, educational policy, teacher training, instructional design, mental health services, and the integration of technology in the classroom.

Instructional design requires the incorporation of evidence-based practices, meeting varied learner needs, and creating engaging content. Effective collaboration requires clear communication and negotiation, allowing team members to address and reconcile differing priorities (Strada et al., 2023). For example, a professor in the education department may prioritize student engagement, while an administrator may focus on compliance with accreditation standards. Through effective interaction, team members develop real-world skills in negotiation and compromise. Differences in pedagogical philosophies and resource allocation can lead to disagreements within these teams, which can impact team productivity. Differing perspectives and internal motivations from team members can generate conflict (Johnson & Voelkel, 2021). In an Adult and Continuing Education Department, program development teams create courses and programs for adult learners. Teams must consider diverse learner needs, career goals, and industry requirements. Conflicts can arise when balancing practical skills training with academic rigor (Foster & Shah, 2020). RPGs can provide opportunities for these varied teams and programs to apply new skills and develop effective collaboration skills needed in the real world. For example, Leadership team members could use RPGs to simulate classroom scenarios that require collaborative problem-solving. Intervention teams could engage in RPGs to practice integrating different strategies. Administrative support

## Table 2.1 Team Type Examples for RPG Games

### Education Focused Teams

- *Individual Education Program (IEP) Teams* are typically multidisciplinary teams that include an administrator, Special Education Teacher, Regular Education Teacher, student and parents who consider student needs, set appropriate goals, and determine services and accommodations necessary.
- *Multi-Tiered System of Supports (MTSS) Teams* help support students who need extra assistance. The teams often include administrators, grade level teachers, mental health professionals, special education teachers, content specialists, school psychologists, counselors, deans, and ELL teachers. The teams review school-wide data, decide on appropriate interventions, monitor progress, and make data-based decisions to help students.
- *Professional Learning Communities (PLCs)* are teams of professionals with similar goals such as the seventh grade teachers or the fine arts department interested in improving student achievement. The teams meet regularly to collaborate on curriculum mapping, teaching practices, student data, and sharing resources.
- *Leadership Teams* may include administrators, department heads, counselors, instructional coaches, and parents or community representatives. The team may be called on to set goals, create plans, and use data to track student achievement, behavior, identify needed professional development and communicate with staff, students, families, and the community.

(Grissom & Condon, 2021; Navo & Williams, 2022)

### Business-Focused Teams

- *Project Teams* often include a variety of different people with specialized skills and have specific goals (such as developing a plan to launch or rebrand a product). The project manager may be tasked to generate plans, schedules or budgets, handle planning, scheduling, costs, and risks. The project supervisor may be asked to continuously monitor the team's progress to be sure what they are doing is in line with the project goals. The business analyst identifies needs by working with stakeholders. Other roles include resource managers, risk managers, team leaders, and coordinators.
- *Quality Improvement Teams* may include supervisors, managers, subject matter experts, and so on. The goal of the team is to maximize efficiency and minimize waste. The Team Leader facilitates the team, Process Specialists and Data Specialists may assist the team to analyze data and better understand problems and trends. Change Management Specialists may be included to help guide transitions and address team resistance while QI Specialists may be asked to design and evaluate improvement initiatives.
- *Risk Management Teams* Risk Management Teams find and reduce risks to business, finances, or reputation. The Chief Risk Officer leads, with Risk Analysts analyzing data and Compliance Officers ensuring rules are followed. Experts in finance, IT, or law provide guidance. The team works together to monitor, avoid, minimize, or manage risks and report them.

(Lee, 2021; Smith & Merritt, 2020)

*(Continued)*

**Table 2.1 (Continued)**

| **Healthcare Focused Teams** |
|---|
| • *Medical Treatment Teams* often include a variety of healthcare professionals from different specialties (e.g., doctors, nurses, therapists, and technicians, etc.) who collaborate to diagnose and treat patients.<br>• *Surgical Teams* work together to make sure surgeries go smoothly and safely. The teams may include surgeons, nurses, anesthesiologists, student doctors, and so on.<br>• *Emergency Response Teams* (or *Rapid Response Team* in hospitals) can include nursing staff, emergency physicians, paramedics, and other specialists trained to handle medical emergencies.<br>(Janssen et al., 2018; O'Donovan & Mcauliffe, 2020; Pritchard et al., 2021) |
| **Service Industry Teams** |
| • *Hospitality Teams* often include front desk staff, concierges, servers, bar staff, house staff, and events coordinators. The team goal is to provide a positive customer experience in their business.<br>• *Sales Teams* may include sales reps, account managers, and sales managers. The team goal is to make money for their company by selling services or products.<br>• *Operations Teams* might include operations managers, workers, and production supervisors who work together to make sure everyone has what they need to do their jobs.<br>(Giousmpasoglou et al., 2021; Hossain et al., 2021) |

teams might use RPGs to simulate school management scenarios, helping them balance efficiency and thoroughness. Technology integration teams might benefit from RPGs that involve implementing new tech tools in a virtual classroom setting. Program development teams in adult education could use RPGs to simulate course design processes, balancing practical and academic priorities in a collaborative environment. In the field of business education, students at IHEs are prepared for diverse careers through a range of specialized programs (Business Administration, Accounting, Finance, Marketing, and Management). Players might work together to develop a business plan for a new startup, navigating challenges like market research, financial planning, and team coordination. In Accounting programs, RPGs can provide hands-on experience in managing financial challenges and collaborating with various teams. A Financial Discrepancy Simulation might have students investigate and resolve discrepancies in a company's financial records while working with finance teams, audit teams, and tax teams. An Internal Audit Challenge can involve reviewing financial statements and assessing internal controls, where students work with audit teams to identify issues and recommend improvements. Tax Preparation and Planning Scenario might require players to simulate preparing tax returns and strategizing tax efficiency with tax teams (Huang et al., 2022). In programs related to careers in medicine, adult learners can benefit from RPG experiences on varied teams across specialties. Medical multidisciplinary care teams bring together professionals from different disciplines such as medicine, nursing, social work, and psychology to provide comprehensive care for patients with complex conditions. Conflicts can emerge from differing approaches to patient care and treatment priorities. Effective interactions within teams require respect for one another and collaborative decision-making. Medical students might be included as a member of a multidisciplinary care team, treatment team, or research team where they must navigate conflicts between different approaches to patient care and practice empathy as they work through a series of tasks related to complex medical scenarios. In all the RPG scenarios above, players can benefit from RPGs simulating real life, content-related challenges, developing policies, analyzing data, identifying patterns, sharing information, and making collaborative decisions (Gaalen et al., 2021).

## How Does Game Theory Shape Team Interactions?

### *Level I (Novice Game Designers)*

Game theory and team theory are important ideas for designing RPG games that are fun and successful. Understanding these theories can help make RPGs more meaningful and relevant. *Game theory* is related to understanding how people make decisions when their choices affect others. Game theory considers how conflicts and cooperation can be analyzed and has been useful in many real-world situations such as designing auction systems and guiding economic negotiations (Barron, 2024). In RPGs, game theory helps designers create a game that simulates how players might interact, create fair challenges, and develop scenarios that reflect real-world strategic decisions that impact the outcome of the game (Bolton, 2002). RPG game designers can incorporate the principles into the game rounds to create challenging and rewarding RPGs. Game designers and game masters can use their understanding of game theory and team theory to create and modify games that reinforce collaboration skills and an understanding of different perspectives (Roungas et al., 2019). In an RPG for criminal justice students, a mock trial might require players to assume roles, such as defense attorneys, prosecutors, and witnesses, and must collaborate to prepare their cases, consider relevant policies and laws needed to successfully strategize, and present arguments. Players learn how to identify and use relevant new learning, communicate effectively, support each other's efforts, and resolve conflicts, which enhances the skills they may need in real-world legal situations (Bolton, 2002). Understanding team roles helps students learn how to communicate effectively, resolve conflicts, and work together to achieve their goals (Bolton, 2002).

## Can Belbin's Team Roles Enhance Collaborations?

### Level II (Experienced—Intermediate Game Designers)

So now that you know game designers can potentially create a more effective team if they have a basic understanding of *Team Theory Principles* (Akhilesh, 2014). Early theorists like Kurt Lewin and Bruce Tuckman developed the foundational models of team theory, such as *Lewin's Change Theory* and *Tuckman's Stages of Group Development*, which analyze how teams evolve through forming, storming, norming, and performing stages (Smith & Knapp, 2011). The theories emphasize the importance of team development and leadership in team success. As the field evolved, *Belbin's Team Roles* offered a more detailed theory. For RPG game designers, beginning with a model like Belbin's Team Roles can offer advantages when building game avatars and scenarios. Although, to be honest, I did not integrate Belbin's framework into my game until after I developed the RPG, and I was interested in refining the team a bit more. Belbin's philosophy identifies nine distinct roles, and we recommend that new game designers consider these roles before team avatar development. Belbin suggests that successful teams benefit from a balanced mix of roles, enabling the team to use the diverse strengths of the group to manage conflicts effectively and complete assigned tasks. Utilizing Belbin's model can improve RPG design by helping to balance roles within a team, and subsequently promoting more effective collaboration among players (Aritzeta, 2007). However, it is important to consider the model's limitations. Concerns about its simplicity and potential role overlap of the team roles have been noted, suggesting that it is not a perfect system, and the framework might benefit from refinement and expansion. Role-Playing Games designers should be aware of the model's limitations and remain open to adapting and integrating additional insights to create effective game scenarios (Roungas et al., 2019; van Gaalen et al., 2021). Belbin's theory is based on comprehensive research into what makes teams work well together. The theory can help game designers improve team dynamics by identifying each team member's strengths and behavior patterns. Belbin's theory suggests that a well-balanced team, with members who have complementary roles, is more likely to succeed and reach its goals (Belbin, 2010; Belbin & Brown, 2022). Belbin's Team Roles are divided into three main categories (1) *Action Oriented*, (2) *People Oriented*, and (3) *Thought Oriented*. While I will talk about specific avatar creation integrating these characteristics into team biographies in subsequent chapters (especially now that we have AI resources to help with this), right now, I would like to focus on a brief description of the varied team role types and their potential impact on the team.

## How Can Shapers Help Teams Overcome Challenges?

### *Level II (Experienced—Intermediate Game Designers)*

Action-oriented team members (Shapers, Implementers, Completer-Finishers) are character avatars that can assist new game designers to create a more balanced team where each avatar on the team has the skills needed to meaningfully contribute to team success. Shapers are often competitive team members with the ability to challenge the team to make positive changes, get things done and figure out how to work through whatever obstacles they may face. The Shaper avatar in a team may be described as a driven personality with strong determination, and shapers often demonstrate the ability to recover quickly from setbacks and perform well under pressure. In RPGs, players taking on the Shaper role may be described as having strong leadership and quick decision-making skills. Challenges this avatar character might experience during the game could include being argumentative, impatient, and aggressive which can lead to team conflicts. Making impulsive choices and difficulty in delegating tasks may cause delays and problems for shapers (Fisher et al., 1998).

## How Can Completer-Finishers Impact Quality Control?

### Level II (Experienced—Intermediate Game Designers)

According to Belbin, Completer-finishers in RPGs can be useful team members because of their strong focus on quality. Team avatars in this role may be described as paying close attention to details, recognizing potential problems, and dedicated to ensuring every part of a team's assigned task meets high standards. The Completer-finisher avatar may be asked to manage the team's schedule as they monitor and track progress toward team goals. Often, these avatars take pride in their work, but they may be overly critical and might struggle with delegating tasks to other team members, as they often believe only they can achieve the desired quality (Pritchard & Stanton, 1999).

## How Do Implementers Help Teams Task Analyze Plans?

### Level II (Experienced—Intermediate Game Designers)

In RPGs, the Implementer avatars are another important member of the team as they are often needed to help the team take ideas and task analyze the needed steps for the team to develop an organized and realistic plan. The Implementer avatar may be described as having the ability to juggle multiple tasks simultaneously and help the team convert long-term and overarching goals into practical action plans that can be achieved within a specific timeline. Implementers can help the team by breaking down complex projects into manageable steps for each team member to complete. Challenges for Implementer avatars might be a tendency to resist alternative ideas, leaning toward traditional procedures with a preference for structured activities that might limit creativity and make unstructured tasks difficult to manage (Aranzabal et al., 2022).

# How Do People-Oriented Roles Strengthen RPG Teams?

## Level II (Experienced—Intermediate Game Designers)

People-oriented avatars on a team are important for managing relationships and keeping the team working well together. The avatars in this category include Coordinators, Team Workers, and Resource Investigators. Although a team may not have all three roles, having at least one person who excels in people-oriented tasks is recommended to maintain team morale and promote effective collaboration. In a project team, a Coordinator avatar might manage meetings, a Team Worker might encourage and support team members, and a Resource Investigator might be good at finding new resources or generating ideas to maximize existing resources. Avatars in these roles can help RPG teams communicate better, stay motivated, and work together (Rahmani et al., 2022).

# How Do Coordinators Help Teams Build Consensus?

## Level II (Experienced—Intermediate Game Designers)

In RPGs, Coordinator avatars can help to lead and organize the team. Coordinator avatars are often described as being confident and experienced with effective diplomacy skills. The avatar can help to facilitate interactions among the team to keep them focused on their common goals. The Coordinator avatars are often comfortable stepping in when needed to help resolve conflicts and clarify communication between team members. The coordinators can help team members feel positive about their unique contributions to the team's goals. Coordinator avatars may be perceived as being manipulative or bossy by other team members. The coordinator might also focus more on long-term goals and miss important details (Monsalves et al., 2023).

## How Do Team Workers Support Cohesion?

### *Level II (Experienced—Intermediate Game Designers)*

In RPGs, a Team Worker avatar may be described as a person with a keen ability to understand the unique perspectives of other team members. Recognizing the unique perspectives of other team members in an RPG round might help the team stay focused on goal mastery and minimize conflicts. The Team Worker's ability to empathize with team members can help the team significantly. If a team member is feeling isolated, unmotivated or neglected, the Team Worker might offer reassurance and encouragement to help the troubled player stay focused and productive. Team Workers can often help to resolve potential conflicts quickly without escalating tensions as they are able to find common ground and facilitate a compromise that works for everyone. Team Workers actively ensure that others on the team feel valued. Challenges specific to this avatar may be addressing conflicts directly, which can sometimes be mistaken for weakness or lack of leadership. Team Workers may neglect their own needs when they conflict with the group's (Belbin & Brown, 2022).

## How Do Resource Investigators Help Teams?

### *Level II (Experienced—Intermediate Game Designers)*

The Resource Investigator avatar may be described as being outgoing, enthusiastic, and persuasive. Resource Investigators often excel at networking and building relationships with people outside the team, which can help the team consider new insights and opportunities. Resource Investigators are often very good at making connections with new people and building resource networks to assist the team with gathering important information. The Resource Investigator avatar may be comfortable organizing meetings and negotiating deals. They are often useful by helping the team to identify useful trends or patterns, secure partnerships, identify new resources when making decisions and developing plans. However, these team members might be easily distracted by new potential opportunities which could lead to missed deadlines and unfinished tasks (Aranzabal et al., 2022).

# How Do Monitor Evaluators Help Make Objective Decisions?

## *Level II (Experienced—Intermediate Game Designers)*

Thought-oriented roles are important to help the team analyze situations and generate ideas. The roles in this category include Monitor Evaluators, Plants, and Specialists, each contributing unique strengths to a team. Monitor Evaluators are often described as being unbiased and having good analytical skills which can help them to carefully examine important information and offer their teammates meaningful insight as they break down complex issues and analyze procedures and methods. In a business-related RPG, a Monitor Evaluator might look at a new product plan, check financial details, and help the team make objective decisions. The avatar character may focus too much on potential problems which could lead to slower decision-making and delays in getting things done. Combining analysis with support can enhance their effectiveness. Monitor Evaluators bring a vital perspective to any RPG team (Fisher et al., 2001; Fisher et al., 1998).

# How Can Plants Help Teams with Creative Solutions?

## *Level II (Experienced—Intermediate Game Designers)*

The Plant avatars on an RPG team are often described as being imaginative and unconventional as they are able to help the team find new ways to solve problems. Plant avatars are often seen as solitary and reserved team members who can help the team solve complex problems by considering different possible solutions. Unfortunately, this team member may be sensitive to criticism, have difficulty communicating their ideas effectively to others, or they may potentially suggest alternatives that may not be practical (Aritzeta, 2007).

# How Do Specialists Help Teams with Specific Expertise?

## *Level II (Experienced—Intermediate Game Designers)*

The Specialist can be very helpful to the team in an RPG because they have specialized knowledge and skills in a specific area that are needed by the RPG team tasked with solving complex problems. Specialist avatars can be detail oriented and focused on matters related to their unique knowledge. However, their focus on their own area of expertise may make it difficult for these team members to be flexible and adjust to unexpected situations and/ or to see the problem from alternative perspectives (Belbin & Brown, 2022).

# What Team Structure Best Fits My RPG Goals?

## *Level I (Novice Game Designers)*

For first-time RPG game designers, your first task is to choose a team type. Your team type should fit your content area and objectives. Table 2.1 offers examples of several different content-related team types with potential team purpose statements. Next, identify the typical roles associated with your selected team type. For example, if your team is a school-based leadership team, each potential member should represent an important group in the learning community (e.g., principal, assistant principal, school counselor, subject matter chairs, athletic director, technology chair, facilities manager, student representative, as well as a community representative). The ideal size for group problem-solving is usually between five and seven members as communication remains manageable and all team members can actively participate. Balanced participation is more likely in smaller groups because larger groups can turn into a situation in which a few key players dominate the conversation and disseminate information and tasks to the larger group without soliciting or engaging input from the others. If the team in your class is too large, consider creating multiple teams with duplicate roles to promote the active participation of all team members (Bonnardel & Pichot, 2020).

# How Do I Create Engaging Avatars for My RPG?

## *Level I (Novice Game Designers)*

For a team to be truly effective, the players must learn to collaborate well and value the contributions of every member. Role-Playing Games designers may want to ensure representation of varied experiences and backgrounds, including different ages, years of experience, knowledge bases, personal experiences, races, genders, disabilities, political affiliations, socioeconomic backgrounds, and educational levels common to the players on your team. We have also found that creating avatar characters with gender-neutral names and varied characteristics is important (Johnson et al., 2023). Using gender-neutral names allows game designers to assign avatars to all team members without creating distractions or discomfort related to gender. For example, if a male player is assigned a female avatar, the potential discomfort of acting like a member of the opposite sex may be needlessly distracting for the player. Using gender-neutral names can help players focus on their roles and contributions without being affected by gender-specific assumptions or biases. Incorporating realistic, multidimensional characteristics into avatar development (varied educational backgrounds, socioeconomic status, cultural backgrounds, language preferences, etc.) can help team members better understand and consider diverse perspectives when making team decisions and interacting with others (Bonnardel & Pichot, 2020). Table 2.2 offers an overview of the characteristics related to each of Belbin's roles for game designers to consider when developing game avatars.

Table 2.3 offers several examples of gender-neutral names along with potential character traits commonly found in different professional teams.

The next step is to develop a set of avatar biographies that include the characteristics and perhaps Belbin's Team Roles that you feel are appropriate for the team type and content demands of your RPG game. Appendix A shows examples of brief avatar biographies that include some of the characters and gender-neutral names we previously suggested. Although we will talk about this more in later chapters, game designers should consider ways to vary the team's perspective when assigning avatars. Consider assigning a player a role that challenges their usual comfort zone to promote diverse problem-solving perspectives (Mirliss et al., 2012). A principal may be a counselor on the leadership team, and a teacher may be

## Table 2.2 Belbin's Team Role Considerations for RPG Development

| Role | Major Category | Powers (Strengths) | Vulnerabilities (Weaknesses) |
|---|---|---|---|
| Completer-Finisher | Action Oriented | These team members in this role usually can be depended on to get things done well and on time. They pay attention to details, find and address potential concerns, and help the team maintain high professional standards. | These team members may have a hard time to delegate tasks because they want to make sure things are done correctly and according to their standards. They may also have difficulty accepting constructive feedback and be seen as critical by other members of the team. |
| Coordinator | People Oriented | These team members often have strong leadership skills and can task analyze project needs and appropriately delegate work among the team. Helping the team stay focused on their objectives and managing conflicts are additional strengths. | Given that these team members can usually recognize what needs to be done, how things might be done and who might be good to do each task, they may have a tendency to take over tasks and be seen as manipulative or miss deadlines because they are overextended. |
| Implementer | Action Oriented | These team members can assist the team by being able to convert abstract ideas and suggestions into action plans with very specific procedures. | This team member may have difficulty considering other perspectives or deviating from the way they think things should be done. They might also be resistant to new or creative ideas. |
| Monitor Evaluator | Thought Oriented | These team members are helpful to the team because they tend to be objective, analytical, and able to help others make informed decisions according to their shared goals. | This team member may not respond well to enthusiastic and idealist comments not supported by facts. They may struggle with making decisions without considering all the facts. |

*(Continued)*

**Table 2.2 (Continued)**

| Role | Major Category | Powers (Strengths) | Vulnerabilities (Weaknesses) |
|---|---|---|---|
| Plant | Thought Oriented | These team members are useful because they are creative idea generators that can help to solve complex problems. They are open to new ideas and opportunities to grow and evolve. | These team members may not recognize their ideas may be correct but not necessarily practical. They may also have difficulty with organization, recognizing and addressing important details, time constraints, and be resistant to alternative opinions. |
| Resource Investigator | People Oriented | These team members are helpful to teams in many ways. They are charismatic, information gathering people with a positive attitude that can be motivating. They are commonly outgoing and enjoy social interactions which encourage and reinforce new ideas. Typically, these team members have solid networks of support that may be useful when soliciting needed ideas or resources for the team. | These team members may become easily distracted as they are constantly looking for new opportunities to build their network and engage socially with others. This tendency may result in them neglecting ongoing tasks, losing track of priorities or failing to follow through with commitments. Their enthusiasm can sometimes lead them to make premature agreements or overlook important details. |
| Specialist | Thought Oriented | These team members are useful because they have unique expertise the team needs and focused problem-solving abilities often needed to solve specific problems or complete complex tasks. They are often independent workers who can offer useful insight analysis and innovative solutions to team challenges. | These team members may struggle to see the potential consequences of their recommendations from different perspectives as they are focused on what is needed in relation to their specialty area. They tend to be loners who might not be open to new ideas or recognize others may have useful ideas. |

| | | | |
|---|---|---|---|
| *Shaper* | Action Oriented | These team members can be competitive and motivated to help the team meet their goals. These team members are often very good at challenging the team to work through difficult and unexpected obstacles. They usually can think and adapt to changes quickly, work well under pressure, and can help teams find solutions when obstacles arise. | These team members can be potentially argumentative and impatient when their ideas are questioned. The drive to quickly resolve challenges can result in them being dismissive of others ideas and making decisions without fully considering potential consequences. |
| *Team Worker* | People Oriented | This team member is very useful because they have useful people skills and they can consider tasks and interactions from different perspectives. They are good at motivating teams, preventing conflicts, boosting confidence and team energy, and helping to encourage others to share ideas. | This person typically prioritizes collaboration and peaceful coexistence so they may avoid confrontation and be potentially too accommodating. They are not comfortable in leadership roles because they may not effectively deal with team members who are unproductive or unkind and they may ignore their own interests or needs to help others or avoid conflict. |

### Table 2.3 Gender-Neutral Names and Character Traits for RPG Development

| Names |
|---|
| • Alex |
| • Angel |
| • Avery |
| • Casey |
| • Charlie |
| • Drew |
| • Ellis |
| • Francis |
| • Harper |
| • Hollis |
| • Jamie |
| • Jesse |
| • Joe |
| • Jordan |
| • Kennedy |
| • Logan |
| • Morgan |
| • Riley |
| • Sam |
| • Taylor |
| • Xavier |

| Character Traits |
|---|
| • Accessibility needs (e.g., wheelchair user, hearing or visual impairment) |
| • Single parent vs traditional family background |
| • Older generation vs younger generation characteristics |
| • Rural versus urban background |
| • Low-income, middle-class or wealthy background |
| • Experience with mental health challenges |
| • College graduate vs non-college graduate |
| • Health concerns |
| • Cultural or religious biases |
| • Experience with disability |
| • Introvert vs extrovert personality |
| • Survivor of trauma or abuse |
| • Experienced or limited experience with technology or social media knowledge |
| • Leadership vs limited/no leadership experience |
| • Experienced or limited experience with the given content area or scenario |
| • Strong political biases |

the principal. Begin with the Belbin's roles, and later adapt them to match the specific needs of your game. Table 2.4 shows a simple (random) example of how to create player avatars with different characteristics that might mirror the roles, experiences, and potential biases common to teams in real-world teams.

Appendix B offers designers another summary of potential strengths and challenges associated with each of Belbin's Team Roles and the characteristics noted above they may want to use when developing avatar characters for RPGs.

## Game Log

*The chapter can be used as a foundational guide for understanding the background knowledge necessary to begin RPG game development. The hope is to help RPG designers begin to create an engaging game. Understanding game theory and team dynamics helps create gameplay where each role contributes effectively. Belbin's model, which categorizes roles into Action-Oriented, People-Oriented, and Thought-Oriented types, offers a framework for assigning distinct functions to game characters (Belbin, 2010; Belbin, 2022). Incorporating this approach into RPGs can help designers develop teams with a balanced mix of skills and perspectives. Utilizing Belbin's roles early in game development can help new game designers develop characters that meaningfully contribute to team success. Selecting the right team type in relationship to the content goals of your class is the most important aspect of new RPG development. We briefly discussed Belbin's nine team roles and how these potential avatar characters are unique and potentially useful to the team. If the game designer already has experience with the selected team type, they can begin by developing a core set of avatars and later adjust them to incorporate Belbin's Team Roles as needed. This was the approach we used for our game, since we knew little about team theory when we first started. We will talk about how to use AI to refine games in Chapter 6. Using AI resources to help you identify the team roles in the characters you created and subsequently using the technology to help you make revisions to your avatars can also be a useful strategy. We recommend team sizes of five to seven members to maximize opportunities for active player engagement and to integrate varied team characteristics which*

### Table 2.4 Example of Simple (Random) Avatar Bios for a Multidisciplinary Care Team

| Role | Name | Bio |
|---|---|---|
| *Certified Nurse Assistant* | Taylor Le | Taylor Le, a 39-year-old Vietnamese-American Nurse Assistant with 5 years' experience on the job. Taylor recently had an accident that resulted in a hurt back at work because they are understaffed and Taylor is a single parent who struggles to afford care for three young children. Taylor recently went back to school and often has difficulty balancing the demands of being a single parent, working full time and being an adult learner which can impact team participation and meaningful contributions to the team. |
| *Clinical Social Worker* | Riley Kim | Riley Kim, a 26-year-old African American clinical social worker with a degree in Social Work. Riley's family was homeless for a time, and Riley is a very devoted social worker and has a strong desire to do what is right for everyone regardless of what they can afford to pay. Riley works hard to manage the needs of a very busy caseload and often finds there are not enough available resources to meet her client's needs. Riley is often discouraged and frustrated in team meetings when this fact is ignored. |
| *Medical Director* | Jordan Howard | Jordan Howard, a 54-year African American doctor from a suburban background with several years of experience in the industry. While Jordan advocates for proactive health measures and useful healthcare solutions, Jordan knows resources are limited, and it is very unlikely that the team will be able to successfully accomplish things that are not clearly funded and documented in the procedures manual. Jordan is reluctant to work longer (or harder) than need be and has little tolerance for people who want to waste the team's time fighting a system that will always win. |
| *Dietitian* | Quinn Edwards | Quinn Edwards, a 58-year-old white dietitian with a degree in nutrition who has 30 years' experience and is ready to retire and start a new career as a pastor. Quinn is deeply religious and maintains an optimistic and enthusiastic attitude in meetings. Quinn is a great listener and is open to new ideas. Quinn is often creative with finding solutions to problems related to dietary advice, meal planning and motivating others to consider healthy eating choices. Unfortunately Quinn can get so excited about nutrition, the comments can be lengthy and more detailed than the team may need which could take up more time than needed for this information. |

*might impact team productivity when it makes sense for your team and content area challenges (Bonnardel & Pichot, 2020). In the next chapter, we will provide a detailed guide for setting up a new game, covering planning, designing, implementing, and evaluating learning experiences, with practical tips, checklists, and peer assessment recommendations for educators to prepare for a successful game implementation.*

# Planning, Designing, and Implementing RPG Games

## Game Master's Prelude

*The last chapter guided you through the first stages of game design. Hopefully, you have selected a course to implement the game along with a relevant team type that aligns with the key constructs of your curriculum. After making these important decisions, core avatar characters have been developed for each of the team roles that you will later assign to student players. The next step involves developing a game framework that can be integrated into your class throughout the semester. When I began my journey into gamification, the goal was to create an experience that would engage students with a variety of professional experiences and help them develop collaborative problem-solving skills needed to effectively apply key concepts from the class in a meaningful way to achieve a common goal. I selected a team type, identified team roles commonly associated with the team type, and then developed character avatars and brief biographies based on my twenty-plus years of experience engaging with similar teams in public schools. As I stated in the last chapter, my first RPG game was for an assessment class. I designed it around what I believed were the most critical outcomes for my students — learning to interpret assessment scores accurately and to use those scores collaboratively with team members so that the data became both meaningful and actionable. Choosing an IEP (Individualized Education Program) team as the focal point of the game provided a structured way to guide students through the branching scenario "problem" that the team needed to solve. My previous K-12 SPED Teacher experiences with IEP teams and their processes proved invaluable in this context. Careful consideration was given to the time teams would need to engage with one another to solve the problem, and the game goals were aligned with the course objectives to ensure that the game was not merely an engaging activity but a powerful educational tool. In this chapter, I will walk you through a potential sequence of steps to design a RPG framework or structure to complement what students are learning that you can readily integrate into your class over the course of a semester. Of course, the initial RPG game development will take some time to develop, but you can always start with a simple game and elaborate more* as your game progresses if desired. Once the game is planned and implemented into your course, we found it very easy to copy the first game and paste it into another course. After you copy the game framework into a subsequent course, you can use the same team of avatars (of course you can tweak the biographies a bit as desired) and adjust the team round expectations according to the learning standards and goals associated with the new class. I think you will find (as we did) that the time put into game development initially is a solid investment in your program because a "good game" can have immediate and positive impact on students (even though my first attempt at game design included several design flaws). Fortunately, the student players didn't even notice . . . they thought it was part of the game design! The goal of this chapter is to help you to design your own immersive and meaningful game experience. By the end of this chapter, you will have the information you need to create a foundational game framework that can be integrated into your course. Implementing this framework will help your students by enhancing their engagement, promoting effective collaboration with peers, and facilitating the practical application of concepts, all of which contribute to a richer learning experience for you and your students.

## What Are My Next Steps?

### *Level I (Novice Game Designers)*

Developing an RPG in a college course begins with the same foundational steps typically used to develop any course or instructional unit. The game designer must first consider the purpose of the course, the curriculum standards that need to be integrated, and the specific skills that should be mastered by learners (Sheldon, 2020). I caution new game designers to carefully consider this aspect of the game. I have been in meetings with professors asking for advice on how to generate a useful grade rubric for a given assignment. When questioned, "What would a good example of this assignment look like to you?" Not all instructors have a clear response to this question. I have heard more than one professor respond, "That is a very good question. I am not sure." The earlier chapters reinforce how GBL can help game designers to create more engaging and effective learning environments (Majuri et al., 2018). In Chapter 2, you were asked to identify a potential team type that might be appropriate for your players to become a part of in order to implement new learning in a real-world scenario to help transition students from being passive recipients of information to active participants who apply their newly learned content knowledge from your courses in realistic scenarios (Costello, 2017). Identifying clear long- and short-term learning goals is the first step. *Short-term Goals (SGT)* in an RPG scenario function like quests or missions. Specific and immediate, these objectives are meant to be completed within a single game round or session. Often focused on discrete tasks or challenges, short-term goals might involve analyzing data, solving a problem, or completing an action based on newly learned content. The Short-Term Goals represent the desired outcome or objective for that particular round. For example, in the first game session or round, the Short-Term Goals may be for players to introduce themselves and discuss the issues related to a real-world problem which would require them to utilize new learning with collaborative skills to solve a problem. While we will talk more about implementing the game into your class throughout the semester, let's stay focused on long- and short-term goal mastery and the *tasks* (steps or activities) that your player teams must complete to achieve the Short-Term Goals. The game rounds or game sessions are the team opportunities to interact with one another and work cooperatively to achieve the given tasks. While there is no set number of game rounds for players, remember your game should complement what you are already teaching. The game should not take over the course or become distracting for the players and the game designer. When designing games, it is important for game designers to consider human nature and the potential for players to be apprehensive about doing something for the first time. For example, in Round 1, the task might be for players to role-play as avatars while introducing themselves and sharing their avatar's unique perspectives (as well as the players own experiences) into the round tasks (Schabas, 2023; Zeng et al., 2020). The Short-Term Goals of the round would be to become familiar with their avatar's background, motivations and responsibilities on the team as they introduce themselves to the team, learn about the other team players and consider the tasks they will be assigned to complete over the course of the game. In a professional team scenario, such goals could include presenting findings, gathering information, or proposing initial solutions to a real-world issue. By providing players with regular feedback and a sense of progression, short-term goals keep them engaged and focused as they advance through the game (Saxena & Mishra, 2021). *Long-term game goals* in an RPG setting represent the broader big picture goals that players work toward over the entire course of the game or several rounds. For example, a Short-Term Goal of a marketing team might be to survey existing clients to determine what social media they use or what internet search terms they used to find information about the program. The team's Long-Term Goals might integrate the key words they generated from the surveys of clients into their business website to increase brand awareness and make changes to increase traffic to their website (Kapp, 2012; Schabas, 2023; Zeng et al., 2020).

# How Do I Turn Course Objectives into Game Tasks?

## *Level I (Novice Game Designers)*

Once you have identified the long-term and short-term goals of your game. Take some time to outline the tasks you would like teams to complete throughout the game. What are the most important objectives or skills students need to be able to understand and be able to demonstrate by the time they finish your class? How will the skills you are teaching them be used in the real world? Once those skills are identified, task analyze each potential skill by determining exactly what teams would need to accomplish to demonstrate they understand the practical application of the new learning? In the context of RPG design, *task analysis* involves breaking down the various activities, skills required of novice players to effectively complete given tasks in the game rounds (Zeng et al., 2020). We will talk more about how to determine the number of game rounds later in the chapter, but game designers must remember to consider the task analysis of the skills you would like teams to demonstrate from a novice player's perspective (Laine & Lindberg, 2020). In a typical semester, which of the skills you teach are most challenging for students? Which of the skills are the most potentially meaningful for learners in the real world? For example, in my initial game, the Short-Term Goals was for teams to accurately interpret standardized test results, and the Long-Term Goals were for them to effectively communicate these findings to others and work collaboratively with a team to identify how the assessment results might positively impact services and student outcomes. While AI tools like ChatGPT, Gemini, etc. were not available when we were developing and enhancing our game, these tools can be potentially valuable "thinking partners" for game designers who to develop goals and game scenarios.

When developing your first RPG, it is important to understand that the game should be a continuously evolving experience because everything changes. In the real-world game of life, situations are constantly evolving, and learning to work collaboratively with others to find new ways to navigate new challenges is key to success. The initial scenario of your game will not be perfect, and that is okay because your players (like mine) will probably not even notice. They may even think you designed the game with flaws and hiccups on purpose. Begin with a simple frame and refine it as your student players work through the tasks and offer feedback on what they learned. Another recommended strategy we will discuss later is seeking feedback from players about what they learned and how the game might be improved as part of the game expectations. Adjustments can then be made based on game master observations, player interactions, and feedback (Roungas et al., 2019; van Gaalen et al., 2021; Sanchez et al., 2020). In preceding chapters, game designers were advised to begin game development by identifying a team type and defining roles within that team, using Belbin's Team Roles and multidimensional characteristics to develop game avatars and bios (Akhilesh, 2014). Once learning goals have been established, attention should shift to designing engaging and educational game scenarios. The scenarios should challenge student players to use, enhance and refine their collaboration skills as they apply the course content to solve complex problems (Bonnardel & Pichot, 2020). Table 3.1 offers guidance to new game designers on how to design an RPG aligned with short-term and long-term objectives in an authentic, content-relevant scenario.

# How Can I Develop an Initial Game Frame?

## Level I (Novice Game Designers)

An RPG game *frame* is a detailed scenario that includes the narrative, setting the rules teams will follow, expectations of players, and the challenges players will address as they progress through the game (Roungas et al., 2019). For a new game designer, creating a game frame that mirrors real-life application of your course content is the easiest place to start. The storyline, the physical and social environment where the teams and players interact, the team roles, and their tasks can and should be related to potential real-life challenges of your selected team type as they are tasked with in potential real-world situations to provide opportunities for teams to engage in collaborative interactions and problem-solving (Toda et al., 2023). Players will interact with the scenario

**Table 3.1 Designing RPGs That Connect Play with Purpose**

| Potential Program Area or Course Title | Overall Game Objective | Short-Term Objectives | Long-Term Objectives | Real-World Applications |
|---|---|---|---|---|
| Introduction to Marketing | Student players work as a team to design a new product that meets market demands and standards within given production costs and distribution channels. | Student players collaborate to identify two key market trends and one identified customer need. | Student players collaborate, consider all perspectives, and identify relevant course content needed to create a plan to launch their product within given time constraints. | Players demonstrate understanding of the importance of collaboration and team decision-making skills, market trends, and customer needs when planning product launch. |
| Interpersonal Communication | Student players work as a team to manage a workplace conflict in which communication barriers have led to misunderstandings. | Student players collaborate to identify communication breakdowns, consider different perspectives, and identify strategies to resolve the issue. | Student players collaborate and develop a conflict resolution strategy to effectively manage the conflict along with follow-up measures to ensure the plan is effective. | Players demonstrate understanding of the importance of collaboration and considering different perspectives for effective communication and conflict resolution in professional environments. |

| | | | | |
|---|---|---|---|---|
| Classroom Management | Student players work as a team to create a school-wide Positive Behavior Intervention and Support Plan for their middle school. | Collaborate to identify common problem behaviors of their students and effective (and ineffective) interventions often used by faculty. | Student players collaborate and design a school-wide plan that teachers, students, and families contribute to and support to maximize student achievement and minimize behavioral disruptions. | Players demonstrate understanding of the benefits of collaborative efforts and group "buy in" when developing and implementing a school-wide behavior plan. |
| Event Management | Student players work as a team to plan a large-scale event based on given customer needs and constraints. | Collaborate to create an event proposal that reflects given customer needs and constraints, considers ideas from the team. The event proposal must include venue selection, a budget, realistic timeline, and clear connections to customer choices. | Student players collaborate and assess the customer's feedback to their proposal and work together to incorporate that information into a revised proposal. | Players demonstrate understanding of the benefits of collaborative efforts in event planning along with the multifaceted details and considerations that go along with planning a large-scale event. |

through their assigned avatar characters, and they will help to make team decisions that influence the game's outcomes (Calvert et al., 2019). As is the case in real life, player choices and team decisions have consequences that can potentially have multiple outcomes. Game designers must remember that player motivation and participation is enhanced when the game tasks are obviously and consistently connected to the skills and knowledge players have learned in the course (Zhan et al., 2024).

Now that you have selected your team type, Short-Term Goals, Long-Term Goals, relevant curriculum objectives, identified the skills, and you have at least a broad idea about what you want the teams to do, it is time to start developing your team avatars. Of course, you can integrate the characteristics of Belbin's Team Roles into the avatar development from the beginning or you can just brainstorm the avatar bios based on your own experiences in such teams. If you are developing avatar bios based on your own experiences, consider the varied member roles on the team along with the personality types and different experiences that may be relevant to team effectiveness outlined in Table 2.1 and Appendix B (Belbin & Brown, 2022). While we will talk more about how to generate these bios using AI in Chapter 6, there are some example bios in Appendix A you may want to use initially and adjust as appropriate according to your game's content needs (Aranzabal et al., 2022; Bell, 2018). Remember that one of the most beneficial aspects of the game is that players are often asked to assume a role they may be unfamiliar with and to consider ways to meaningfully contribute to the team from a different perspective (Bonnardel & Pichot, 2020). The next chapter will explore game mechanics in detail. When designing your first game, start with manageable tasks for the team to ensure a smooth introduction to the game design process. Integrate your own background and experiences related to the team and content-related challenges to create a more authentic game and be sure to offer teams challenging (but attainable) opportunities to problem solve and collaborate in order to complete assigned tasks within the game round timelines (Adare-Tasiwoopa ápi & Silva, 2024; Irwanto et al., 2023).The goal of the book is to help instructors or new game designers in higher education (regardless of what content you teach) understand how to develop a basic game frame to improve their instructional delivery and better meet the needs of their adult learners (Daul, 2014). We have created numerous tables, charts, and appendices with examples and suggestions to help you visualize how a game can be developed or even use some of the examples that you can tweak according to your needs. However, we will also add some examples into the narrative to demonstrate how concepts may be applied in different programs. In a business education course, student players on an Investment Management Team might be asked to work collaboratively to create or manage a marketing budget for a new product. The game scenario might include examining or generating a limited budget and developing performance indicators. In this game frame, the student players would be required to use what they have learned in class related to budgeting, marketing, and so on. In a course about Healthcare Administration an RPG game round might require student players to be part of a Medical Treatment Teams (doctors, nurses, therapists, and technicians) whose task is to develop an appropriate rehabilitation plan for a client with dementia and aggression who has recently undergone major surgery. The round tasks could include reviewing a fictitious medical history, progress reports, and being able to skillfully coordinate available resources to generate a realistic and individualized rehabilitation plan. The game designer might consider including some frequently encountered real-life obstacles into the game activities (e.g., delays in obtaining necessary approvals for treatments, limited access to medical equipment, understaffing or policies that complicate the coordination of care). Role-Playing Games require practical application of newly learned information as well as strategic problem-solving, effective communication and productive team collaboration (Mirliss et al., 2012).

## How Can I Add an RPG into My Existing Course?

### *Level I (Novice Game Designers)*

Designing an RPG may seem like a huge task at first, and my first thought for advice on this aspect of game development is to remember what my favorite HS English teacher (Ms. Brown) used to ask us when we started a multifaceted task. *"How do you eat an elephant? One bite at a time, y'all"*. Integrating an RPG into an existing course does require you to consider many factors to be sure the game enhances the learning experience without overwhelming the players or the instructor (Romera & Ustart, 2013). The timing and frequency of the game rounds must be thoughtfully integrated into the course calendar in a manner that aligns with the presentation in your course. The *backward chaining method* is a useful way to set up the game. The backward chaining method begins with defining the final goals or outcomes you want players to achieve and then works backward to identify the intermediate steps and tasks needed to reach those goals (Björk & Zagal, 2018). Planning out the game milestones in reverse order can help as you plan your game because you are able to keep the end goals in mind as you move the teams through the game rounds. Start by identifying and then defining the specific skills you want your student players to develop and be able to use and demonstrate by the end of the game. The skills might include application of course content as well as any related collaboration, critical thinking, problem-solving your players and teams may need to be able to use in order to achieve the goals (Janssen et al., 2018). Visualize then define clearly what success looks like in the game for individuals as well as teams. How will they demonstrate the learning (game round) goals? How will you know they met the goals (Campillo-Ferrer et al., 2020)? After you have identified the goals, then think about where your learners are in relation to the content knowledge and professional skills they are likely to have at the beginning of the game. Consider their backgrounds as well as your typical experiences with your student players. Identify the prior knowledge and resources they will need to complete the task (e.g., reports, presentations, examples, forms, agendas, background information, etc.). With these outcomes in mind, estimate the time required to achieve these goals and the number of game sessions needed. Consider mapping out the course structure in detail, possibly using a spreadsheet, to effectively integrate RPG elements. A spreadsheet calendar might include the number of weeks in the course, current assignments, assessments that are due each week and important academic or skill milestones students should be able to demonstrate throughout the course. The next step would be to consider ways the game assignments could be added to or potentially replace existing assignments or assessments as appropriate. Understanding which assessments are already in place and when significant content should be covered is important when choosing when and how to add in the game to the course. In my eight-week minimester courses, I integrated three game rounds (weeks, 3, 5, and 7). The first round in my games is an introduction type round in which the players introduce their avatar personalities, experiences and skills to the team and they learn about the overall game tasks and review the material and resources they will need to complete tasks throughout the game. They also learn how they will be assessed, and so on. The second round is the action round in my game in which players work cooperatively with their team to complete the tasks or quests they must complete in the round. The third round is a reflective round in which the players are asked to think about what they learned about applying the content and working as part of a team from a different perspective. All the rounds are recorded and shared with the team so they can reflect on their experience and individual contributions to the team. However, the number of rounds can vary based on the course structure and content. In a sixteen-week semester, the game designer may integrate the game into weeks six, ten, and fourteen or they may choose to add in an additional game round. You may want to start simply and then elaborate on the game as you think it is appropriate later. Decide when it makes the most sense to introduce game sessions, considering student workload to ensure that students can engage with the game effectively while balancing their other academic responsibilities (Barron, 2024; Camilleri, 2023). To ensure students had enough time to digest and then apply the new learning, the first round of our game was an introduction round, the next round was strategically placed around the middle of the course to ensure they had been exposed to the concepts they would be using and the last round was near the end of the course which was mainly reflective in nature. Realistically estimate the time required for each game round task, including any prep and follow-up tasks. In a traditional sixteen-week semester, consider how it might be best for your course to schedule game sessions at regular intervals, such as every three or four weeks, to align with key course content-related milestones. For shorter minimesters, consider planning for more frequent sessions while ensuring they fit well within the course schedule. Integrate these game sessions with existing course components. Consider replacing or complementing weekly discussions or assessments with game sessions to seamlessly incorporate them into the learning process without adding extra workload or major course revisions (Daniau, 2016). New game designers might consider sharing information about the game early to provide student players with information about the game, its purpose, and how it benefits them as learners in the academic and real world. Explain how the game connects to your institution or industry's professional standards, mission, or value statements (Foster & Shah, 2020). The timing of the game rounds and spacing between game sessions is important to help players and teams adequately prepare for the game, collaborate with team members between sessions if needed and subsequently integrate player and team reflections on their experiences (Franco & DeLuca, 2019; Jaramillo-Mediavilla et al., 2024). If you are an instructor—who also serves as game designer and game master, you will naturally identify areas for improvement and recognize how to improve the game as your students work through the process (Toda et al., 2023).

Role-Playing Games game rounds must be directly aligned with the academic content of the course. For new game designers, each game round scenario must be linked to a content-related dilemma that requires players to collaborate and use their knowledge to find solutions. For example, in a business management course, a scenario could involve teams working together to rescue a failing company, applying principles of finance, marketing, and organizational leadership learned in the course. In a nursing program, players might work in teams to develop a care plan for a patient with complex medical needs, integrating knowledge of patient care, community resources, and communication. In a law course, players could be tasked with solving a legal dispute, requiring them to research case law, develop arguments, and negotiate settlements as they tap into and utilize their understanding of legal principles. In each example, RPG scenarios can support critical thinking, ethical reasoning, teamwork, and problem-solving. Players receive immediate feedback on their decisions, helping them reflect on what they know, tap into their experiences and build skills needed to better address real-world challenges in their discipline (Laine & Lindberg, 2020). In a school leadership team round, players might assume roles like principals, school counselors, teacher leaders, and district administrators, working together to tackle challenges such as policy implementation or crisis management. The RPG requires effective collaboration, as players must balance diverse viewpoints and make strategic decisions that influence the educational environment. Through this RPG, team players showcase their leadership skills, conflict resolution abilities, and strategic thinking, revealing how well they function within a team and handle complex, real-world challenges (Lee, 2021). Interactive RPG scenarios can promote ongoing reflection and professional development. By engaging with these scenarios, instructors who also serve as game masters can gain deeper insights into students' strengths and identify areas needing improvement which can help the course designer to make needed adjustments to the game or content presentation to better support student players (Kim & Maloney, 2020). Game rounds must be structured to require students to demonstrate their understanding of new knowledge in simulated environments that reflect real-life situations that mirror actual professional contexts (Franco & DeLuca, 2019). In a medical ethics related game scenario, player avatars (e.g., physicians, nurses, and social workers) might need to consider and resolve a situation related to an ethical dilemma in their field. Player avatars would need to use their skills in communication and conflict resolution as they apply the theoretical knowledge learned in the course to a practical situation. In a school leadership team, player avatars (e.g., principal, counselor, teacher, or district administrator, parent representative) might be tasked to work cooperatively to review and revise the school's crisis management plan after a school shooting incident). The RPG scenarios help student players to consider a realistic situation from a different point of view and then work successfully with a team of people with different experiences, biases and priorities to negotiate solutions, and make strategic decisions. In all of these examples the interactive nature of the RPGs can become a powerful mechanism to assess students' performance and offer *immediate feedback* and opportunities for reflective learning (Jaramillo-Mediavilla et al., 2024; Kapp, 2012). Table 3.2 offers an example guide of a potential process for planning, designing, implementing and assessing a new RPG. Table 3.3 shows how the game can be implemented across synchronous, asynchronous, hybrid, and vignette formats in an eight week minimester timeline.

# How Can I Keep Players Focused and Involved?

## Level I (Novice Game Designers)

The *game master* plays an important role in RPG design and implementation as the game master is tasked with building teams, assigning avatars, and participating in each of the game rounds to facilitate the flow of events and guiding players through the round tasks as needed. Balancing structure with flexibility is very important when designing new games (Plass et al., 2020). Often, the game master is the instructor who designed the game and teaches the class. However, this role can also be assumed by an instructor who is teaching a class designed by someone else or an adjunct instructor, graduate teaching assistant, and so on. I will elaborate on this more later, but it is important for game designers to remember that the game masters who will be facilitating the games will need detailed guidelines to effectively assist players through the process. In advanced games, student players might take on the game master role, or the game master might even become one of the game avatars.

While the game designer is responsible for setting up the RPG scenario, including establishing the game environment, defining challenges, and outlining objectives based on learning goals and scenario requirements, during gameplay, the game master will be tasked with setting the dates/times for the rounds, assigning avatars, facilitating game round task completion, and

### Table 3.2 Guide to Designing Educational RPGs

| | Planning The Game |
|---|---|
| Identify Course | Identify a course that includes content and/or skills students can apply in real-life scenarios. |
| Define Educational Objectives | Identify short-term and long-term learning goals for the game including skills players are expected to demonstrate, such as analytical thinking, teamwork, or practical application of course content. |
| Identify Content-Relevant Game Tasks | Decide and then define the specific problems or challenges your student teams should be able to solve by the end of the game. The tasks should directly relate to course content, requiring players to apply their knowledge collaboratively and reflect real-world scenarios. |
| Develop Game Objectives | Identify game objectives that can be reasonably completed given the needed and available resources, time constraints and demands on your students. Be sure the objectives are challenging but not overwhelming and students clearly understand the benefit of engaging with the game. |
| Identify Game Structure and Sessions | Identify how and when to implement the game into the course (maybe an excel sheet of how many weeks are in the class, and when existing assignments are due). Given what students must complete (in addition to the game tasks), identify how many game sessions can be realistically added to complement and enhance instruction. Consider when students will have access to needed content and skill development. Plan the overall structure of the game, considering the number of sessions and their duration. Include a first-round introductory session to familiarize players with their avatars and main tasks, along with a final reflection session to assess learning. Establish the length of each game round session and goals of each game round. |
| | **Designing the Game** |
| Identity Appropriate Team Type | Choose a content-related team type related to potential professional or real-life teams students might interact with or apply content-related skills. |

*(Continued)*

**Table 3.2 (Continued)**

| | **Designing the Game** |
|---|---|
| Develop Teams and Avatars | Consider Belbin's Team Roles to develop a realistic team with different personality types, backgrounds, experiences, ages, genders, educational levels, beliefs, and so on, that are commonly represented in professional teams. Create detailed avatars with gender-neutral names and typical bios for players based on identified personality types. Include common challenges these types face, which will help prepare players for teamwork and allow them to connect with their roles during gameplay. Link avatar descriptions, and so on, to game rules and expectations in several places so players are familiar with team types. While this may be a bit time consuming at first, once the avatars are created, they can be reused to address different game scenarios in future games and/or different classes. |
| Design Game Mechanics and Elements | Consider adding in game mechanics as desired (some of these will be added naturally and others you can clarify and define later). Align mechanics with educational objectives and integrate milestones for player progression. |
| Prep Game Master and Gather Necessary Game Materials | Identify and prepare all content materials, resources, and background knowledge needed for the game master to understand the purpose of the entire game, how the game is set up, what resources are needed by the game master and players, how game rounds should be structured, how players will be assessed, and what the game master's role is in the game as well as how and when the game master may need to intervene in the game. Consider developing a game master manual that game masters can use to prepare for the game. Include a way for the game master to communicate with the game designer if needed if they have any questions or suggestions for improvement. |
| Establish Rules and Procedures | Develop comprehensive rules and procedures for the game, explaining what players need to do before, during, and after the game, how they will be assessed and how they should ask for help. Post individual and group norms. Clearly define the game master's role in supporting players and facilitating the game experience. |
| | **Game Implementation** |
| Integrate Game into Course Structure | Plan how to incorporate the RPG into the course syllabus, clearly explain the game's personal, professional and content-related benefits (purpose, long- and short-term goals, etc.) to students. Align the RPG with major assignments and milestones to reinforce its relevance in the educational context. "Sell" the game at the beginning of the class (several weeks before the game starts so they can prepare and know what to do, how to do it, when the game sessions will be held). |

*(Continued)*

**Table 3.2 (Continued)**

| | **Game Implementation** |
|---|---|
| Plan Game Round Tasks | Identify the game round quests—what the teams will be expected to do during each game round. Create a detailed agenda with time estimates for game task progression. The agenda should include specific tasks, avatar interactions, and suggestions for minimum responses. All avatar experiences and perspectives should be integrated into the agenda to ensure everyone has an opportunity to share and respond. The agenda should be VERY detailed so each player knows exactly what they will be responsible for doing and when they will need to do it during the game. Share the agenda with the players before game rounds so they can prepare along with their avatar bios. |
| Assign Avatars/Teams | Assign individual avatars and share avatar bios. Be sure players understand what they need to do and how to use improv skills to interact with other players in the game. |
| Explain Game Mechanics and Elements | Provide a comprehensive explanation of the game mechanics and elements at the beginning of the course (in writing and/or video review). Be sure players understand how to proceed through the game, what resources are available, how they will be assessed and how they can successfully progress through the game round sessions. |
| | **Game Assessment and Continuous Improvement** |
| Identify Assessment Method and Procedures | Outline methods for assessing the effectiveness of the game in meeting educational objectives. Develop a clear assessment strategy for player experiences with specific methods (such as grade rubrics) to evaluate how well players and teams met game objectives. Be sure the players have access to the assessment methods prior to game rounds so they know how to prepare. |
| Collect Feedback and Refine Game | Keep records of the entire game revision needs based on issues that may occur during the game and/or feedback from players in their reflections. Consider adding questions about game implementation, mechanics, and procedures to the self-reflection questions players fill out at the end of a round or at the end of the game. The provided feedback can be used to improve the game. |

Table 3.3 Implementing Game-Based Learning Across Synchronous, Asynchronous, Hybrid, and Vignette Formats

| Timeline | Synchronous Game | Asynchronous Game | Hybrid Game | Game Vignettes |
| --- | --- | --- | --- | --- |
| Definition | Players are assigned avatar characters and placed on collaborative teams to address a content-related problem; all players are present during the game rounds in person or online via video meeting. | Players are assigned avatar characters and placed on collaborative teams to address a content related problem; players engage with the game asynchronously prior to each game round as scheduled by the game master. | Players are assigned avatar characters and placed on collaborative teams to address a content related problem; players have a choice to engage synchronously or asynchronously on/before each game as scheduled by the game master. | Players are assigned avatar characters and placed on collaborative teams to address a content related problem; players review materials and engage with the game in traditional discussion forums via video clips or written responses asynchronously on/before each game as scheduled by the game master. |
| Week 1 | Intro to Game Project; students share related background and game preferences via game survey the first week of class. | Intro to Game Project; students share related background and game preferences via game survey the first week of class. | Intro to Game Project; students share related background and game preferences via game survey the first week of class. | Students Intro to Game; students share related background the first week of class. |
| Week 2 | Game Master reviews Survey; Sets Up Teams/Logistics; Students notified via class announcement; Players review avatar bios, game tasks, begin crafting avatar responses and contributions. | Game Master reviews Survey; Sets Up Teams/Logistics; Students notified via class announcement; Players review avatar bios, game tasks, begin crafting avatar responses and contributions. | Game Master reviews Survey; Sets Up Teams/Logistics; Students notified via class announcement; Players review avatar bios, game tasks, begin crafting avatar responses and contributions. | Game Master reviews Survey; Sets Up Teams/Logistics; Students notified via class announcement; Players review avatar bios, game tasks, begin crafting avatar responses and contributions. |

(*Continued*)

**Table 3.3 (Continued)**

| Timeline | Synchronous Game | Asynchronous Game | Hybrid Game | Game Vignettes |
|---|---|---|---|---|
| Week 3 | Game Round 1; All players meet synchronously and follow the game round agenda to work through team tasks by the end of the game round. | Game Round 1; All players submit video or written avatar contribution to team; all players review avatar contributions and use that information to prepare for the next round. | Game Round 1; Asynchronous players submit a written or video avatar contribution. Synchronous players review these during their live meeting and use them to guide discussion. Meeting minutes are recorded and shared with asynchronous players to prepare for the next round. | Game Round 1; All players access the game vignette, problem, and materials in the shared discussion forum. Players engage fully asynchronously by (1) posting their avatar's initial response by the first deadline, (2) responding to at least one other player's post, and (3) replying to someone who responded to them. All contributions remain visible so players can build on one another's ideas and prepare for the next round. |
| Week 4 | All players complete the post-round reflection of the game and prepare for the next round. | All players complete the post-round reflection of the game and prepare for the next round. | All players complete the post-round reflection of the game and prepare for the next round. | All players complete the post round reflection of the game and prepare for the next round. |
| Week 5 | All players review the discussion from Round 1, read the new game vignette and tasks for Round 2, and prepare their next avatar-based contributions. | All players review the discussion from Round 1, read the new game vignette and tasks for Round 2, and prepare their next avatar-based contributions. | All players review the discussion from Round 1, read the new game vignette and tasks for Round 2, and prepare their next avatar-based contributions. | All players review the discussion from Round 1, read the new game vignette and tasks for Round 2, and prepare their next avatar-based contributions. |

| Week | | | | |
|---|---|---|---|---|
| Week 6 | Game Round 2; All players meet synchronously and follow the game round agenda to work through team tasks by the end of the game round. | Game Round 2; All players submit video or written avatar contribution to team; all players review avatar contributions and use that information to prepare for the next round. | Game Round 2; Asynchronous players submit a written or video avatar contribution. Synchronous players review these during their live meeting and use them to guide discussion. Meeting minutes are recorded and shared with asynchronous players to prepare for the next round. | Game Round 2; All players access the game vignette, problem, and materials in the shared discussion forum. Players engage fully asynchronously by (1) posting their avatar's initial response by the first deadline, (2) responding to at least one other player's post, and (3) replying to someone who responded to them. All contributions remain visible so players can build on one another's ideas and prepare for the next round. |
| Week 7 | All players complete the post-round reflection of the game and prepare for the next round. | All players complete the post-round reflection of the game and prepare for the next round. | All players complete the post-round reflection of the game and prepare for the next round. | All players complete the post round reflection of the game and prepare for the next round. |
| Week 8 | Round 3: All players meet synchronously; reflect on the effectiveness of the collaborative problem-solving process; shares what they learned about applying course content in practice and/or about working collaboratively; discuss changes to improve future collaboration or outcomes | Round 3: All players submit video or written avatar contribution to team; reflect on the effectiveness of the collaborative problem-solving process; shares what they learned about applying course content in practice and/or about working collaboratively; discuss changes to improve future collaboration or outcomes | Round 3: Asynchronous players submit a written or video avatar contribution; reflect on the effectiveness of the collaborative problem-solving process; shares what they learned about applying course content in practice and/or about working collaboratively; discuss changes to improve future collaboration or outcomes | Round 3: All players access the game vignette via asynchronous discussion forum; reflect on the effectiveness of the collaborative problem-solving process; shares what they learned about applying course content in practice and/or about working collaboratively; discuss changes to improve future collaboration or outcomes |

supporting players and teams as they navigate their tasks (Fraguas-Sánchez et al., 2022). Feedback from the game master during and after each round helps players reflect on their performance and evaluate their impact on the team. While the game master remains in the background unless needed during the game rounds, they may also be needed to prompt players to apply their knowledge and skills using from the avatars' bios and provided resources and also to provide positive and constructive reinforcement to help players feel comfortable in their new roles. To effectively support player development and ensure that collaborative problem-solving is grounded in evidence-based practices, the game master must be familiar with the course content as they work behind the scenes to enhance the game experience (Dorożyński & Dorożyńska, 2022). So, if you are a game designer who is creating a game in an LMS that can be copied and shared with other instructors, please be sure to take some time after your game is developed to write down what subsequent game masters may need to know about the game purpose, setup, expectations, timeline, and so on, to be able to facilitate an effective game meaningfully support the players through the game.

During gameplay, the game master facilitates interactions, offering guidance and support as needed to help players navigate through their tasks effectively as needed (Fraguas-Sánchez et al., 2022). After each round, the game master can offer feedback to players, encouraging them to reflect on their performance and evaluate their impact on the team. In online (Zoom-type) game rounds, game masters can utilize the chat function to offer reinforcement, remind players of key aspects of the game scenario, make character suggestions, provide information that is not in the scenario, or answer questions the team has about their given tasks. Managing breakout rooms is another effective strategy, as the game master can assign players to these rooms for focused discussions on specific tasks to give smaller groups on a team an opportunity for collaborative problem-solving while minimizing direct supervision. Sharing visuals or documents via screen sharing can help to make sure all players have equal access to important information, such as maps, clues, or game rules, which can keep the team on task and working toward meeting round objectives. Using online polling tools can help the game master to gather player opinions or decisions on organized decision-making or other important game moments. Facilitating debriefings after game rounds can help the game master to get a better understanding of what occurred from the player's perspective and help them to more effectively provide constructive feedback and discuss strategies, helping players reflect on their actions without disrupting the live game flow (Sanchez et al., 2020). When facilitating in-person game rounds, the game master can use visual aids such as smart boards, whiteboards, flip charts, or physical props to keep the game flow moving forward. An effective game master can help to keep players visually oriented and informed while avoiding verbal interruptions. By circulating around the room, the game master can offer support and answer questions discreetly, assisting players as needed while remaining unobtrusive (Dorożyński & Dorożyńska, 2022).

## How Can I Assess Student Skills Effectively?

### *Level I (Novice Game Designers)*

Although we will touch more on how to assess players in Chapter 5, it is important to note that individual and group assessment can be naturally integrated into the game rounds in both an instructor and player friendly way. Reflecting on my own experiences as a learner, I sincerely appreciated it when I knew what I was supposed to do, how to do it and how I would be graded. As an instructor, course designer, and game master, I think it is important to be clear about this to new gamers (especially since they are likely to be nervous at first). For each of my game rounds, I include a post-round self-reflection form in which the player responds to key round milestones related to their practice with specific examples of how and when their avatar meaningfully contributed to the team in the round. Players can reference the game round video when needed to assess themselves, their team, and so on. The point rubric for the round is aligned with the player reflection form, so players know exactly what they must do or demonstrate to earn full points in each aspect of the rubric. As an instructor, all I need to do is review what the player shares on their avatar along with my observations of what happened in the round. While this is not a perfect system, it is more objective when the instructor considers the player's self-assessment along with their own observations when assigning scores. In addition, many LMS programs allow the instructor to develop a rubric within the gradebook with preassigned points for each aspect to make grading very easy (Daniau, 2016). When using the game as an assessment tool, plan the frequency of sessions to align with grading requirements and ensure a fair evaluation of student progress, gain insights into player strengths and identify areas needing improvement (Kim & Maloney, 2020). Table 3.4 is an example rubric for guiding players and assessing individual performance.

**Table 3.4 Example Self-Assessment Rubric for RPG Game Progress**

| Category | Highest Level (20 pts) | High Level (15–19 pts) | Moderate Level (10–14 pts) | Low Level (6–9 pts) | Lowest Level (0–5 pts) | (Examples) |
|---|---|---|---|---|---|---|
| *Avatar Connections* | Exceptionally well-developed Avatar interactions with strong connections to avatar bio. | Well-developed Avatar interactions have good connections to avatar bio. | Adequate Avatar interactions somewhat connect to avatar bio. | Inconsistent Avatar interactions minimal connections to avatar bio. | Poor storytelling; lacks coherence or connections to avatar bio. | |
| *Game Thinking* | Skilful application of content applications that assist the team with understanding or addressing game round team concerns. | Good demonstration of understanding content but lacks meaningful connection to understanding and addressing application of content in the game round. | Basic understanding; of content application applies concepts with limited success. | Minimal understanding; of content application attempts are often incorrect or irrelevant. | No effort to apply content concepts; lacks understanding. | |
| *Analysis and Strategic Problem-Solving* | Highly effective analysis of content and/or appropriate strategies help the team to problem solve and complete game tasks. | Effective analysis of content and/or appropriate strategies to help the team solve and complete game tasks. | Moderate analysis of content and/or strategies; some success but often lacks coherence. | Limited strategies; poor implementation and inconsistent problem-solving. | No effective strategies; little to no attempt to address challenges. | |

| | | | | | |
|---|---|---|---|---|---|
| **Communication and Team Dynamics** | Excellent communication and collaboration; actively contributes to team goals and supports others effectively. | Good communication; provides helpful input and contributes to team efforts. | Inconsistent communication; occasionally contributes to the team. | Poor communication; rarely contributes to team goals. | No communication or teamwork; completely disengaged. |
| **Player Engagement (Participation)** | Highly engaged; consistently active, enthusiastic, and motivated. Always participates and contributes meaningfully. | Moderately engaged; participates regularly with some enthusiasm and motivation. | Sporadic engagement; participates occasionally but without enthusiasm. | Rare engagement; minimal participation and enthusiasm. | Completely disengaged; no participation. |
| **Creativity and Adaptability** | Highly creative and adaptable; demonstrates innovative thinking and adjusts strategies effectively. | Creative with good adaptability; adjusts strategies when necessary. | Limited creativity; occasional attempts to adapt but often struggles. | Minimal creativity; struggles to adjust to changes. | No creativity or adaptability; rigid approach to gameplay. |

# How Can My RPG Accommodate My Adult Learners?

## *Level I (Novice Game Designers)*

Integrating an RPG into your course can help to better accommodate the different needs and social-developmental characteristics of adult learners who bring a huge variety of life experiences and preferences with them which can influence their engagement with your course content (Fallahi, 2019; Franco & DeLuca, 2019). Keep in mind that the comfort levels with the course content differ with some learners feeling apprehensive about unfamiliar material and learning experiences. Start by incorporating introductory materials and designing the game with varying difficulty levels. Begin with simpler tasks to prevent overwhelming players and help them build confidence gradually—also helps the game designer to create, refine, and assess player and group performance. Tutorials or practice rounds can provide additional support—although I have not done this myself. Posting videos or script examples of previous teams engaging in game rounds can potentially help new players to see the game in action and understand expected outcomes. As players gain confidence with RPGs, game designers can gradually add in more complex tasks—if needed (Huang et al., 2022; Irwanto et al., 2023).

Remembering that players have diverse communication skills and cognitive abilities is important when designing a successful game. For new players who may be apprehensive about communicating but need to participate in *real-time team activities*, the game master can strategically assign avatar roles based on a student player's strengths while simultaneously helping players to understand how the game will also provide them with opportunities for growth. Motivating students to explore different perspectives, engage with the content, and develop or enhance their collaboration skills can be achieved through this approach—if you effectively get "buy in" from the players as they recognize the potential value of the experience (Jaramillo-Mediavilla et al., 2024).

As a new RPG game designer, you can promote interaction and collaboration within a team by integrating *structured frameworks* into your game, which can offer players clear guidelines and processes that can help them with decision-making and generating ideas. A *decision-making model* (often in the form of a flowchart or other visual diagram) can give teams a specific, structured problem-solving strategy to help guide players through the round decision-making and task completion. These types of resources (which can be integrated into the game resources) can help student players to stay focused and more carefully analyze their choices and make informed decisions. The *SWOT Analysis model* is a more specific decision-making model that can help teams identify and consider relevant internal and external factors that the team should consider in relation to the team's goals as they carefully consider potential decisions and mutually agree on a consensus. As a game designer, you can integrate *brainstorming protocols* into the game rounds to guide players in generating and refining ideas that may contribute to the team tasks. The *Round-Robin Brainstorming* strategy is commonly used in RPGs as each player takes turns sharing information relevant to the task and suggesting ideas. All of the avatar perspectives are considered using this strategy, and a variety of ideas are considered and shared (Parshuram & Ramesh, 2020; Plass et al., 2020).

Providing specific *meeting agendas* is important for clarifying what is expected of individual players and teams during each game round. The agendas should indicate when players need to participate and what information they need to be able to share with the team when they are scheduled to participate. An effective agenda might include sections such as "Introduction," "Discussion of Options," "Decision-Making," and "Next Steps," along with estimated time demands for each task. Again, we will learn more about grade rubrics in Chapter 5, but the rubrics are important so players have a solid understanding of how they will be evaluated. The rubric might include criteria such as "Contribution to Discussion," "Quality of Ideas," and "Effective Collaboration," helping players understand what is required for success in each round (Saxena & Mishra, 2021; Toda et al., 2023). Table 3.5 shows an example of an agenda for an initial game round that guides this team through an authentic, real-world, and content-relevant scenario. The agenda shows clear roles, tasks, and expectations for each avatar player, making sure everyone knows their part and how to contribute.

## What Factors Shape a Positive Player Experience?

### *Level I (Novice Game Designers)*

One of the most important aspects of creating engaging and effective RPGs is establishing clear milestones. *Milestones* are key goals or achievements that

**Table 3.5 Example Agenda for Round 1**

| Game Round 1 Agenda |
|---|
| **Introduction and Role Immersion** |
| Welcome to the Game! Are You Ready to Play?<br>**Gaming Subject Theme for the Course Here**<br><br>The mission of our organization is to teach and prepare our students to be leaders and practitioners in the field and help them develop skills needed to meet their needs. The game addresses all parts of this goal by immersing students in an adventure in which you will have opportunities to consider varied roles on a content-relevant team, experience the human elements involved in team related professional decision-making, and gain new insights into the complexities of team challenges and content-related professional responsibilities.<br><br>The game requires you, as a player, to integrate research with practice, as you consider varied perspectives and scenarios related to the game tasks. Participation in the game requires the game master (your instructor) to work cooperatively with your avatar and your teammates to establish and reinforce a foundation of mutual trust, active engagement, and respect for all players.<br><br>Game Benefits:<br>- Actively engage players by presenting them with complex, authentic scenarios that would require creativity, critical thinking, negotiation, and cooperation.<br>- Supplement the learning experience with challenges that enable students to apply content expertise and personal experiences.<br>- Enhance thinking and reasoning skills, problem-solving, strategic reasoning, and creative thinking.<br>- The purpose of these activities is to provide opportunities to consider varied scenarios from different perspectives and to work collaboratively as a member of a content-related professional team.<br><br>The game master (your instructor) will strategically assign your avatar to a student team. You will operate *as* your assigned avatar, with a specified role in the support team during all game-related activities in the course. Your avatar status grants you the capacity to rapidly acquire new knowledge and strengthen your power to make a positive difference on a collaborative team to resolve an important real-world challenge.<br><br>- While avatars should represent the background and beliefs in the avatar descriptions, as members of a team avatars are expected to demonstrate the ability to work collaboratively, actively listen to one another, consider different perspectives, be flexible, and willing to negotiate to ensure the best decisions are made in a timely manner so the team can achieve game round goals. |

*(Continued)*

Table 3.5 (Continued)

### Task One Overview (Module 3)

The purpose of task one is for players on an Student Support Team (SST) to introduce themselves to one another and share relevant information to the team in order to address current concerns identified for ninth-grade Joey, a fifteen-year-old male student who is not being successful in his courses despite numerous tier one interventions attempted by his teachers.

### ** PRIOR to Meeting **

*What is going on with Joey?*

- Joey has been diagnosed with ADHD. He has a history of making satisfactory progress in grades K-8.
- He is currently failing all his classes.
- He has been suspended for skipping class three times.

** PRIOR to Meeting **

- Ensure the team meeting date, time, and link are noted in your personal calendar.
- Principal or Assistant Principal should review the suspension reports, and school related standardized data relevant to the team's concerns.
- Find your AVATAR on the avatar description page and learn more about the avatar's background, experiences, and motivations.
  o Adopt and role-play your Avatar's perspective and position in all aspects of the game moving forward.
  o For this activity, merely review and consider the information needed on the form in conjunction with your avatar's background, experiences, and motivations.
  o Review the team-building activity (below), and draft a response to the prompts based on your avatar's profile.

### ** DURING the Meeting **

Introduce your Avatar to the Team
  o Players will need to review the following information to make the decision.

- Joey's suspension reports (lined or hard copies)
- Joey's attendance reports (lined or hard copies)
- Joey's standardized test data (lined or hard copies)
- SST Team Referral Form and Procedures (lined or hard copies)

### Follow the MEETING AGENDA

  o **Administration Avatar (team leader)** should thank the team for coming, and ask them to adjust their names on their name tags to include their last name, and role on the team.
  o **Administration Avatar** should read the details of the *MTSS Referral form completed by Joey's English teacher.* The team will then ask the team to share relevant information the team may want to consider.
  o **Administration Avatar** should introduce self to the team and ask all the team members to go around the table and briefly introduce themselves (name, role on the team, and association with Joey). Each Avatar should briefly review their name, and role and provide some background about experience and understanding of what might be going on with Joey.

(Continued)

**Table 3.5 (Continued)**

- *Note each avatar can use evidence from the avatar's background, internal motivations, and so on. Avatars should reference course materials, case study, or their own experiences to "make up" details and stories to supplement the evidence presented. Avatars are encouraged to connect fictitious Joey with other individuals they may be familiar with in real-life experiences. Avatars should "sell" a sincere connection to Joey and actively engage with the team regarding the current issues and meeting purpose.
- **Special Education Avatar** should introduce self to the team and introduce self as the special education teacher and Joey's case manager, share a bit regarding any background as with reference to Joey's general academic and behavioral strengths, concerns, and primary IEP goals (Joey's IEP), provide a brief overview rather than a detailed outline of Joey's strengths and needs here. *Note each avatar can use evidence from the avatar's background, internal motivations, and so on. Avatars should reference course materials, case study, or their own experiences to "make up" details and stories to supplement the evidence presented. Avatars are encouraged to connect fictitious Joey with other individuals they may be familiar with in real-life experiences. Avatars should "sell" a sincere connection to Joey and actively engage with the team regarding the current issues and meeting purpose.
- **English Teacher Avatar** should introduce self to the team and share relevant details regarding any background, and knowledge of Joey's academic, communication, and social demands related to English Language Arts *Note each avatar can use evidence from the avatar's background, internal motivations, and so on. Avatars should reference course materials, case study, or their own experiences to "make up" details and stories to supplement the evidence presented. Avatars are encouraged to connect fictitious Joey with other individuals they may be familiar with in real-life experiences. Avatars should "sell" a sincere connection to Joey and actively engage with the team regarding the current issues and meeting purpose.
- **Math Teacher Avatar** should share relevant details regarding any background, and knowledge of Joey's academic, communication, and social demands related to math *Note each avatar can use evidence from the avatar's background, internal motivations, and so on. Avatars should reference course materials, case study, or their own experiences to "make up" details and stories to supplement the evidence presented. Avatars are encouraged to connect fictitious Joey with other individuals they may be familiar with in real-life experiences. Avatars should "sell" a sincere connection to Joey and actively engage with the team regarding the current issues and meeting purpose.
- **Science Teacher Avatar** should introduce self to the team and share relevant details regarding any background, and knowledge of Joey's academic, communication, and social demands related to science. *Note each avatar can use evidence from the avatar's background, internal motivations, and so on. Avatars should reference course materials, case study, or their own experiences to "make up" details and stories to supplement the evidence presented. Avatars are encouraged to connect fictitious Joey with other individuals they may be familiar with in real-life experiences. Avatars should "sell" a sincere connection to Joey and actively engage with the team regarding the current issues and meeting purpose.

*(Continued)*

**Table 3.5 (Continued)**

- **Parent Avatar** should introduce self to the team and share relevant details regarding any background knowledge about Joey's prior school academic, communication, and behavioral challenges as well as concerns about the quality of the programming available to Joey. *Note each avatar can use evidence from the avatar's background, internal motivations, and so on. Avatars should reference course materials, case study, or their own experiences to "make up" details and stories to supplement the evidence presented. Avatars are encouraged to connect fictitious Joey with other individuals they may be familiar with in real-life experiences. Avatars should "sell" a sincere connection to Joey and actively engage with the team regarding the current issues and meeting purpose.*
- **School Psychologist Avatar** should share relevant details regarding any background, and knowledge of Joey's academic, communication, and social demands related to detailed information about the linked psych report *Note each avatar can use evidence from the avatar's background, internal motivations, and so on. Avatars should reference course materials, case study, or their own experiences to "make up" details and stories to supplement the evidence presented. Avatars are encouraged to connect fictitious Joey with other individuals they may be familiar with in real-life experiences. Avatars should "sell" a sincere connection to Joey and actively engage with the team regarding the current issues and meeting purpose.*
- **Guidance Counselor Avatar** should walk through the SST process and share information about strategies and next steps to collect data on Joey for the team to review at the next meeting. The team should take a moment to review the documents and ask any questions.
  - **Principal Avatar**
    - Ask any of the team members if they have any questions or concerns about the next steps in the process.
    - Confirm the next meeting day and time while all players are present.
    - Thank the team for participating and asking them to complete the meeting reflection.

**\*\* AFTER the Meeting \*\***

**Post Round \* Post-Round Avatar Reflection Form**
- Reflect on your performance through the post-round Avatar Reflection Form
- Specially evaluate your immersion and contributions. Identify specific contributions to the collaborative efforts and decision-making among players (cooperation, problem-solving, and teamwork).

guide players through the game and measure progress. The milestones can be categorized into two primary types: short-term and long-term. *Short-term milestones* are content-specific goals players should be able to demonstrate within a single game round. A short-term milestone might require players to use their assigned roles to introduce themselves and discuss an issue related to the content. Communicating how these tasks connect to real-world applications and the benefits of understanding different perspectives enhances player engagement. By making these connections explicit, players are more likely to see the immediate value of their efforts. *Long-term milestones* involve broader objectives which may be developed throughout the game and often highlight the importance of collaboration and different viewpoints in solving intricate issues. By clearly defining and consistently reinforcing milestones and their relevance you can help to make sure your game remains purpose driven. Players will better understand how their progress contributes to their academic and professional growth and also recognize the benefits of their collaborative efforts (Adare-Tasiwoopa ápi & Silva, 2024; Toda et al., 2023). Table 3.6 shows RPG game designers examples of content-relevant milestones that potentially align with real-world tasks.

## How Is Planning Related to Engagement?

### Level I (Novice Game Designers)

Developing a compelling RPG includes careful planning and strategic thinking when outlining team tasks and academic milestones (Dymek & Zackariasson, 2016). Effective task planning begins with defining clear, actionable objectives for players to accomplish during and between sessions. Actionable objectives should be closely linked to each player's assigned role and unique perspective. Tasks must be specific, realistic, and achievable within the given timeframe (e.g., ninety-minute game session or two-hour in-person session). Complex tasks must be broken down into manageable steps to prevent players from feeling overwhelmed. In a RPG round for a college history class, the game round might require teams to work collaboratively to solve a historical mystery, the initial game tasks might include reviewing historical documents, conducting interviews, and discussing findings with their team. Subsequent game round tasks might require the team to present a solution based on their collected data. The game round tasks should help players gradually build their skills and content knowledge (Irwanto et al., 2023).

## How Can I Ensure Tasks Are Challenging and Achievable?

### Level I (Novice Game Designers)

When developing RPGs, balancing the complexity of tasks is an important consideration in conjunction with player engagement and collaboration.

## Table 3.6 Milestone Examples for RPG Gameplay

| Team Type | Milestone Name | Description |
|---|---|---|
| Safety and Security Teams | Safety Protocol Implementation | You and/or your team successfully designed and rolled out safety protocols that made everyone involved in the game scenario feel more security and confident. Keep up the great work! |
| | Emergency Drill Completion | You and/or your team organized and completed a realistic, full-scale emergency drill that helped everyone in the game scenario be ready for anything. Nice attention to detail! |
| | Community Collaboration | You and/or your team partnered with law enforcement to run training sessions to improve your team's readiness. Impressive problem-solving skills! |
| | Safety Audit Completion | You and/or your team conducted a safety audit, identified concerns and resolved them like professionals. Way to go! |
| Business-Related Teams | Project Kick-off Meeting | You and/or your team gathered information about your assigned new product and worked together to plan a successful and motivational project kick-off meeting. Outstanding effort! |
| | Milestone Review | You and/or your team regularly checked in with your game master to assess your progress, accepted constructive feedback and made needed revisions to keep the team moving through the project tasks. Very nice! |
| | Final Project Presentation | You and/or your team delivered a polished presentation of your project which clearly indicates an understanding of the relevant content objectives and mastery of project goals. Good job! |

(*Continued*)

**Table 3.6 (Continued)**

| Team Type | Milestone Name | Description |
|---|---|---|
| | Budget Management Achievement | You and/or your team stayed completed all assigned project tasks and expectations within the given very challenging budget constraints. Nicely done! |
| Quality Improvement Teams | Process Mapping Completion | You and/or your team mapped out existing processes to identify problem areas and also suggested realistic ways to make improvement. Excellent team work! |
| | Quality Initiative Launch | You and/or your team launched a new quality improvement initiative that is creative, includes important course content, and effectively meets customer needs! |
| | Data Analysis Report | You and/or your team successfully presented a straightforward, data-focused report with suggestions for needed improvement. The report is well written, objective, and convincing. Great work! |
| | Improvement Assessment | You and/or your team effectively measured the impact of changes and determined what's working and what's not for your assigned company, and you created a simple and practical plan to meet the company's needs. Way to go! |
| Task Forces | Crisis Response Plan Development | You and/or your team developed a practical and useful crisis response plan for your assigned company that incorporates course content in a useful way. Outstanding work! |
| | Stakeholder Engagement Meeting | You and/or your team met with the relevant stakeholders in your company to gather information, consider different perspectives, and make sure your project meets their needs. Excellent work! |

*(Continued)*

**Table 3.6 (Continued)**

| Team Type | Milestone Name | Description |
|---|---|---|
| | Communication Strategy Implementation | You and/or your team successfully designed an effective communication plan for your team to keep everyone informed and on task throughout the project. Good job! |
| | Final Report Submission | You and/or your team delivered a comprehensive report summarizing your project goals, decision-making steps, data analysis, and recommendations for the company moving forward. Excellent work! |
| Hospitality Teams | Guest Satisfaction Survey | You and/or your team completed an easily accessible and useful guest satisfaction survey using a QR code that customers can quickly use to share experiences and give your company useful information for improvement. Well done! |
| | Service Training Completion | You and/or your team trained everyone to deliver quality service to our customers. Thanks for working together to make us better! |
| | Event Coordination Achievement | You and/or your team planned a major event and your report showcases your attention to details and consideration of the budget of your assigned customer needs. Congratulations! |
| | Cross-Training Completion | You and/or your team made sure everyone could step into different roles when needed, enhancing flexibility and service quality for your assigned company. We need more people like you! |
| Sales Teams | Sales Target Achievement | You and/or your team met the sales goals of your assigned company. Your team effectively implemented what you learned in class in a practical and effective way. Nicely done! |

*(Continued)*

**Table 3.6 (Continued)**

| Team Type | Milestone Name | Description |
|---|---|---|
| | Product Knowledge Training | You and/or your team worked together to demonstrate you mastered new product knowledge and customer profile which ensured your marketing project recommendations were very effective at meeting your consumer's needs. Excellent work! |
| | Customer Relationship Development | You and/or your team generated a project that included strategies for your assigned company to build strong, lasting relationships with clients that will likely improve sales in the future. Very good work! |
| | New Client Acquisition | You and/or your team successfully marketed your product on social media and you generated several new clients. Way to go team! |

The first round might focus on introducing the team and defining the tasks, reviewing available resources, tools, and timeline expectations. Designing simpler tasks that allow avatars to practice interactions can help players become more comfortable with the game expectations and embrace their assigned roles. Integrating opportunities for avatars to engage with and receive feedback from the game master can also help student players build confidence (Jaramillo-Mediavilla et al., 2024). As players progress, gradually increasing task complexity can potentially improve the experience and motivate players to stay engaged as the assigned tasks can evolve to require deeper collaboration and strategic planning (Kapp, 2012). A round might require teams to work together to develop a comprehensive plan to address a complex issue, such as creating a sustainable urban environment, involving detailed research, strategic planning, and group discussion. To avoid player fatigue, consider following this with less demanding tasks, like summarizing the plan or creating a presentation outline (Liberona et al., 2021). Tasks involving extensive collaboration should be paired with opportunities for individual contributions to help motivate players. In a game round where players must design a marketing campaign for a new product, allowing time for individual brainstorming before regrouping can promote a more cohesive team effort. Be sure to integrate strategies that encourage individual contributions to help each player express their unique perspective and promote effective teamwork throughout the game (Leaning, 2015).

Providing players with needed background information and materials is vital for successful gameplay in each round of an RPG. Preparation sets the stage for an immersive experience, enabling players to better understand the game tasks, their avatar roles, and specific scenarios (Majuri et al., 2018). Acknowledging the diverse professional and personal experiences that players bring to the game and integrating these elements into the game can motivate players and make each round more meaningful and relevant (Plass et al., 2020). Ensuring that needed preparatory materials are available to players well in advance can give players an opportunity to review and consider the information prior to the game rounds and may help them feel more confident about their game interactions when the game begins (Saleem et al., 2022).

# What Role Do Incentives Play?

## *Level II (Experienced—Intermediate Game Designers)*

When designing an RPG for a course, it is important to consider that adult learners often manage multiple responsibilities, forcing them to prioritize their tasks. Think about your own "to-do" list. Typically, we put more energy into what we consider our most immediate needs as well as the consequences and rewards associated with meeting those needs by a specific deadline. Our adult student players can also be expected to focus on activities they perceive as most essential and time sensitive. If students believe their lack of preparation will go unnoticed or have little or no consequences, they choose to spend time on what they consider more important tasks and might not put much effort into preparing for the game (Croxton, 2014). Providing players with clear, meaningful tasks that require active participation while simultaneously connecting their preparation and participation with what intrinsically motivates them can potentially motivate them to actively engage with the game (McKeithan et al., 2021). Game designers should note that upcoming chapters will explore how to enhance player motivation in RPGs. For now, consider linking motivation to grades based on effort and preparation. Helping players understand the broader purpose of the game—whether preparing for real-world challenges, making a positive impact in their profession, or deepening their knowledge of course content—cannot be overstated (Saxena & Mishra, 2021). When these aspects are clearly connected to gameplay, players are more likely to engage fully and take their roles seriously. Initiating and maintaining player motivation is important for a successful game. A common issue in group assignments (in the classroom and in real life) is that some people we work with may tend to contribute more than others in group-related tasks. The unequal workload can be frustrating for those who feel as if they carry the workload and can minimize engagement from those who contribute less (Ambrose & Wankel, 2020). When designing an RPG for a course, it is important to consider this potential concern and be sure that all players are provided with the necessary information they need to be successful, given meaningful roles that require active participation and clearly understand how they their preparation and participation will be assessed to motivate players to engage with and interact with the content and their teammates throughout the game (Leaning, 2015). Assigning specific tasks to each player ensures accountability and prevents passive participation, as each round demands individual input and effort. Consider creating tasks that promote collaboration while simultaneously incorporating individual responsibilities—making each avatar's role indispensable.

Consider making sure the game assignments are clearly integrated into your course syllabus. In your course, the game rounds might replace traditional module discussions or a large cooperative group project. The grading of these assignments should reflect the complexity of the tasks and the collaborative nature of the game round activities. Role-Playing Games assessments can easily include individual and group assessments. You can develop rubrics (similar to the one referenced above) that evaluate players based on their active involvement in the game (e.g., contributions to discussions, problem-solving efforts, and role-playing activities). The rubrics can make it clear to student players how you will assess individual contributions as well as the completion of academic content related to game tasks, such as developing a treatment plan, analyzing patient data, or reflecting on the game's progress (Adare-Tasiwoopa ápi & Silva, 2024). The first round of the game can be challenging for new players who may be unfamiliar with role-playing or uncomfortable with the idea of improvisation or pretending to be someone else so remember to be supportive and intentional when assigning avatars and creating tasks so all student players have an opportunity (and responsibility) to participate. Starting the game with low-stakes tasks may help students ease into their roles (Barron, 2024). Game designers must remain open-minded and flexible to the diverse needs of students, especially as they may feel intimidated by the first game. While Chapter 5 will address unusual implementation scenarios and special player circumstances, it is important to consider strategies to ease initial apprehensions (Bell, 2018). Game designers must be willing to adjust expectations, when necessary, a topic that will be explored further in later chapters. Offering alternatives to direct role-play, such as written reflections or strategic planning tasks, can help reluctant players engage meaningfully without feeling overwhelmed. Pairing less experienced players with more confident ones, assigning mentors, role playing one on one prior to the game to allow a reluctant student an opportunity to practice their avatar and holding pre-game round group meetings for students to ask questions and clarify expectations are additional ways you might want to build in support structures for your first game experience (Best & Conceição, 2017; Plass et al., 2020).

# How Can I Plan an Effective First Game Round?

## *Level I (Novice Game Designers)*

Once you have decided on the essential skill you want players to be able to apply or demonstrate in a real-world scenario as part of an appropriate team type (instructional objectives of the game), you are ready to build out your game round activities. While there is no true "right way" to do this, you can potentially start with an "Introduction and Role Immersion" theme for the first round. The goal of this round would be to introduce players to the game and ask them to review their assigned avatar's bios, motivations and potential contributions and biases in relation to the overall game activities. Asking them to start simply by introducing their avatar character to the team by citing relevant details from the avatar's background (in conjunction with the content-related game tasks) that can help them to become more familiar with the RPG format in a lower stakes game round. You may even want to use AI to generate digital, visual aids such as character cards that detail avatars' special skills, experiences and weaknesses for players to easily reference throughout the game (Martin & Bolliger, 2018). A time frame of sixty to ninety minutes game sessions can support meaningful interaction and problem-solving without overwhelming players. Consider the whole group and small group options including breakout rooms within the online platform to facilitate focused group work. The first round focuses on establishing a strong foundation for gameplay. Players are encouraged to prepare by reviewing relevant documents, such as character backstories and game mechanics, before the meeting. Preparation for the round should enhance engagement during the session. Spending time getting familiar with the materials and thinking through ideas or questions allows players to fully participate and enjoy the experience together. During this round, the game master would be needed to facilitate a clear agenda, guiding players through their tasks and ensuring they stay on track. Emphasis should be placed on collaboration and communication, providing opportunities for group discussions where players can share perspectives and feedback. Clear expectations for game conduct, such as maintaining character consistency and respecting fellow players, contribute to a smooth session and can be added to the agenda or round directions. The first game session might focus on introductions, background sharing, and an overview of upcoming tasks and sets the tone as well as the academically related expectations for collaboration and task completion throughout the game. After the round concludes, participants complete a reflection form to evaluate their performance on an individual basis as well as their contribution to the team's progress toward round task mastery (McKeithan et al., 2021). Subsequent sessions should encourage active participation. For instance, in a round requiring players to develop a crisis management plan, use breakout rooms to address different aspects, such as strategy development and resource allocation. In-person sessions might last two to three hours to promote deeper engagement and complex problem-solving activities. Physical presence enhances collaboration through real-time discussions and hands-on activities, such as using props or whiteboards for brainstorming and group discussions. Whether the game is in person or online, be sure to make the necessary materials accessible to players as they need them for all game sessions (Monsalves et al., 2023).

While the number of game rounds can vary according to course and player needs, we are suggesting that an initial RPG might include four distinct rounds throughout a semester. We completely made up these names based on major team tasks in the rounds in conjunction with opportunities to use game vocabulary into the process. Round 1 is the *Introduction and Role Immersion*, Round 2 we call the *Strategic Quest Challenge*, Round 3 is described as the *Critical Decision Round*, and Round 4 we simplified into the *Debrief and Reflect* final game round. Each round is designed to build upon the previous round's activities to encourage student players as they work collaboratively with their team to convert theoretical knowledge into practical (real-world) application (Ramic-Brkic & Balik, 2023). The following sections will provide examples of rounds two to four and how they can be created and integrated into your course (Toda et al., 2023). Appendix C provides an example of an educational Multi-Tiered System of Supports (MTSS) Team RPG scenario, focusing on goal progression and tasks, with potential goals and tasks outlined for rounds one through four.

## What Might Be Included in the Second Game Round?

### *Level I (Novice Game Designers)*

In round two, what we are calling the Strategic Quest Challenge, the players are asked to prepare for the round ahead of time, to carefully consider how their assigned avatar character's background, motivation, and characteristics can meaningfully contribute to the team task in the round. They are required to also consider what they have learned in the course so far and to appropriately help the team apply what they are learning to complete given task(s) as outlined in the game round agenda using the resources provided. The focus is on strategic decision-making and the practical use of theoretical knowledge from the class. Remember to keep in mind the varied backgrounds and experiences of your learners. To set up the round effectively, consider providing teams with detailed background information relevant to the challenge, such as case studies or situational reports. Including details necessary for informed decision-making can offer enough complexity to challenge players while supplying the data they need. In my own game, first game, I had to remember that not all my students were teachers or had experiences on IEP teams. So, I had to consider the tasks from a novice perspective. I linked a glossary of IEP terms, short videos from YouTube related to special education laws and procedures and links to important resources and forms they would need to complete throughout the game (Zhan et al., 2024). Structuring the round into distinct phases related to clear game tasks (academic objectives) and required work products can help individual players and teams synthesize the information to develop a plan of action. Include an outline of the action plan you would like them to complete along with examples of completed plans with clear connections to contributions from each team member. Be sure the plan includes team insights related to the initially shared resources as well as the team member's insight related to the content and team discussions as players are encouraged to share what they know about a task and also improvise information that avatar may have that could help the team to complete tasks. Integrating estimated time limits into the game round agenda can help teams to stay on task and make progress. For example, a sixty-minute game round might allow for twenty minutes for the initial review, fifteen minutes for consultations, and twenty-five minutes for developing and presenting the final plan to the team to prepare for the next round (Rivera & Garden, 2021).

## What Might Be Included in the Third Game Round?

### Level I (Novice Game Designers)

Keeping in mind that the game might have any number of game rounds, and in fact, you might choose to only have three rounds instead of four, we are offering potential planning guidance if you would like a fourth round. The *Critical Decision Round* builds on the team insights gained from the previous round, and teams are potentially asked to complete and report on their final game round tasks. They would need to have prepared individually for the round (while remaining in character) and meaningfully contribute to the academically relevant tasks presented in the game round agenda as teams work through the round and make final decisions and complete final products (McKeithan et al., 2021). The round highlights the importance of teamwork, as players must rely on one another to navigate challenges and achieve shared goals. Throughout the round, the game master should provide ongoing guidance and support to help players stay in character, referencing materials and guidelines and working toward meeting the game round objectives (Plass et al., 2020).

## How Can a Reflection Round Enhance Learning?

### Level I (Novice Game Designers)

While this round may seem unnecessary, I strongly encourage game designers to include this in their game for several reasons. The most important reason is that reflection helps students connect the game to real world learning. When players consider how they apply content, collaborated as a team, or approached a conflict from a new perspective, the experience becomes more meaningful. The process encourages deeper learning for students who might not otherwise take the time to think about what they gained. Sharing what they learned with the team and listening to the thoughts and experiences of their classmates, adding to the thoughts and extending the conversation as a group can be very reinforcing for the players and the instructor! In the final round, what we are calling the *Debrief and Reflect* round, as I previously mentioned, the round can meaningfully contribute to the overall game experience. The activities in this round offer players the opportunity to reflect on their gameplay, share insights, and provide constructive feedback, while consolidating their learning and evaluating the effectiveness of their strategies (McKeithan et al., 2021). During this round, the game master or instructor has the opportunity to gather and review actionable insights that can help you enhance the game for future students. Data collection can effectively occur during a final round "debriefing" session between the game master and the players. During this round, the game master can pose surveys with questions such as, "On a scale of 1 to 5, how well did you apply academic content in the scenarios?" and "To what extent did the game foster collaboration among team members?" Open-ended questions like, "What challenges did you face in understanding the tasks?" can generate valuable insights. The game master might further explore players' experiences with questions such as, "What aspects of the game did you find most effective in promoting teamwork?" The debriefing round discussion can reveal in-depth observations about gameplay dynamics. Game designers may also choose to send out surveys or conduct interviews in a different format after the game. Game master *observation logs* can be used to record often players collaborated, methods of communication, and any moments of confusion or difficulty. Feedback sessions between the game master and the Game designer can facilitate dialogue about key observations. Game masters might highlight successes, such as, "Players effectively utilized each other's strengths during problem-solving," while also identifying areas for improvement, like, "The instructions for task three were unclear, leading to confusion" (Monsalves et al., 2023). The qualitative or quantitative data can be used to continuously improve the game (Li & Tsai, 2013). Focus on gathering feedback related to the effectiveness of the game's objectives, the appropriateness of the challenges, and how well the avatars' abilities and backgrounds influenced decision-making. Be sure the adjustments align with your learning objectives (Roungas et al., 2019). I have revised our game numerous times according to this player feedback. Piggybacking on the "we are smarter together" theme noted in the last chapter, when a game designer sets up a game, even if they are purposefully considering the tasks (assignments) from the student player's perspective, there is always the potential for a miscommunication in the reader/writer relationship. So, listening to players share ideas about what worked, what they learned and how the game might be improved can help game designers continuously refine the game. Players feel valued as their opinions are solicited and considered as they openly discuss the challenges they faced during the game and how they worked through them (Plass et al., 2020). Players are asked to contemplate and share what they have learned individually about applying the course content in a real-world scenario. The challenge encourages players to consider how their avatar's perspectives and experiences differ from their own, fostering a greater understanding of diverse viewpoints and enhancing empathy (Toda et al., 2023). As a game designer, you can easily ask players to connect theoretical knowledge with practical application, emphasizing how the game has informed their understanding of key concepts. Players might also be asked to consider how their thinking has evolved over the course of the game and the semester in relation to the practical application of course content particularly in relation to real life scenarios. Players complete statements such as "I used to think . . ." and "But now, I think . . ." to articulate specific changes in their understanding and the reasons behind those shifts in thinking. Sharing these reflections promotes a collaborative environment where players can learn from each other's experiences and insights (Roungas et al., 2019). Listening to and considering the thoughts from players can be very rewarding and motivating to instructors (game designers) as well. Table 3.7 is an example of an agenda for a final game round that shows how to include structured reflection and feedback in RPGs.

Given that I had no idea where to begin when I first started developing my game round, I have created several practical examples of RPG scenarios across many different higher education programs for you to consider that are located in the appendices. The examples include an education-based School Leadership Team Game in which the team is tasked with developing a plan to improve school and community relationships (Appendix D). Another potential education-based team RPG example involves an Individualized Education Team that must determine educational placement for a student (Appendix E). Appendix F shares an example of a university marketing

### Table 3.7 Example Agenda for Round 4

| Game Round 4 Agenda |
| --- |
| **Debrief and Reflect** |
| Congratulations on reaching the final task of our game challenge for this course! Now that you have leveled up your knowledge about assessments, the referral process, and teamwork in making informed and collaborative decisions about a featured student, it is time for the ultimate quest: reflection and consolidation. |
| **\*\* PRIOR to Meeting \*\*** |
| To prepare for the final quest, take some time to reflect on your journey. Consider what you have learned about the practical applications of the course content. Recall your avatar's background and experiences, thinking about how they differ from your own. Summarize the key insights and lessons you have gained, and reflect on how your thinking has evolved throughout the course. Set up a quiet, distraction-free environment with your notes and materials ready. Approach this final task with an open mind, prepared to reflect and share your thoughts. |
| **\*\* DURING the Meeting \*\*** <br> **Final Quest** |
| **Reflection Challenges** <br> *Your assigned team leader will begin the discussion by answering the first question, setting the tone for engagement. After that response, the team leader will call on team members individually to share their thoughts on the same question, allowing each person to contribute their unique perspective. Once everyone has had the opportunity to respond, the team leader will introduce the second question and encourage the entire team to share their ideas. This process will continue for any additional questions, with the team leader facilitating individual responses followed by team collaboration for each question.* <br> • **Player Reflection**—Reflect on what you have learned about the specific application of your course content in this simulated real-world scenario. How did your avatar's perspectives and experiences differ from your own? <br> • **Quest Insight**—What insights have you gained from this role-playing adventure? <br> • **Game Feedback**—What aspects of this game experience would you like to change or explore further? <br> • **Mind Shift**—As you reflect on the game and your content learning and the importance of meaningful collaboration throughout the semester, consider how and why your thinking has changed. Share your thoughts by completing the following prompts: <br>   ○ "I used to think..." <br>   ○ "But now, I think..." <br>   ○ Follow each statement with an explanation |
| **\*\* AFTER the Meeting \*\*** |
| Upload your responses on the *Post-Round Reflection FORM* by the end of the module to complete your final quest. Good luck, and may your reflections be insightful! |

team who are tasked to enhance brand awareness and increase student enrollment. Marketing Campaigns and Rebranding. Another potential game scenario for that marketing team is to design a campaign to launch a new business (Appendix G). The next example (Appendix H) is a potential RPG challenge for members of a Medical Treatment Teams related to challenges with patient care.

# Why Is Beta Testing Important?

## *Level II (Experienced—Intermediate Game Designers)*

Including a first practice test or "*beta test"* of your newly designed game can be an important part of the RPG development process. Beta testing allows a group of players (who were not involved in the initial game design) to play the game, work through the tasks, and provide valuable feedback related to potential areas for improvement prior to implementing the game with your students. Beta testing can help to validate the game's mechanics and ensure that all elements—from the storyline to the rules—work together smoothly (Sari et al., 2021). During the beta test players can help to identify whether the objectives are clear, and how effectively the game incorporates course content. The feedback can help game designers potentially adjust difficulty of tasks, provide additional resources for teams to use, adjust the timeline, offer more examples, be more specific about assessment methods and resolve any other types of inconsistencies (Anagnostopoulou, 2023). The game master role is important during this beta test phase. The game master must be well-versed in the game's purpose and desired outcomes, serving as the facilitator who guides the gameplay while remaining observant. The game master's responsibilities can include setting meeting dates, assigning avatars, sharing information about the game with players, explaining the game round objectives, enforcing rules, and providing real-time support to players before, during, and after the RPG. During gameplay, the game master should observe player interactions closely, noting how players navigate challenges, collaborate as a team, and apply their knowledge. The game master can interact with players and the team to keep them moving forward—consider taking notes on any issues that might be refined later or potential ideas for improvement (Hammer et al., 2018a; Leow et al., 2016). The tables in this chapter offer several examples that illustrate key game elements and task analyses. The examples serve as practical guides, helping to clarify how to structure game tasks, develop avatars, and define both short-term and long-term milestones within the game rounds (Ambrose & Wankel, 2020).

## Game Log

*The purpose of this chapter is to guide future game designers in developing their first RPG to integrate into their courses. The chapter begins with a discussion about the importance of identifying and setting clear game objectives along with suggestions about how to create a structured plan for each game round. We offer suggestions about how to structure four different rounds into the game with the first being an introduction round and the final focusing on generating data related to the usefulness of the game from the player's perspective. Each of the game activities is linked with course-specific learning activities and provides meaningful real-world scenarios for player teams. The chapter also covers practical aspects of launching the game, including choosing an appropriate space for students to work comfortably and ensuring that all necessary resources are readily available as needed by teams. Effective integration of game assignments into the course is another focus of the team because adding a game to the course should not require the instructor to completely revise the syllabus or grading policy. One suggestion was to use the game rounds to replace traditional discussion, participation grades, or group project grades with game rounds. While we will talk more about extremely reluctant players in Chapter 5, we did briefly suggest that instructors or game masters who were familiar with student needs might want to consider them when assigning avatars to new players—potentially starting with smaller roles and offering alternatives such as written reflections. Finally, we suggest that beta testing your new game could be beneficial—although I didn't do this for my games. The research does suggest that beta testing even with a small group of people can help the game designer to gather feedback needed to potentially create a better game experience for your students. Communicating the benefits of the game to students helps them understand the value of their participation. In Chapter 4, the focus will be on game mechanics and we will share ideas about how to effectively incorporate game elements such as points, levels, and badges to increase student engagement.*

# 4 Game Mechanics for Meaningful Learning

## Game Master's Prologue

*My journey into the world of education comes with a different twist than most. I graduated from college over thirty years ago with a bachelor's degree in finance and accounting. Upon graduation, I embarked on a career in the world of business, accepting a position in Procter & Gamble's Financial Management program at the time. Fast-paced, competitive and all time consuming, I learned strategies of business, time management, leadership, and strategic thinking. I worked sixty-hour-work weeks in a fast-paced challenging career. However, I knew I needed something more. As challenging, exhausting and financially rewarding as this career was, I knew I was designed to be something different. When I made this change, the first step of my life's true career calling was put in motion. I returned to school to study Speech-Language Pathology (SLP), obtaining my Masters degree. As with life's twists and turns, I did not return to start my SLP practice in the schools for several more years. Staying home for ten years as a full-time mom of three delayed starting my SLP career but gave me invaluable insight into child raising, child management, and patience. It was one of my most rewarding but exhausting careers yet. Shifting gears, let's move forward to here and now. Why do I share all of this as we embark on the topic of gamification? I want to ground you a little into who I am. As an author exploring gamification in higher education, my perspective is shaped not only by my role as a speech-language pathologist (SLP) within the school system but also by a unique blend of experiences across various professional landscapes. At this point in my life, I am more than an SLP who returned to school for a clinical doctorate. I am an adult learner with successful experience in the fast-paced business world. I understand the value and necessity of skills in adaptability, collaboration, and problem-solving in real-world environments. In a post-pandemic world, where remote and face-to-face learning are regularly a part of our professional lives, and as an educator (and student) in higher education I understand the need for skills that extend beyond traditional academic knowledge. Navigating multiple careers has reinforced the power of empathy, perspective-shifting,* and people management (qualities that are required in every industry). My professional and personal experiences have shown me that understanding others' perspectives, anticipating unexpected challenges, and being able to use what you know to effectively collaborate with others to find actionable solutions to common problems must be the future of our field if we want to stay relevant to contemporary learners. When I was a doctoral student, Glennda was one of my professors and a major influence in my learning. It was her classes, where I had my first experience with gamification as a student and later as a Graduate Teaching Assistant and game master. As you'll discover throughout this book, introducing GBL into your courses can be a powerful catalyst for student engagement and growth. My experience was that most students will embrace RPGs, while others may be less enthusiastic because they are stepping outside their comfort zones. As a game master, my student players applied the knowledge they learned during the course and developed skills to help them in their own practice and future interactions with others. Chapter 4 will guide you as you design and enhance your game experiences by using game mechanics such as goals, challenges, feedback loops, and collaborative roles to create your own RPG that brings your curriculum to life. I encourage you to approach this chapter with an open mind. Consider new ideas gradually, one step at a time, and incorporate them as your confidence with RPG elements increases. In doing so, you can create experiences that help players master content and build valuable, transferable skills.

# Why Are Game Mechanics and Elements Important?

## Level II (Experienced—Intermediate Game Designers)

To be honest, I had to do some research myself to prepare to write this chapter. *Game mechanics* are the rules and systems that guide player interactions, create challenges, and help teams achieve long- and short-term learning goals and milestones (Barron, 2024). For new RPG designers, understanding at least the basics of game mechanics is important because these tools can help you develop effective RPGs that promote learning (Bell, 2018). How are they different from game elements? When comparing the game elements and their relationship to game mechanics, the proverbial expression comes to mind . . . "The frame holds the painting, but the brushstrokes tell the story." In other words, the game mechanics (the frame) provide structure and boundaries, while game elements (the brushstrokes) bring the experience, creativity, knowledge, and narrative that define the RPG mechanics maintain order and drive learning objectives, while elements create immersion and connect students to the course content in a way that promotes active, sustained engagement (Lameras et al., 2017). Both mechanics and elements can help game designers to build an RPG that is educationally rigorous and interactive (Bowman, 2010). Both are needed to ensure successful gamification implementation into practice.

Broadly defined, *game elements* are the components that make up the game to create the overall experience (Campillo-Ferrer et al., 2020). Game elements answer the "What" when creating an immersive game which includes primarily the visible interactive aspects of the game the players engage with. Game elements in RPG-based learning include characters (avatars) and their roles, narratives and background story, points and goal mastery based on player performance, RPG challenges, rewards choices and decision-making (Gatzidis, 2012). Specific to RPGs, game elements involve players assuming the role of an assigned character (avatar) as they actively participate in game round activities (scenarios) which require critical thinking, collaboration, decision-making, and practical application of new learning to achieve common goals (Cullinan & Genova, 2023). As stated repeatedly in the previous chapter, when incorporating RPG game elements into a new course, the most important aspect of the RPG is to align the game tasks with learning objectives to promote player engagement and motivation (Christopoulos & Mystakidis, 2023). Once you, as a new game designer, have identified specific game (course) goals and objectives (to be achieved by the end of the game) you can use game elements to help your players achieve educational targets. Be sure to develop avatar roles and teams that are relevant to the subject matter (with unique, realistic skills and abilities) that evolve as needed as the players progress through the RPG (Daniau, 2016). Game elements can help you create meaningful game round tasks (missions or quests) and allow players to explore cause and effect, use strategic thinking and work collaboratively as a team (Dymek & Zackariasson, 2016). In a business class, players might simulate making marketing choices to demonstrate their understanding of market trends. Rewarding team and individual progress with badges or points can potentially motivate players to demonstrate effort and skill rather than just showing up (Lameras et al., 2017). Encouraging players to take initiative in an RPG game task can also enhance a student's curiosity and self-directed learning (Featherstone, 2016). In a communications course, an RPG might require players to examine and manage miscommunication related conflicts in a professional setting as they implement newly learned strategies from your course while simultaneously honing their teamwork and problem-solving skills. Game mechanics can help you provide regular feedback on player performance and help them to recognize their strengths and opportunities for potential growth (Franco & DeLuca, 2019). Thoughtful design of RPG game elements can increase the likelihood that the experience nurtures creativity, critical thinking, and collaboration (Gatzidis, 2012; Lameras et al., 2017). Table 4.1 gives examples for new game designers to show how game mechanics and game elements can be used to complement RPG experiences in higher education.

Okay, full disclosure again, when we created our RPG games initially, we did add in mechanics and elements, but they needed lots of revisions as our games evolved. In fact, it would have been great to have known much of this before we got started. In RPG design, knowing the difference between mechanics and elements can help you design more effective RPGs. Think of game mechanics as the rules and systems that guide how players interact with one another to achieve learning goals. Points are one example, and we will explore assessments and rubrics in more detail in Chapter 5. Points can be used to assess individual and team players and keep them motivated. If you are designing a technical writing RPG, players might earn points for finishing writing assignments and actively engaging in collaborative discussions. *Levels* are another important mechanic commonly used in RPGs as they can represent progression in the game. In a statistics RPG, your student players might be tasked with applying basic curriculum concepts such as calculating means and medians or they might work collaboratively to gather and analyze data and create visuals of the results to present to the group for team decision-making (Hartt et al., 2020). *Quests* (game round tasks) must be clearly connected to the curriculum, relevant to real-world application as well as interesting and engaging. In a college level statistics RPG, players might be asked to gather data on campus resources, analyze the information, and present their findings to faculty. The collaborative team effort should enhance analytical skills and promote collaboration and effective communication. In these RPG game round examples, the elements of the game shape the overall tone and meaningfulness of the tasks for players (Kelly, 2020). By blending effective mechanics like team quests and skill progression with engaging elements such as immersive storylines and interactive characters, you can design RPGs that meet learning objectives and inspire players. The combination

## Table 4.1 Elements and Mechanics Comparison

| RPG Aspect | Game Mechanics (How the Game Functions) | Game Elements (What the Game Consists Of) |
|---|---|---|
| *Avatar Roles and Player Interaction* | Players assume assigned avatars' perspectives, motivations, and experiences to maintain consistency during game rounds as they contribute information and help the team work toward meeting goals. | Avatars are assigned roles such as Principal, Special Education Teacher, Parent, School Psychologist. |
| *Collaboration and Problem-Solving* | Teams work together to solve problems and negotiate decisions according to the team assigned game round task (problem scenario). | The narrative of the game round task (real-world simulation) related to the course content. |
| *Information Review and Sharing* | The process players go through as they review information, and incorporate their avatars' perspectives to contribute meaningfully to the team's progress and achieve common goals. | Documents such as background information, resources, timelines, examples, and so on. The teams need to understand what is expected and achieve tasks. |
| *Meeting Structure* | The procedures and rules that clarify how the players in the game interact with one another before, during and after game rounds such as introducing themselves; linking comments and feedback with avatar biographies, participating actively in the game in an organized manner, and so on. | The agenda that guides the flow of activities and discussions during the game round. |
| *Reflection and Assessment* | The system for evaluating performance through reflection forms that assess cooperation, decision-making, and contributions. | Reflection forms, rubrics, leaderboard, that are used as tools for post-round evaluation. |
| *Game Master* | Facilitates gameplay by establishing rules, monitoring interactions, and guiding the discussion to help teams progress through game tasks. | The game master's role as the facilitator and authority figure in the game. |

creates an impactful and enjoyable educational experience (Topîrceanu, 2017). Table 4.1 presents a visual comparison of game mechanics and elements to better understand the distinction between the two.

# How Do Game Mechanics Influence Learning Outcomes?

## Level II (Experienced—Intermediate Game Designers)

*Gamification strategies* involve integrating game-like elements into non-game contexts, such as education, business, or healthcare, to make learning and training more engaging, motivating, and fun. A gamification strategy is the specific plan of how to incorporate elements (e.g., points, badges, or leaderboards) into the game you are creating to make the overall experience more successful (Hartt et al., 2020). Acting as the backbone of any game, mechanics define player interactions and the relationships between game components (Christopoulos & Mystakidis, 2023). Mechanics like point systems, levels, badges, and structured challenge are widely used in educational settings and they can be adapted across grade levels and subjects to create engaging and immersive, goal-oriented learning environments (Zhang, 2024).

# How Can I Assess Individual Student Learning?

## Level I (Novice Game Designers)

While we will elaborate on this aspect of RPGs on a deeper level in the next chapter, we felt it was important to address this initially in this chapter because assessment and instructor feedback are important and potentially difficult for new game designers to understand. Of course, assigning points to students according to content mastery is a traditionally used assessment method in education across content areas. The good news is that assigning points in an RPG can be just as easy to do (if not easier) than grading a traditional student assignment. A *point system* in an RPG is often a foundational game mechanic that provides students with a clear and quantifiable method for tracking their progress in completing tasks, mastering skills, or achieving specific objectives. Accumulated points (grades) allow students to see their subject matter mastery over time. Points can be used in an RPG as part of a comprehensive *feedback loop* (between student players, instructor game masters and even peer team players) to support continuous improvement by allowing students to reflect on their performance and adjust their strategies accordingly (Hartt et al., 2020). Role-Playing Games designers can use points to assess and offer feedback related to how far a player has advanced through game tasks, and points can be awarded for including participation, accurate answers, and game preparation and team interactions that meaningfully contribute to team decision-making. In a marketing course for example, players might earn points for developing successful campaign strategies and for their ability to effectively "channel" their assigned avatar's perspective and experiences in game round discussions and collaborative projects (Salman, et al., 2024). Preparing for a game requires effort, and accountability plays an important role in enhancing motivation among players. When players recognize that their game preparation translates into real-world skills (for which they will be held accountable), they are more likely to invest time and energy into the experience (Gallardo, 2020). RPG grading approaches have shown a positive impact on student motivation and engagement in higher education. Role-Playing Games grading involves transforming traditional assessment methods into interactive experiences where students earn points and levels by completing tasks, demonstrating mastery, and engaging with course material in meaningful ways (Jaramillo-Mediavilla et al., 2024). Role-Playing Games grading is associated with a reduction in course failure rates in higher education as players feel more supportive and encouraged by other players and the game master (Kelly, 2020). Many students report feeling a greater sense of content-related self-confidence, problem-solving and decision-making when RPG assessments include meaningful feedback. In fact, a majority of adult learners reported a preference for RPG grading methods over traditional grading practices often leading to heightened anxiety, avoidance of challenging courses, and students disengaging from the coursework (Chamberlin, 2018; Jaramillo-Mediavilla et al., 2024). In contrast, the RPG evaluations can potentially better support your student player's basic psychological needs, encourage cooperation, build trust, resulting in higher levels of intrinsic motivation of content learning (Kelly, 2020). *Leaderboards* can be used in games with a competitive element to offer a visual of individual and team performance by displaying rankings based on earned points (Laine & Lindberg, 2020). RPG elements (experience points or *leveling up*, leaderboards, levels, etc.) have been validated as effective strategies to enhance student motivation and engagement (Abdool et al., 2017). Just as is the case with traditional academic grading, accumulated points can lead to tangible rewards, including recognition, enhanced learning opportunities, or access to exclusive resources. *Recognition* can take various forms such as *shout-outs* (verbal acknowledgments) of a player's contributions or achievements and leaderboards, which display rankings based on points earned and accomplishments achieved (Lameras et al., 2017). Another potential form of recognition is the assignment of *special roles* within the game, where players may be designated as leaders, strategists, or experts in specific areas (Leow et al., 2016). New RPG game designers can utilize tools like digital recognition boards or shout-outs during (or between) game rounds to highlight individual or team accomplishments and maintain player enthusiasm. Recognition has the potential to validate player efforts and make the learning experience to improve academic outcomes and greater student satisfaction (Topîrceanu, 2017).

## How Can I Use Badges, Levels, and Milestones to Improve My RPG?

### Level II (Experienced—Intermediate Game Designers)

*Opportunities for advanced learning* can help RPG game designers provide rewards to players with challenging tasks and specialized content that support academic and career goals. The opportunities might include complex projects or content related to field simulations. Providing opportunities for advanced learning, such as skills workshops can enhance your student player's curriculum knowledge and help them to connect what they are learning with practical application to reinforce the importance of continuous learning and skill development (Hammer et al., 2018b). Access to content via advanced learning opportunities that align directly with career goals can further enhance RPG scenarios by connecting authentic learning opportunities into your game that enables players to build valuable, transferable skills (Dowling-Hetherington & Glowatz, 2017). *Vital rewards* can be used to improve player motivation in RPGs. Examples of vital rewards that can be integrated into your RPG are status achievements (earning the title of "team lead" or other specialized title) during collaborative projects.

*Status achievements* are game- (and content-related) milestones that your players can potentially work toward during the RPG rounds (tasks, skills, or experiences that players have not yet completed or mastered) to motivate players to explore different parts of the game. The achievements may involve combat, exploration, crafting, or social interactions. Think about what actions players can take and what skills they can develop (Plass et al., 2020). *Achievements* (similar to *skill badges*) are another advanced reward you can integrate into your RPG to reinforce players and promote social interaction. You can reward players as they complete tasks that require teamwork or competition, like an achievement for "Fastest Quest Completion" to potentially generate a friendly rivalry (Bell, 2018). Once you have a clear idea, create a diverse list of long- and short-term goal achievements and set clear criteria for each achievement so players know exactly what they need to do to earn them. For example, to achieve "Master Researcher," a player might need to find and document reliable and peer reviewed resources to help the team meet their game round tasks (Lin et al., 2015). Badges and achievements add another layer of motivation. Often awarded for reaching specific milestones or completing unique tasks, badges serve as visual markers of success. When designing unique achievements or badges for an RPG be sure they are closely related to the application of course content and content areas that are most relevant to the course so players understand their value (Sousa-Vieira et al., 2021). The design should also include visual representations that resonate with the course theme. Table 4.2 provides examples of twenty-five potential badges that can be incorporated into your RPG to enhance player motivation. To integrate these badges into your RPG, consider mapping each badge to particular tasks or challenges within the game, and introduce the badge system early in the game to create opportunities for players to achieve shared goals and receive group recognition (DeGloria et al., 2014). Table 4.2 shows a variety of potential Achievement Badges RPG game designers might consider adding into their games.

Level-ups are another potential motivational element in RPGs, but they work a little differently and serve slightly different purposes. Leveling up refers to the process by which players gain experience points to advance to higher skill levels. The progression (moving from novice to expert or beginner to advanced) is motivating for student players (Manzano-León et al., 2021). Level-ups are a way for players to progress their character or role usually tied to completing tasks, overcoming challenges, and they often come with new abilities, increased stats, or expanded access to resources or challenges.

### Table 4.2 Examples of Achievement Badges for RPG Gameplay

| Badge Name | Description and Game Criteria |
|---|---|
| Puzzle Master | You have been awarded the Puzzle Master Badge because you solved a complex challenge in the game round tasks and/or presented an innovative solution during the team rounds that helped with problem-solving skills needed by your team to achieve game objectives. Great work! |
| RPG Oscar | You have been awarded the RPG Oscar Badge because your avatar has consistently exhibited exceptional role-playing skills by staying in character and enhancing the game experience for all players. Very well done!! |
| Team Diamond | You have been awarded the Team Diamond Badge because your avatar character has consistently demonstrated the ability to maintain composure under pressure and during conflicts to assist your team with achieving their game tasks. Outstanding personal effort! |
| Avatar Player Expert | You have been awarded the Avatar Expert Badge because your avatar character has consistently demonstrated a thorough understanding of its own strengths and weaknesses. Your avatar has used their characteristics strategically throughout the game to assist the team in meeting their mutual goals. Excellent work! |
| Course Knowledge Connector | You have been awarded the Knowledge Connector Badge because your avatar character has consistently demonstrated the ability to connect course content into relevant team discussions and decision-making. Outstanding Effort! |
| Support Specialist | You have been awarded the Support Specialist Badge because your avatar character has consistently demonstrated a willingness to help other players, showing empathy, encouragement, motivation, and commitment to team success. Your skills have helped ensure the game experience was meaningful and relevant to all players. Thanks so much! |
| StoryTeller | You have been awarded the StoryTeller Badge because your avatar character has consistently made the game rounds more interesting by sharing significant, useful and creative (perhaps not accurate) details to the game round tasks that make the game experience more interesting and engaging for the rest of your team. Thanks so much for the extra effort here! |

*(Continued)*

**Table 4.2 (Continued)**

| Badge Name | Description and Game Criteria |
|---|---|
| RPG Rebound | You have been awarded the RPG Rebound Badge as your avatar character has recently shown they were able to recover from a setback in the game and ultimately help to meaningfully contribute to team success. Nicely done! |
| Resource Locator | You have been awarded the Resource Locator Badge because your avatar character has been able to find relevant information, resources, and use course materials effectively to help their team complete game round tasks. Your extra effort is appreciated! |
| Game MVP | You have been awarded the Game MVP Badge because your avatar character has consistently been recognized by the game master and your peers as a standout player who has made significant contributions to the team's progress and learning experience throughout the game. Outstanding contributions! |

Leveling up can occur in RPGs as the game round missions or quests are goal-oriented tasks. A *mission* usually includes a content-related team challenge or task to complete, while a *quest* can integrate a series of smaller, scaffolded tasks leading to a larger goal (Shoenberger, 2024). For instance, in a teacher education course, a mission might involve developing a comprehensive lesson plan that incorporates curriculum knowledge with innovative teaching strategies, related theories, independent research, technology, and developmental knowledge of their students. The goal of the RPG game round tasks is to provide players with defined goals, clear steps to achieve them, and rewards upon completion (mirroring the quest structure). Similarly, *milestones* are significant points in the learning process that represent a player's journey toward mastery (Saxena & Mishra, 2021). Table 4.3 shows potential examples of milestones for different types of teams, emphasizing their roles and achievements that RPG game designers may want to consider. Appendix F outlines gameplay across four rounds, emphasizing tasks, game mechanics like Recognition and Status Achievements, and concluding with a reflective debrief on teamwork and strategy development outcomes. Table 4.3 offers a visual of several Level Up Achievements game designers may want to consider adding to their RPG.

**Table 4.3  Level-Up Examples for RPG Gameplay**

| Achievement Title | Course | Description |
|---|---|---|
| Brand Builder | Marketing | Your avatar has developed skills in creating and managing brand awareness and identity through strategic messaging. You have earned the distinction of Brand Builder and you are now eligible to unlock new modules, and achievements to reflect your growing expertise. |
| Customer Specialist | Marketing | Your avatar has developed skills in customer satisfaction using marketing channels (email, social media, podcast, website optimization, etc.). You have earned the distinction of Customer Specialist and are now eligible to unlock new modules and continue to build on your academic and professional achievements. |
| Achievement Title | Course | Description |
| Lead Teacher | Educational Leadership | Your avatar player has demonstrated superior skills in planning and delivering quality instruction. You have earned the distinction of Lead Teacher and are now eligible to unlock new modules and continue to build on your academic and professional achievements. |
| Policy Influencer | Educational Leadership | Your avatar player has demonstrated superior skills in supporting and explaining educational policies and their impact on your community. You have earned the distinction of Policy Influencer and are now eligible to unlock new modules and continue to build on your academic and professional achievements. |

# What Are the Core Principles of Effective Game Design?

## Level I (Novice Game Designers)

When it comes to designing RPGs for educational settings, it is important to have clear design principles and mechanics (rules, procedures, etc.) in place to create an engaging experience for your student players. Many instructors already use basic game mechanics via rewarding students for completing assignments or recognizing outstanding efforts to reinforce positive behavior and promote achievement (Jennings, 2021). We must warn you, once your game is designed and you learn more about GBL options, it is easy to potentially go overboard with the game-related vocabulary and features. The goal is to find that sweet spot between fun and educational value, so game elements compliment the learning instead of becoming a distraction. While these ideas are discussed continually throughout the book, we cannot say too often that it is important for game designers to establish and reinforce clear goals and objectives of the game including the overall, big picture objectives as well as the smaller, more targeted, short-term objectives of each game session. A VITAL element of effective game mechanics is the game designer's thorough task analysis of each step in the game and how the smaller steps (activities) are connected to the long-term instructional milestones of the course and the RPG (Kapp, 2012). So, here is where your content and student related knowledge can help you develop an effective RPG. Game designers must consider the game progression from the novice player's perspective and successfully break down the game into clear, understandable stages that guide players from the beginning to the end. Think about it, what content-related constructs in your course do students generally struggle with as they progress through your courses? What do they need to know to complete each task and what resources are required to complete tasks in a timely manner? Keeping this in mind as you develop your game round tasks is so important (McKeithan et al., 2021). By doing this, you are more likely to ensure that players are able to grasp what they need to do at every point in the game, making their journey toward success more straightforward (Laine & Lindberg, 2020). When players clearly understand each step, they are more likely to stay engaged and motivated. The structure helps players navigate challenges and reinforces their learning and skill development throughout the game. Table 4.4 provides a potential overview of recommended steps for RPG game designers to consider when developing an RPG game and implementing game mechanics to maximize the potential for players to successfully complete tasks and access relevant content and background knowledge for their roles.

# What Are Some Common Mistakes in Game Design?

## *Level I (Novice Game Designers)*

Preparing for and participating in a multifaceted, team-based RPG game can be challenging and intimidating for players, so game designers must consider the tasks they are asking their players to perform in conjunction

### Table 4.4 Game Master Preparation Basics

| Preparation Essentials | Description |
|---|---|
| Session Objectives | Make sure the game master knows the purpose of the game, the long- and short-term content-relevant objectives as well as the overall personal and professional collaboration and problem-solving communication skill related benefits of the game. Be sure to explain exactly how the game rounds will be conducted and that the game master has access to all the materials they need to facilitate the game. Consider making and posting a Game FAQ to address common questions, provide clarifications, and avoid potential obstacles during the game. |
| Game Timeline | Be sure the game master understands when the game rounds should be integrated into your course assignment calendar and what to do if the timeline needs to be adjusted due to holidays, and so on. If your game sessions are in person, outline steps are needed to set up the game environment prior to game rounds. If the game is virtual, make sure the procedures related to what software program to use, how to set up teams, notify players and generate appropriate communication to the players. Consider a game round survey early in the course assignments in which players provide relevant information such as their current roles, experiences with the content, time zone, dates/times they are available, and contact numbers so the game master can use that information to set up teams and communicate with players as needed if the team dates/times, and so on, need to be adjusted. Also be sure the game master knows what to do if a player needs an alternative assignment or make up assignment. Keep that information in a readily accessible place. |
| Avatar Familiarization | Ensure the game master knows who the avatar characters of your RPG are and how the information you have created about each avatar should be used by the players and integrated into the game in relation to game round task completion and player preparation and assessment. |
| Scenario Clarification | Make sure your game master familiarizes themselves with the game round tasks and expectations. Have them consider and review the tasks to make sure the materials teams might need to complete tasks are readily accessible so the teams can meet objectives within the given time constructs of the game round. Consider leaving instructions on how to edit and make needed revisions to the game directions, timeline, or add additional resources, and so on, to help make sure the game rounds run smoothly. |

*(Continued)*

## Table 4.4 (Continued)

| Preparation Essentials | Description |
|---|---|
| Gameplay Mechanics | Encourage your game master to be familiar with the rules or guidelines of the game (which should be stated in the game round directions) and to review the game round directions, expectations, time constraints, and team norms with the players before the game round starts. |
| Player Communication | Be sure the game master understands when and how they can and should interact with players during game rounds. The goal is to minimize disruption of the game but keep the team progressing toward common goals. If the RPG is an in-person game, share needed resources to players prior to the game rounds. The game master may want to use visual signs to guide and redirect players when needed (e.g., pause, try again, review objectives, stay on task, break, etc.). Another potential nonverbal communication method would be to use index cards with messages or prompts as needed. Facilitating teams can be much easier in virtual games as the game master can use the chat function, polling and break out rooms. |
| Leaderboard Management | If your RPG has a competitive component, be sure your game master knows how to assess players and teams as well as how and when to and post updates on the course leaderboard. If you are using a rubric, consider making it very easy for your game master to use and if you are using other methods of assessment. Be very specific about your expectations with players and the game master. Avoid general or ambiguous evaluation terms, and be sure your game master knows how to access the needed documents (consider sharing examples). |
| Game Flow Management | Be sure your game master knows how to facilitate the session according to the agenda, guiding players through gameplay. If your game round directions, tasks, time constraints, resources, and assessment expectations are clearly evident in your game rounds, the game master may not need to do more than monitor and gently guide the teams. However, there may be unexpected situations such as if the team leader does not show up or prepare fully, the discussion gets off task, avatars conflict or there may be an emergency in the middle of the game. Consider an "if/then" chart of tips for the game master to think about ahead of time. If you are designing a game for someone else to teach, they may not have your experiences or natural abilities to guide and manage the team. Set your game master up for success! |

**Table 4.5 Taxonomy of Gamification Elements for Educational Environments (TGEEE) RPG Design Principles**

| TGEEE Element | Application in RPGs for Higher Education |
|---|---|
| Goals | Be sure your RPG includes content objectives for players that clearly define what players must do (and when) to be successful and connect to course outcomes as well as personal and professional goals when possible. |
| Challenges | Be sure your game round tasks include content relevant, realistic scenarios in which players work cooperatively to apply what they are learning and communicate what they know to others from their avatar's perspective in order to solve problems, consider the potential benefits, and consequences of their decisions. |
| Feedback Systems | Be sure your student players understand what is expected of them, how they will be assessed, and build in a variety of feedback mechanisms (game chats, visuals, scoring rubrics, debriefing sessions, leaderboards, etc.) to let players know how they are doing and provide suggestions for improvement as needed. |
| Rewards | Make sure your game is motivating, and student players have access to extrinsic and intrinsic rewards. Make the game fun but also work in recognitions when individual players or teams achieve content-relevant milestones. |
| Levels | Consider player comfort and experience when designing game rounds tasks and content mastery levels. Start with less rigorous game rounds and progress to more difficult levels or challenges as players become more comfortable with the RPG. |
| Social Interaction | Take advantage of opportunities for players and teams to collaborate with one another, share ideas, consider other opinions, and recognize the experience of how your course content is relevant in real life. Encourage them to think outside the box and consider the benefits and consequences of all potential game task related strategies and insights while simultaneously managing varied personalities and meeting deadlines. |
| Storytelling | While the goal of many RPGs in an IHE setting is to have players practically apply new learning, when developing the game task, consider making the problem in the narrative (or the avatars) interesting and potentially controversial to draw players into the story and motivate them to engage with the other players. |

*(Continued)*

**Table 4.5 (Continued)**

| TGEEE Element | Application in RPGs for Higher Education |
|---|---|
| Immersion | While the players should be encouraged to use their improv skills when appropriate to add details and character to their assigned avatar characters, remind them to stay in character and make sure any elaborations are in line with the avatars' motivations and experiences. Encourage them to really "channel" or connect with their avatar and the content on an emotional level. |
| Choice | Be sure your RPG provides players with many opportunities to make choices as they prepare for the game, participate in the game and interact with the content and other players. Players must feel as if their actions are valued and useful. Consider ensuring ways for very prepared players to be recognized and rewarded in the game to enhance motivation. |
| Time Constraints | When developing your game, be sure you set a realistic number of game sessions and time limits for each round. Also be sure the game master sets reminders and communicates time constraints to motivate players that they must be prepared, engaged and be familiar with the required tasks so they are able to think about and quickly respond to team interactions in real time during the RPG. Consider posting an agenda for the team with clear time estimates and perhaps assigning a time keeper. |

with the potential difficulty of the content, the players prior experience with gaming and the content demands, comfort and communication skill levels as well as the time demands of their adult learners (who often have competing responsibilities). When players do not see the connection between the game tasks, course content, and relevant real-world application of learning, motivation can be impacted. A common design flaw occurs if game designers do not clearly communicate this connection to players (Plass et al., 2020). Designers can address this concern by clearly linking game round activities to educational, personal and/or professional goals (Rivera & Garden, 2021). If the task of analyzing each step of the game is not executed properly, players may find themselves confused or frustrated rather than feeling supported and motivated to take initiative to fully prepare for and participate in game tasks (Sheldon, 2020). The misalignment can lead to *game collapse*, where the RPGs ability to reinforce content learning goals is at risk and as players or teams may become disengaged (Plass et al., 2020). When developing an RPG, game designers must consider each session scenario and agenda from the perspectives of novice and advanced player experiences. Assuming players have needed background information and/or an understanding of common professional language associated with the team's task, can be a potential barrier to player success (Salman et al., 2024). Do not assume your players have the accurate background knowledge or understand (or remember) the professional lingo needed for their game tasks. To avoid this common error, make sure to link all relevant materials to the game resources, even the basics. In our games, we added relevant professional vocabulary and acronyms the teams might need and links to short video clips related to basic content for players to review as desired. We made sure players could easily find the materials they need and they know how to access needed and relevant resources like tutorials, manuals, or in-game items (Toda et al., 2023).

Another game design flaw might occur when expectations and deadlines are unclear. If players are unsure of what they need to accomplish or when tasks are due, they can quickly become disengaged (Saxena & Mishra, 2021). To prevent this from happening, game designers can establish clear game round task objectives, outlining what is expected of players (from beginning to end) and the timelines for completing tasks. As we talked about in the previous chapter, we developed specific game round agendas in our games to help player avatars know exactly what they were expected to do and about how often they should expect to be given opportunities to interact in the round. Implementing in-game reminders and checkpoints (via weekly announcements or posted reminders) can help players stay on track and ensure they understand their responsibilities (Bell, 2018). Game designers might consider providing detailed checklists or preparation guides that offer guides and examples for players before engaging with the game (Castillo-Parra et al., 2022). Remember to assume that your players (or game master) will benefit when the game mechanics you choose to include in your game are clearly explained and resist the temptation to integrate new gaming words into your game directions unnecessarily. We will talk about how you might be able to use AI to help you do this, but remember to use clear and simple language and consider incorporating visual aids, such as diagrams or flowcharts, can also clarify complex mechanics, making them more accessible (Roungas et al., 2019).

Although this was mentioned earlier, it is important to emphasize that a realistic timeline for task completion is very important. Without clear and achievable deadlines, players may struggle with time management, feeling rushed or unable to complete tasks satisfactorily. To prevent this, designers should establish reasonable deadlines with built-in flexibility. As a game designer (and course instructor), think about mapping out your course assignments and be sure the game task assignments are included in your course maps and appropriately weighted according to the task difficulty and time demand. Consider including an assignment timeline within the course syllabus and LMS, course calendar, assignment modules, and regular announcements can help players stay informed, better manage their time and potentially reduce stress (Cullinan & Genova, 2023). Player support (before, during and after each game session) must be considered in game design. Players may feel isolated and struggle if they are unsure of how to seek help or what resources are available to them if they have questions at any point in the game (Cheng et al., 2017). Designers can provide an in-game support system that includes easily accessible FAQs, a help menu, and a community forum where players can ask questions and receive assistance. Offering tutorial missions or practice scenarios can also give players a chance to familiarize themselves with gameplay mechanics without the pressure of advancing the main storyline. Although we have found this is rarely needed after the players experience the first game round, we suggest that course instructors aka game masters should be sure players know they will be available throughout the course and during game sessions to provide guidance and support to apprehensive or confused players (Majuri et al., 2018).

## How Can I Promote Skill Development and Knowledge Application?

### *Level II (Experienced—Intermediate Game Designers)*

While the previous chapters addressed game learning objectives, we would like to emphasize again that game designers must always know and be able to explain how the short- and long-term content learning goals are related to each game round task and real-world applications of the knowledge your players will need. Players interested in developing their professional skills will feel more motivated when the game master and game scenarios present authentic, real-world challenges (Dymek & Zackariasson, 2016). By ensuring every decision, challenge, and interaction within the RPG has a purpose, you can align the game with broader educational goals and also allow you to measure progress, provide targeted feedback, and adjust the RPG as needed

(Foster & Shah, 2020). Table 4.6 presents examples of potential RPG tasks that game designers can review to use as ideas for getting started on your RPG (or making revisions) across various higher education disciplines.

Who or what is the game master may be asked. The game master in an RPG is part storyteller, part referee, and part puppet master of chaos. The game master in RPGs is primarily considered a game element (though they also include characteristics of a game mechanic). As a game element, the game master serves as the game round architect, guiding and assisting players through assigned game tasks or quests (Plass et al., 2020). The game master must monitor player and team progress, enforce rules, assess outcomes, and facilitate the game flow. We have found that often in the initial rounds, this requires the game master to be encouraging and reinforcing to players as they get comfortable assuming their avatar's role and providing team input from a different perspective (Fraguas-Sánchez et al., 2022). A game master is the ultimate multitasker, ensuring the rules are followed (mostly), keeping the narrative flowing, and serving as both guide and trickster, often with a knowing grin. Game Masters are, in essence, universe guidance with a sense of humor. Game masters set the rules, present challenges, and facilitate the overall flow of the game, ensuring that players' actions align with the story and objectives (Dorożyński & Dorożyńska, 2022). The game master needs to be strategic and knowledgeable about the content and the entire game's purpose and activities to ensure the objectives of the game are being met as teams progress. The game master can also work behind the scenes to interact with players and teams to make the game a bit more exciting by encouraging players to channel their avatar's powers or vulnerabilities as they engage with the team. For example, in our IEP team rounds, the principal avatar's biography may state they are working with a tight budget or concerned about what parent groups may think if they are not a tough disciplinarian. In the game round, if the avatar mentions funding, the game master may want to prompt the parent avatar to be upset that political factors may be influencing services for their child and another avatar may be prompted to point out that those statements may be illegal. You can see how the game master in this game round can potentially manipulate the play to immediately change the tone of the game round and which can quickly engage the rest of the team.

For game designers who are building games into classes that may be taught by other faculty or Graduate Teaching Assistants, be sure your game

### Table 4.6 Examples of Different RPG Formats

| Character-Based RPGs *Focus on Content Role-Play and Perspective Taking | |
|---|---|
| **Course Content** | **Potential RPG Scenario** |
| Chemistry | Student players are assigned avatars on an Environmental Impact Assessment Team to find out what is causing the pollution of a local river and suggest a solution to the problem. |
| Statistics | Student players on a Performance Analytics team are asked to analyze player performance and strategies over the past two years and generate a report to the new owners of a baseball team. |
| Elementary Education | Student players are assigned elementary school teacher avatars on a Professional Learning Community (PLC) Team are tasked with identifying evidence-based practices and sharing relevant information from their course to improve teaching practices and student learning outcomes for English Language Learners in fourth grade by developing a series of interdisciplinary projects to share with faculty. |
| **Collaborative RPG * Focus on Content-Related Teamwork** | |
| **Course Content** | **Potential RPG Scenario** |
| Chemistry | Player avatars on the Environmental Impact Assessment Team must work together during game rounds to consider the perspectives of all members of the team to address the problem. |
| Statistics | Student players on a PLC Team must work together during game rounds to research evidence-based practices appropriate for the students and consider the perspectives and information from all members of the team and share strategies to complete their tasks. |
| Elementary Education | Student players on the PLC Team must work together to share ideas and avatar knowledge to identify and integrate evidence-based practices into a series of interdisciplinary projects. |
| **Problem-Solving RPG * Focus on Solving Content-Relevant Challenges** | |
| **Course Content** | **Potential RPG Scenario** |
| Chemistry | Player avatars on the Environmental Impact Assessment Team must complete tasks in which they apply course content (scientific inquiry processes to determine the impact of the pollution) to identify and solve their game task. |

*(Continued)*

**Table 4.6 (Continued)**

| Problem-Solving RPG * Focus on Solving Content-Relevant Challenges ||
|---|---|
| **Course Content** | **Potential RPG Scenario** |
| Statistics | Student players on a Performance Analytics team must identify the appropriate statistical testing needed to complete their tasks and come up with a plan to make it happen within given time constraints. |
| Elementary Education | Avatars on a PLC team research and apply strategies learned in class to create materials to improve student outcomes for a specific student group. |
| **Scenario-Based RPG * Focus on Immersing Players in Real-Life Scenarios** ||
| **Course Content** | **Potential RPG Scenario** |
| Chemistry | Student players assigned avatars on an Environmental Impact Assessment Team engage are asked to practice chemical safety and laboratory safety protocols as they progress through their game task of responding to a potential chemical spill in the river. |
| Statistics | Student players on a Performance Analytics team must gather the information they need and complete the analysis. |
| Elementary Education | Player avatars on the PLC committee assume the roles of teachers, media specialists, ESL teachers and consultants to help students whose first language is not English in fourth-grade classes by identifying and sharing recommendations for evidence-based practices and examples of materials that might be used to help them (interdisciplinary projects). |
| **Simulation Based RPG* Focus on Replicating Realist Environments** ||
| **Course Content** | **Potential RPG Scenario** |
| Chemistry | Student players are assigned avatars on an Environmental Impact Assessment Team apply chemistry knowledge in practical contexts to complete game tasks. |
| Statistics | Student players on a Performance Analytics team recognize how the statistical methods they are learning about in class are related to real-world decision-making. |
| Elementary Education | Student avatars on a PLC team work together to resolve a simulated real-world project in which they apply what they are learning in class to help fourth-grade English Learners. |

master has a thorough background in the subject matter and field-related relevance to the course content and game round tasks as they may need this information to ensure they can guide discussions and narratives effectively (Sanchez et al., 2020). Consider creating a detailed *Game Manual* which clarifies this information just in case it is needed (e.g., summarizing historical events, theoretical frameworks, short/long-term goals, game timelines and expectations, resources for players, game rules, game master duties, etc.) Familiarize the game master with the avatars players biographies, how to assign player avatars and assessment procedures (Dorożyński & Dorożyńska, 2022). Again, we talk more about assessment in Chapter 5 but we encourage you to use game round assessment rubrics to clearly communicate game round expectations during each game round session. Outline the discussion points that will guide the dialogue during the session. The points could include questions that prompt critical thinking, themes that need exploration, or connections to the course material that players should make during their interactions. The resource will allow the game master to plan and facilitate sessions that keep players engaged (Sanchez et al., 2020). Consider sharing what you know about the diverse needs of your student players with regard to the RPG goals, curriculum content, varied backgrounds and experiences. If possible, the game designer might meet with the game master before the game starts to answer questions and/or record a brief video to provide relevant information. Sharing videos of previous team rounds can also help the game master to better prepare and be more effective as they support players. After each session, encourage the game master to gather feedback from players about their experiences. The game master plays an important role as guide and enforcer of game rules, but their identity can be assumed by the course instructor, game designer, or, in more advanced scenarios, even a player within the game (Kelly, 2020). Table 4.4 outlines basic information game designers may want to make sure they share with their game masters.

# What Framework Might Help Me Create My RPGs?

## *Level II (Experienced—Intermediate Game Designers)*

Creating engaging and effective RPGs requires understanding how to incorporate various gamification elements. The *Taxonomy of Gamification Elements for Educational Environments (TGEEE)* can be a valuable resource for new game designers (Toda et al., 2023). TGEEE can help game designers create their RPG by organizing game elements based on the game's purpose (e.g., motivation, learning, assessment). The resource can help game designers select elements to promote student player engagement, skill mastery, and provide valuable feedback. TGEEE was developed by a group of researchers and educators who provided feedback on different game elements to create a comprehensive framework that effectively represents the basic elements needed for GBL (Toda et al., 2019). The basic elements (e.g., learning goals, challenges, feedback systems, and rewards, etc.) are task-analyzed into manageable parts to help game designers better understand how the different game elements can help to facilitate learning. As we have repeatedly noted throughout the book, when you begin designing a game, it is important to identify the game's purpose and align the game rounds with specific learning objectives. TGEEE can be used as a resource to help guide you in selecting appropriate game mechanics that align with your curriculum goals. If your objective is to improve teamwork skills as well as content, incorporate collaborative challenges where players must work together to solve problems. The strategy encourages interaction among players and keeps the game focused on goal mastery. The idea of immersive educational experiences is another trend IHEs often promote to recruit and retain adult learners and it is also an aspect of the TGEEE framework helping game designers design educational tasks that require active (rather than passive learning) from their students (Halabieh et al., 2022). Using role-playing games (RPGs) takes immersion a step further. RPGs allow players to step into the shoes of various avatars within a structured narrative (Huang et al., 2022). The resource can provide game designers with guidance on how to explore different perspectives, make decisions in complex game scenarios, and promote content-related and professional collaboration (Toda et al., 2023). The effectiveness of an RPG relies heavily on its design; scenarios, game mechanics, and reward systems all must be crafted carefully to ensure the game remains both engaging and educational. One of the strengths of TGEEE is its focus on enhancing student engagement because contemporary adult learners tend to value interactive experiences in which learners are encouraged to actively participate in personally relevant learning activities (Helmefalk et al., 2023). Table 4.5 provides examples of how game designers can integrate the ten core elements of the TGEEE when designing RPGs.

# Which RPG Format Best Fits My Educational Goals and Classroom Environment?

## *(Level I—Novice Game Designers)*

Integrating RPG mechanics into higher education courses can provide opportunities for engaging and immersive learning experiences, and there are several options available to game designers and each type of RPG can offer unique benefits and learning opportunities. While the RPGs we have described throughout the book integrate a variety of elements from several different types of RPG formats, it is important for you to understand there are other options. *Scenario-Based RPGs* immerse students in specific contexts, allowing them to explore complex situations and decision-making processes. *Simulation RPGs* are considered immersive because the student players have an opportunity to connect theory to life as they are faced with a realistic, content-relevant scenario, and they have to consider varied factors and make important decisions which enable them to apply what they have learned in the course and recognize the potential benefits and consequences of their choices (Björk & Zagal, 2018). *Character-based RPGs* require student players to assume different avatar characters and help them to see the scenario and problem from a different perspective. These RPGs help student players to build empathy and understand different viewpoints as both content as well as personal and professional social skills, cultural awareness, and ethical decision-making are reinforced (Bowman & Schrier, 2018). *Collaborative RPGs* include the need for effective communication and teamwork skills into the game. Student players in these RPGs must actively listen to and consider input from their team members to achieve shared goals. The previously described RPGs give game designers the option of focusing on individual player decision-making and contributions, but Collaborative RPGs are team focused and can be used to reinforce communication, cooperation, team productivity, and achievement of common goals (Campillo-Ferrer et al., 2020). *Problem-based learning RPGs* also require student players to resolve authentic, content-related real-world challenges. The game tasks might require students to research, ask questions, and identify multiple potential solutions. Problem-based learning RPGs focus on the critical thinking and task analysis needed to find realistic and appropriate solutions (Christopoulos & Mystakidis, 2023; Martins et al., 2018). Our game easily integrates all these aspects into our game design as the games are Scenario-Based RPGs that require individual player avatars (Character Based) and teams to work together (Collaborative) to resolve a content-relevant real-world (Simulation) problem (Problem-based) as a team. Table 4.6 presents examples of different role-playing game types and their applications across various content areas.

## How Can Player Feedback Help Me Improve and Refine My Game?

### *Level II (Experienced—Intermediate Game Designers)*

As RPG designers, the right game mechanics for your RPG are important and related to what kind of game you want to create and why. Role-Playing Games mechanics are typically categorized into three types: immersive mechanics, non-immersive mechanics, and cross mechanics (Ioannidis & Kasapakis, 2022). *Immersive game mechanics* are useful if you want your student players to feel as if they are really involved in the game and their interactions and decisions in the game are important. Student players become invested in the game tasks as they are drawn into the game round because they are considering a different perspective and developing meaningful skills (Lameras et al., 2017). *Non-immersive game mechanics* are related to measuring student player progress toward learning milestones in the game and providing players with meaningful feedback to help them to recognize their strengths and opportunities for growth. Non-immersive mechanics help to provide players with structure and promote learning goal achievement. Students might be asked to analyze their experiences through activities such as debriefing sessions, where they discuss strategies and outcomes. The sessions can promote a deeper understanding of the content, helping students connect their in-game actions to real-world scenarios and concepts. *Cross Mechanics* can integrate immersive and non-immersive game elements into an RPG because they can help to make the game engaging and also assist with structure and clear pathways to achieving measurable learning objectives. The combination of mechanics can be used by game designers to align in-game experiences with specific skills and relevant content knowledge (Loup et al., 2016). Role-Playing Games designers do not need to incorporate all game elements and mechanics into the initial design. Consider starting more simply and gradually introducing additional elements as the game evolves. Feedback from players and inspiration gained from gameplay can guide the

**Table 4.7 Comparison of Immersive, Non-Immersive, and Cross Mechanics**

| Potential Program or Course Title | Immersive Mechanics | Non-Immersive Mechanics | Cross Mechanics |
|---|---|---|---|
| Introduction to Engineering | Character-based RPGs where student player engineers work collaboratively on a design project (building a house). | Post-game round debriefs and reflection assignments in which the players consider the importance of teamwork, engineering challenges, and game choices. | Players identify engineering concepts from the class and the team collaboration required by game tasks are related to real-world engineering situations. |
| Introductory Psychology | Collaborative RPGs in which student players assume the roles of psychologists who need to design and test theories through experiments. | Post game round debriefs about the psychological principles applied and what they learned. | Players learn how psychological concepts learned in class can apply in real-life situations. |
| General Chemistry | Immersive simulations RPG in which student players assume the role of a scientist and conduct lab experiments which apply chemical principles to cause chemical reactions. | Post-game round debriefs about the scientific method, the experiment, and their findings. | Players learn real-world applications of chemical principles and reactions. |
| Introduction to Nutrition | Scenario-based RPGs where student players work as nutrition experts to create meal plans for specific dietary needs at a group home. | Post game round debriefs about the nutritional science behind their choices and how well their plans might be received. | Players learn how dietary planning (or the lack of good planning) may be connected to health problems in the real world. |
| Introduction to Statistics | Role-playing scenarios where students work as analysts to interpret data sets and make predictions. | Post-game round debriefs on statistical methods used, interpretations of data, and any biases. | Players learn how statistical information is used by business and other organizations in real life. |
| Introduction to Education | Collaborative RPGs where students assume roles of teachers on a school leadership team trying to help a teacher with inadequate teaching and classroom management skills. | Post-game round debriefs about teaching strategies used, their connection to course content, and their effectiveness. | Players learn how the theories and practices learned about in class are applicable in real life. |

designer in refining and enhancing the game. Table 4.7 offers examples of immersive, non-immersive and cross mechanics.

## Game Log

*Chapter 4 is designed to help new game designers better understand how to use game elements and mechanics to develop an appropriate RPG aligned with your course objectives. The goal is to enhance your course by using GBL to reinforce key skills and constructs instead of simply providing a fun distraction. Throughout the chapter (and book), we stress the importance of clear, measurable and content-relevant learning goals. Whether the course covers business, psychology, or a technical field, your RPG must challenge your student players to apply what they've learned in an authentic and meaningful way. We encourage game designers to look at their course content through the eyes of today's learners. Revisiting how the field has changed can be an energizing way to make sure students are engaging with ideas and skills that reflect today's professional standards. The world is constantly changing, and if IHEs are to remain relevant and useful to our students and our society, we must teach the content that is useful to our students in today's world. Developing RPGs to address our student's needs can potentially help us to meet this challenge. While every instructor has probably had the experience of students not particularly enjoying an assignment, it is important to remember that student player "buy in" for RPGs is important. So, build a game that really connects with your student's interests, experiences, personal and professional goals. RPGs can be developed to address varied preferences and content experience by offering a variety of game mechanics and game elements to enhance the RPG experience. Player feedback is another aspect discussed in the chapter. We know, as instructors, the usefulness of (positive) constructive feedback, so build that into your game description and game rounds as often as possible to help your student players understand what worked and where they can improve. Looking ahead, in Chapters 5 and 6, readers will learn how to promote effective player engagement and identify potential challenges associated with implementing RPGs. The last two chapters offer readers practical strategies to integrate RPGs into your courses, information about many technology tools that might be helpful in developing avatars and teams, designing branching scenarios, and evaluating learning outcomes.*

# 5 Maximizing Engagement and Minimizing Problems

## Game Masters Prologue

*If there's one thing I've learned from working in finance, education, and everything in between, it's this: People are unpredictable. No matter how much you plan, structure, or task analyze, things will go sideways at some point. And honestly, that's what keeps learning (and life) interesting. Outside of work, I'm an avid yogi. After more than twenty years as a student and teacher, I've come to appreciate the importance of fluidity, flexibility, knowledge, and balance—things I strive to master every time I step on the mat. Each practice is different, bringing new challenges, but I show up ready. I learn something new every time, just like in an RPG. Every student player comes to your class with a different level of experience, yet together, you can create a truly meaningful learning environment and connection to your course content. The same principles that guide a great yoga class, adaptability, engagement, and growth, are essential when designing and facilitating an RPG experience and if all else fails ... just breathe. Players assuming the roles as their assigned avatar characters will second-guess their choices, overanalyze a simple task, or go completely rogue and throw the team off task. Game masters may find themselves playing referee, therapist, and motivational coach all in the same gaming session. What about game designers? They'll quickly realize that no matter how well they thought they constructed the game, players will still find a way to do the unexpected and potentially lead to a surprising outcome. At this point, as a game designer, you've got some basic knowledge and should feel ready to start thinking through the design of your RPG. This chapter isn't about creating a perfect game—it's about embracing the challenges and the evolving needs of your student players. The goal for the game designer and game master is to guide players, manage personalities, and keep players and teams moving forward without losing sight of the learning goals. Some strategies work, some don't, and sometimes you just have to roll with it. But that's the beauty of it—because real learning happens in the classroom (and in life) when we stop expecting perfection and adapt to the unexpected.*

# What Challenges Might I Encounter?

## *Level II (Experienced—Intermediate Game Designers)*

Next, we will explore some of the unexpected challenges we encountered in our roles as game masters and game designers. As we have repeatedly noted in the preceding chapters, GDs must align content goals and develop game round scenarios that promote individual and team achievement (Belbin & Brown, 2022). Managing student expectations is an important focus, as GBLs in IHEs must communicate clearly with players and structure the RPG experience (Björk & Zagal, 2018). In this chapter, we will share feedback from players and insights from game masters and game designers that such as the potential impact of extrinsic motivation (reliance on rewards) which can detract players from intrinsic learning (Campillo-Ferrer et al., 2020; Dowling-Hetherington & Glowatz, 2017). We will discuss the importance of designing RPGs that motivate students through meaningful engagement with content, rather than through superficial rewards and incentives (Chamberlin et al., 2023). We will share practical strategies for overcoming these challenges such as integrating reflective practices, encouraging open communication, and designing collaborative tasks that allow for diverse contributions (Daniau, 2016). Imagine a classroom (virtual or in-person) that feels more like a long-awaited gaming event than a typical classroom. As we have previously stated, creating a RPG learning experience allows our student players a different way of learning as we reinforce curriculum objectives while simultaneously building soft skills, teamwork, collaborative problem-solving and more (DeGloria et al., 2014). One of the most common themes we have consistently noted in our player reflection game rounds was the realization of how rapidly changing, unpredictable and multifaceted real-world content-relevant team decision-making can be. Many players report that while the course provided theoretical knowledge, the RPG experience enabled them to actively engage with the material in a way that required practical application. Rather than simply discussing concepts in a classroom setting, they had to apply them in a time-sensitive, interactive environment where decisions had immediate consequences. Another insight often expressed by our student players is that initially they may have assumed that decision-making in professional settings was primarily a linear process (following a straightforward series of steps). However, the RPG game round tasks that required them to work collaboratively with their team helped them to better understand how professional decision-making might involve competing priorities, multiple stakeholders, and the need for negotiation. Players may have had to assess incomplete or ambiguous information, consider different perspectives, and justify their choices while considering potential risks and outcomes. Another common insight shared by student players is the value of role-playing different perspectives. Many players found that stepping into an avatar's role helped them understand the multifaceted complexity of decision-making challenges and constraints faced by different professionals (team leaders, finance managers, parents, caregivers, lawyers, etc.). The game-round tasks helped them to understand that effective decision-making isn't just about individual expertise—it requires collaboration, communication, and an understanding of different team roles and content priorities within a system (McFarland, 2024). Although the potential benefits are undeniable, as is the case with any new approach to teaching, anticipated and unanticipated considerations and challenges are likely to surface and can impact students engaged in play (Dorożyński & Dorożyńska, 2022).

One of the unexpected benefits of being able to assume the role of instructor and game master is the potential power of the RPG experience to inspire and motivate us as well as our student players. While the majority of student feedback about the RPG experience is positive, there have been a few incidents in which student players did not find the game to be a meaningful experience. Game designers must remember that change can be difficult (for some more so than others). Change can be difficult for all of us as we are naturally more comfortable repeating familiar routines which includes how we design our curriculum related learning activities. Teachers and students have their own ideas about what education experiences are appropriate and worthy of their time, and when we feel as if we are being asked to do something that may be uncomfortable or time consuming, it is natural to consider resisting or avoiding the task (Bell, 2018; Camilleri, 2023). Finding the time (or making the time) to learn a new skill as an instructor to improve our practice can be its own challenge (who has time for this?). The reality is that we must make time to meet the needs of our evolving students if we want to stay relevant , but we will elaborate more on this in the next chapter (Franco & DeLuca, 2019). We must keep in mind that our students may also struggle to fully engage with role-playing elements (i.e., step into their avatar roles), working cooperatively as part of a team and considering a given content-related problem from a different perspective). Some students may still prefer the more structured classroom style learning approach as the RPG "open-ended scenario" learning may feel unpredictable or uncomfortable (Alismail & McGuire, 2015). Prior GBL experience, content knowledge, interpersonal communication skills, confidence and digital literacy can affect how your student players engage with game round mechanics, task objectives, and game satisfaction. In addition, players who are apprehensive about professional communication, actively listening to or sharing ideas or who are experiencing adverse personal challenges may have difficulty fully engaging with the game and working effectively with their teams (Anderson & Krathwohl, 2020; Ashcroft & Foreman-Peck, 2013). Group-based RPG rounds may include potentially uncomfortable or unpredictable social interactions resulting in communication challenges, uneven player participation, or conflicts between collaborative and competitive elements (Hammer et al., 2018a; Hammer et al., 2018b). For RPGs to be truly effective in education, thoughtful design, clear instructions, and ongoing student feedback are needed (Castillo-Parra et al., 2022). Over the years, we have identified the challenges and benefits of using RPGs in higher education. Some of the most important areas of focus include how players take on avatar roles, the impact of communication and group dynamics, the emotional and professional growth that happens as players work through game round tasks, and the balance between competition and cooperation (Dotson, 2020).

## How Can Role Conflicts Impact Teams?

### Level II (Experienced—Intermediate Game Designers)

It makes sense, of course, that a well-developed avatar character aligned with Belbin's Team Roles can positively impact team productivity and individual player satisfaction. Fortunately, even a skeletal bio for an avatar can be useful for players if the relevant characteristics and perspective motivations are clear (e.g., strengths/powers and weaknesses/vulnerabilities) as long as the student player understands what the avatar needs to do, and how to use the game resources, how to meaningfully collaborate with their team to complete their given tasks (Dorożyński & Dorożyńska, 2022). Players need to know how to identify and use relevant avatar information (backgrounds, experiences, biases, etc.) in conjunction with the required content knowledge to meaningfully contribute to the game round. One challenge a few of our players have shared is the potential difficulty with RPG *role immersion*. Role immersion in a RPG occurs when players embrace and feel comfortable assuming their characters role, interact with others, share ideas (experiences, biases). They make choices from their avatar's perspective and respond to fellow players as if they were truly in the game setting (Dymek & Zackariasson, 2016). Role immersion can make an RPG more fun and believable. For this reason, it is important to create avatar personalities which include enough relevant personality and motivation details to make it easy for your student players to assume those roles (Franco & DeLuca, 2019). We have found it is important to make clear to student players that they can be creative and draw on their own real or imagined experiences—so long as they align with the avatar's bio—to channel their inner avatar. By improvising and filling in gaps from the avatar's perspectives and experiences with relevant information, players can better support their teams. Encouraging players to be creative and add in unexpected details and knowledge can help to motivate them to be more actively engaged as they are making independent and unique choices that may relate to their own (content-related) experiences (Jaramillo-Mediavilla et al., 2024). We have found that most of the time, the freedom to be creative and improvisational can be a positive aspect of the game, but some players are not as comfortable filling in the gaps, which can sometimes feel forced or unnatural. Without a strong foundation, it's easier for players to revert to their own perspective and just play as themselves rather than stepping into a different role. Plus, if the team doesn't recognize or react in a meaningful or expected way, the player may feel like they are doing something wrong, making it tougher to fully immerse in the game tasks (Hartt et al., 2020). One way to prevent this is to develop clear assessment expectations for players prior to game rounds so they are aware of how they will be evaluated and are motivated to prepare better for the role ahead of time knowing, for example, they will need to reference specific examples of how they used information from their avatar's bio as they interacted with the team during the round to help the team achieve round tasks, but we will elaborate more on assessment later in the chapter (Kapp, 2012; Kelly, 2020). Another potential issue that is somewhat related to role immersion is role conflict. *Role conflict* can arise when a player's assigned avatar or role within an academic game round doesn't align with their expectations, if a player considers themselves as a strategist or analyst but they are assuming a role requiring them to be a persuasive communicator. If the RPG tasks do not emphasize the need for and value of each avatar's participation the players may struggle to engage or even disengage from the round tasks (Bowman, 2023). We found these instances created an interesting dynamic where players had to step outside their comfort zone and work within the boundaries of their assigned role. For some, this was a challenge; for others, it was an eye-opening experience that deepened their appreciation for team-based problem-solving.

While this has not happened very often in our games, another potential concern with RPG teams for game masters is knowing when to step in and help manage social interactions of players if they delay team progress or become a barrier to team success. One reason it may be difficult for game masters to know when and if to intervene in a game round is that professional team behaviors can mimic RPG team challenges. So, recognizing when the team may need game master assistance can be difficult. Team schisms can occur when smaller groups of players form factions during conflicts over resources, timelines, leadership decisions, or personal disagreements which may prevent the team from moving forward. The game master must know how to manage the team when this happens to be sure the schisms do not lead to complete game breakdowns (Bowman, 2010). Online communication can make things worse, as tone is often misinterpreted, emotions run high, and arguments can escalate more quickly than they would face-to-face. Since many educational RPGs rely on digital tools for coordination, designers need to think carefully about how to facilitate productive discussions and prevent conflicts from spiraling (Thomas, 1992). Another potential issue that the game master and game designer should keep in mind is the reality that each game round can lead to unique results and final products as players and teams may not always approach the game tasks the same way. Some teams and players may focus on storytelling, while others may be more strategic and competitive. Some players may choose to focus on brainstorming and problem-solving, while others just want to move quickly onto the tasks and resolve issues as soon as possible (Bowman, 2023; Yang et al., 2024). Balancing individual decision-making with group consensus can also be problematic in RPGs. Players may struggle when they feel motivated to advocate for their own perspective versus when to compromise for the benefit of team cohesion. Some noted that they initially wanted to push their own solutions forward, but later realized that truly effective collaboration requires listening to others, recognizing diverse expertise, and finding common ground. Another challenge was dealing with time constraints and uncertainty. Unlike a classroom discussion where players have unlimited time to reflect on their responses, the RPG scenario mirrored real-world pressures by requiring players to make decisions within a limited timeframe (Bowman, 2023). Some players noted that they felt overwhelmed by the need to quickly process information, consult teammates, and reach conclusions without having all the data they wanted (Bowman, 2010). The experience forced them to rely on critical thinking, adaptability, and prioritization skills—important takeaways for their professional growth. We have been able to resolve most of these issues with very detailed agendas with suggested time expectations while we simultaneously prompt players as needed throughout the game to help them stay on track. Emphasizing the need to stay in character and work productively with their team to complete tasks in the game round instructions and assessment rubric can help as well.

Competition is another potential RPG game mechanic that can adversely impact the game experience (Lameras et al., 2017). Game designers should remember that GBL does not require competition, but competition can be one component of the game that enhances the experience and reinforces related academic concepts (Kelly, 2020). We have found that although competition is often motivating for our graduate students, they are typically invested in the experience of applying the content areas and working with their teams. Most of our student players thrive in competitive environments, while others may not. If your RPG relies too heavily on winning, players might start focusing more on doing better than their peers rather than working collaboratively to achieve common goals, which can make the experience frustrating especially if more confident or more experienced players seem to take control or dismiss less experienced players (Leaning, 2015). For future game designers creating RPGs in higher education, understanding these potential concerns is important. Your RPG must balance collaboration with competition (if that is part of your game), provide clear role expectations, and offer room for different playstyles to contribute meaningfully toward team achievement. Although the competitive nature of RPGs can be advantageous, remember the focus for our adult learners should be related to intrinsic motivation—mastering a relevant skill, solving real-world content-related problems, or engaging with peers to complete interesting tasks—rather than direct competition (Hartt et al., 2020; Majuri et al., 2018) In our courses, the first game does not include competition. Players and teams have tasks, and they are awarded points based on their own engagement and assistance in helping the team be successful. Encouraging open communication, setting, posting, and discussing *Team norms* for respectful interaction and incorporating debriefs can help to prevent or minimize conflicts before they disrupt the learning process (Liberona et al., 2021; Loup et al., 2016). Most importantly, the game round directions and player expectations (noted in the directions as well as the agenda) should always bring players back to their shared goal—working together to solve real-world content-related challenges.

Game designers and instructors can take proactive steps to help teams function smoothly. One key approach is to build flexibility into role assignments. The game should also encourage diverse contributions, ensuring that every role has meaningful ways to participate in challenges beyond a narrow skillset. *Role authority* in RPGs can impact how players interact, make decisions, and solve problems throughout the game. *Role authority* is related to how power is distributed among player avatars and how that impacts team engagement. Some teams have a clear hierarchy, where one player takes on a leadership role (e.g., principal, hospital administrator, CEO, chairman of the board, president of a company, etc.) and the other team players may see themselves in more supporting roles. Sometimes, authority shifts based on the game tasks (e.g., legal expert leads contract negotiations, data analyst leads with data analysis). If one avatar has too much power, other players may disengage. To avoid this, game designers can be sure the agenda for team rounds clearly states when each avatar is responsible for leading the meeting, facilitating game activities and each player should be clearly involved in the decision-making (Khair, 2022). In addition (although we spoke about this in Chapter 3), try to keep the teams smaller than seven people if you can to minimize the potential that less obviously in charge players do not feel as if their character's input is useful or needed. Also, (again we will talk about assessment later), integrate active listening, and responding to finding information from other players into the assessment for all avatar characters. Conflict is another factor. Players may push back against authority figures, disagree on who gets the final say, or struggle with feeling unheard in group decisions. Another challenge is reliance on the instructor. When players constantly turn to the facilitator for direction, they miss out on a learning opportunity (and life skill)—figuring things out for themselves (Jaramillo-Mediavilla et al., 2024).

Although asking student players to switch avatars within the same game in different game rounds is asking them to research and consider the new avatar's perspective in conjunction with the content-relevant game tasks, one way to prevent power imbalances is to rotate roles between game rounds and give everyone a team the chance to assume a leadership role.

We are fortunate because students take numerous classes in our department with RPGs so we can easily rotate these roles in different courses so students experience the entire game in their assigned perspective (Laine & Lindberg, 2020). Competition is added to the game after the first course, and we have found students feel very motivated to assume and explore the new avatars after the first game round. Collaborative decision-making keeps all voices in the mix, making sure authority isn't concentrated in just one or two players. Some games introduce checks and balances, like requiring a team vote before major decisions or setting up peer feedback systems (Campillo-Ferrer et al., 2020). Training students on leadership and communication before the game begins can also make a big difference but most of the players have had enough experience with authority figures to be able to channel their inner boss in conjunction with their avatar bios and game round agendas to assume these roles initially. Experience, instinct and guidance from the game master has been useful in helping them manage team conflicts and unexpected incidents constructively. Again, if a team vote is required, be sure it is noted in the agenda (Lameras et al., 2017). Well thought through strategies to reduce players' stress and emotion can help navigate such challenges. Game masters need to be equipped to help talk through possible stress and emotions attributed to gameplay. Game designers can incorporate pre-game discussions to set expectations, provide structured decision-making guidance during gameplay, and facilitate post-game reflections to process experiences. Providing team feedback via social feedback loops also helps to clear up potential challenges as they arise. Feedback loops will be addressed later in this chapter.

Making decisions in an RPG can be overwhelming for students as they navigate complex information, leadership challenges, and uncertainty about their authority within the game. Multifaceted expectations for those experiencing RPGs, especially for the first time, can lead to game play challenges. Our experiences have highlighted the following decision-making challenges. Processing large amounts of complex data building on course knowledge/goals while making real-time avatar driven decisions. For example, RPG players acting as administrators had to analyze reports, consider policies, and make decisions quickly to be prepared for team meetings (Dymek & Zackariasson, 2016). The pressure to make decisions while meeting course goals often resulted in cognitive overload. Clear guidance, preparation, and awareness of the anticipated time commitment helped, but some still experienced decision fatigue (Franco & DeLuca, 2019).

*Decision fatigue* may occur if students are assigned avatars for which they did not have essential background knowledge. These students did not feel well equipped with knowledge needed for success. Team leaders may struggle to manage conversations, keep discussions on topic, and ensure inclusivity (i.e., all team members were heard). Balancing differing viewpoints, keeping the conversation focused on ethical decision-making, and ensuring all team members contribute to the final resolution are important for success (Helmefalk et al., 2023). RPGs can present an array of challenges and watchouts—decision fatigue, role confusion, or debating policy with a stressed-out avatar.

## How Can Game Masters Guide Teams without Taking Over?

### *Level II (Experienced—Intermediate Game Designers)*

We have mentioned the important role of the game master in game rounds (in almost every chapter) because the relationship between the game master and student players is tightly connected to team productivity and game success. The game master should actively engage with the entire team only when necessary, and when the game master does stop the game, the emphasis should be as a guide rather than a referee. At the same time, if the game master does not monitor and hold players accountable for active participation and team productivity, or if the game master is too rigid, players may feel like they do not need to fully prepare for or participate in the game. If the game master interacts too often or the players may feel like the game master is controlling the game and undermining the player's autonomy or decision-making (Bowman, 2023). The game master's knowledge of player backgrounds is important when they assign avatars to avoid Bleed. In an RPG, *bleed* can happen if an avatar player's personal experiences and emotions are triggered during the game activities. When this happens, the student player may feel personally attacked or defensive. The tension in the game round can escalate and schisms may occur. The tension in the game round can escalate, and schisms may occur. Although such experiences also happen in real life professional decision-making, it is important for the game master to monitor and guide players when this seems to be happening. However, the game master should not necessarily prevent instances of emotional connection to team rounds. Bleed can be an effective learning tool that shapes how teams function and conflicts unfold (Hugaas, 2024).

While the designer is responsible for initially creating the gaming experience, the game master must ensure all information is clear and accessible to the players. In our experience, avatar roles and player expectations need continuous updating and player education to strike the optimal balance. As we ran the game, avatar roles were modified based on player and game master feedback. Small changes such as adjusting personality traits or expanding background details for avatars (e.g., adding Belben personality traits) and modifying agendas for game rounds, when needed, helped clarify player expectations. Each time the game was played, student feedback was incorporated into the game design to help make avatar expectations and game tasks more clear. Managing player and team interactions during the game can be complex (Hammer et al., 2018b). Game masters must ensure every student has the necessary background knowledge to participate fully in the RPG. In one course, a student lacked the foundational content expertise, even though they were qualified to enroll for the course. This knowledge gap made it difficult for them to contribute effectively based on experience and team progress. The game designers or instructors quickly provided other learning options (i.e., supplementary materials, brief refresher sessions). By recognizing and correcting this issue, the student player felt more prepared in the game. Some players may try to take control of discussions, while others hesitate to contribute. Some players need more support based on individual needs—before, during, and after the game. Competition between players can create tension, requiring the Game master to carefully monitor interactions and step in as needed (Kapp, 2012). Managing and facilitating team productivity isn't a one-size-fits-all task—it shifts with each game session. Each game round can bring a unique mix of personalities, perspectives, and skill levels, shaping how avatars interact and make progress toward learning goals (Laine & Lindberg, 2020). From subtle guidance to more active involvement, the game master's role continuously adapts to keep the game running smoothly and maintain a productive learning environment.

Managing player dynamics extends beyond the RPG—what happens outside of gameplay within the classroom is just as important. The game master plays a significant role in providing support and feedback which helps players grow and refine their skills in and off the gaming field. Keeping in mind the potential power of a teacher's words on students, constructive criticism must be tactful and individualized according to each player's strengths, challenges, and role within the RPG. The feedback should be objective, meaningful and actionable (Majuri et al., 2018). Independent evaluations after each round allow the game master to track progress and identify areas for improvement, while structured feedback loops create opportunities for ongoing assessment and refinement. We found this to be true when using social feedback loops to support our RPG. As part of our assessment and player feedback process, players, team members are asked to observe and fill out rubrics to assess peer game participation after each round which are submitted for points (a grade). The game rounds were recorded for players to refer to later. We originally started with vague and open-ended rubrics, but we found that the game master and peers became very generous giving full points to everyone in every category, and in some instances they were very punitive and took considerable points without explaining their reasoning (Plass et al., 2020). We changed the rubric guidelines to include connections to each player's avatar bio linked to specific instances of how the information was integrated and shared with the team at appropriate points in the round. We require avatars to identify how they contributed unique information to the team that helped them to achieve team goals, and we ask for examples of how they identified key information shared by other avatars and elaborated on that information to again, help the team keep moving forward toward goal mastery. Establishing very clear and specific rubric rating guidelines which included citing supporting examples from the game helped us to develop a more objective assessment method with an improved feedback system for all players (Rahmani et al., 2022). Being flexible, adaptable, and organized are important for the game master to successfully support players and avatars as the game progresses (Rivera & Garden, 2021). For some gaming experiences, the game master will be needed to keep the game on track to meet goals and objectives. In our gaming experience, the game master used the Zoom chat to offer players personalized support and advice throughout the game. This could be guidance on the game's topic or a prompt to encourage more or less participation, depending on the player's engagement. Game master advice was given to all players at some point during play. All players were aware the game master was present, providing direction, and watching the game unfold. In one gaming scenario (e.g., a meeting involving education professionals), the team members went so far off track of meeting objectives, a game restart option would have been implemented if available (Romero & Usart, 2013). Afterwards, a *Game Restart Option* was created and implemented from that point forward. As illustrated, game master's role is to keep team discussions productive and centered on learning while being flexible and handling unexpected occurrences. By paying attention to group dynamics, stepping in when discussions go off track, and encouraging teamwork, the game master helps create a balanced, educational and engaging RPG experience (Roungas et al., 2019).

Flexibility and scheduling was another challenge when the game is synchronous and/or online. Coordinating RPG meeting times for hybrid and synchronous games can be tricky when juggling time zones and player schedules. One semester in an online class, I had a student in Iraq who agreed to meet at 3:00 am, one in South Korea who participated via phone on her way to work at 5:00 am, and one in Taiwan who was willing to play at 6:00 am. For individuals who could not attend, a hybrid game was set up so they could interact with their team.

An additional note regarding challenges and student schedules. When establishing gaming dates and times, remember to consult the calendar to ensure holidays will not impact your scheduled gaming dates. Having the team meet without an expected avatar character was also beneficial for the team in some ways as they needed to readjust their expectations in real time because that person and their contributions were not available. In some instances, the avatar who was not present could have shared information with the team leader ahead of time. Overall, this experience helped to reinforce the importance of active participation from the entire team. When players make comments related to how the missing team member "didn't even bother to show up," the entire team feels more motivated to contribute to the team's goals as they respond to that concern and comment. The game master manual should help the game master be prepared for potential gaming emergencies. Have a plan for managing student cancellations or avatar no-shows on game days. If we knew a player was not going to be in a round ahead of time, we also asked students on different teams (and even students who were no longer in the class) if they wanted to step in and play the game again to help the team. We have found previous gamers are typically very willing to volunteer. The game master must be ready to step in as a player/avatar on a moment's notice. Two heads are better than one—a statement that holds true for game masters as well. If this is an option, you may want to try it. Having two game masters participate in play and post-round reflections can enhance the overall gaming experience creating additional benefits as they identify potential ways to improve the game and make real-time adjustments to the current or future rounds (Saxena & Mishra, 2021). Players receive more support, ensuring smoother gameplay and quicker guidance. As is the case with player avatars, different game masters bring unique perspectives, enriching discussions and facilitation skills. When we tested this approach, the benefits were clear—improved gaming flow, and a more dynamic learning experience (Zhan et al., 2024). Being a RPG game master is more than keeping the game running—it is about keeping players/avatars on task to the game round learning goals. A game master has to know the game inside and out—learning objectives, mechanics, avatar roles—while also reading the room (or the Zoom) to keep things on track. Clear role descriptions, guided discussions, and feedback loops can keep players on track with rubrics helping to provide structured feedback too. Scheduling can be a challenge. But with strong communication, a little flexibility, and a backup plan for when things go off the rails, a game master can turn an RPG into a dynamic, engaging learning experience. Traditional teaching methods establish a solid foundation. In RPG design, this means linking academic content and objectives with in-game success. Simply put, when students successfully complete the game, their player experience should directly reflect targeted educational outcomes relevant to course material that has been effectively taught, absorbed, and experienced (Anderson & Krathwohl, 2020; Campillo-Ferrer et al., 2020). But this is just the beginning. How can the game designer make sure this is accomplished? There are many ways to design and implement strategies to ensure students are meeting the intended goals and objectives. Most importantly, assessments tailored to capture the unique aspects of RPG-based learning should be used (Castillo-Parra et al., 2022).

## **How Can I Effectively Measure Learning?**

### *Level I (Novice Game Designers)*

As a game designer, several key areas require discussion: game content and learning assessments, player motivation, player teamwork, and the use of feedback. Let's explore these topics to design (or refine) an RPG that truly supports student learning. Assessing player success in RPGs presents unique challenges, as it involves capturing individual and team performance within interactive and often multifaceted game rounds over time (Gallardo,

2020). Some of the more advanced assessment methods can be effective and generate some informative data, but they are also more complex and potentially challenging to set up and maintain. Table 5.1 shows examples of common assessment methods that can be used in RPGs.

*Data tracking* is all about gathering useful information (e.g., time on tasks, decisions made, contributions to the team, connections with their avatar, etc.). While this may seem very time and instructor intensive, there are technology resource tools that you may be able to use such as Twine or Unity to help you collect and analyze the data (Abdool et al., 2017). *Feedback loops* are potential RPG assessment methods that can be used to offer your student players regular updates on their progress. To build effective feedback loops, you need to decide when players will receive feedback, whether it's immediately after tasks or at the end of missions. Encouraging players to assess their own progress and incorporating peer feedback when relevant provides even more insight especially if you keep a record of feedback and improvements over time (Cheng et al., 2017). *Outcome mapping* is another assessment tool that you might want to consider to assess whether your student players are achieving their learning objectives. Once you identify the learning goals and game round objectives, you link those with game round milestones to keep your student players on track and informed about their progress (Grande-de-Prado et al., 2020). While outcome mapping, feedback loops and data tracking can be valuable resources, we used grade rubrics (that needed to be modified often) to simplify the assessment process (Nawrin & Sadek, 2022). Table 5.2 shows some examples of Data Tracking, Outcome Mapping and Feedback Loop Assessments that might be used in RPGs.

Assessing player success in RPGs feels "easy" once you have done it, but we have found you might initially feel like this is a challenging task. While we will talk about this more in the next chapter, using AI can help you to generate scoring rubrics that are in line with your game objectives and player expectations (Dyer et al., 2018). Assessing gameplay often requires capturing individual and team performance. Other, more traditional approaches might include direct observation, self-assessment, peer reviews, or even informal feedback sessions. While these methods can provide valuable insights, they often fall short in terms of consistency, clarity, and structure. *Grade rubrics* can offer a more systematic and transparent way to evaluate performance in RPGs (Mrangu, 2022). We found rubrics to be effective with assessing individual and team performance-based tasks requiring players to actively

### Table 5.1 Common RPG Assessment Methods

| Data Tracking |
| --- |
| Data Tracking Assessment requires the game master (course instructor) to collect a variety of data from players and teams throughout the game rounds. Data collection opportunities would be related to the overall game round objectives and course content. Examples of game measures that might be collected are things like the time spent in game rounds, the number of decisions made during the game, the number of interactions with the team, or attempts to assist the team as they progress through game tasks. An example RPG in a healthcare course might require players to use available information to diagnose a patient within forty minutes. The game master might record data related to the time the players spend researching the problem, collaborating with others and attempting to share relevant information. Game designers may want to use tools like Google Sheets or Excel to create forms or tables where players or observers can manually record actions, choices, or progress throughout the game. The advantages of this assessment method are that the data can provide insight into player understanding of course content and give the game master insight into how to help the players or team as needed. However, the set up can be somewhat time consuming and players would need to stay on top of this so game masters would need to ensure players understand how the materials are used for assessment. |
| **Feedback Loops** |
| Feedback Loops require the game master (instructor) to monitor player and team progress throughout the game and provide ongoing, structured feedback to players about their progress and areas of improvement. Feedback must involve two-way communication between the game master and players and should be given after each game round aspect to guide continuous improvement and growth. In a Teacher Education RPG example, the players may be asked to develop and defend an appropriate classroom management plan that integrates team support and caregiver supports. The team may be asked to defend how their plan is in line with newly learned content related to effective evidence-based practices and educational theory. The feedback should be targeted, specific, and aligned with clearly stated expectations. The feedback might be through automated messages, instructor comments, or peer reviews in which the strengths of the program are recognized and opportunities for improvement are explored. This assessment method often helps players to meaningfully reflect on their practices and be open to constructive criticism. However, the feedback loops can be time consuming and difficult to manage in very large classes. |
| **Grade Rubrics** |
| Grade rubrics are an assessment method option for RPGs. The game designer can make these rubrics with very detailed expectations to help players and game masters understand exactly what is expected of players (what do they need to do, how long should it be, how many times should they do it, what format should it be in, etc.). In an educational RPG about historical debates, players may be assessed on argument quality, evidence use, creativity, and teamwork. Rubrics can be used to emphasize different categories of an assignment such as accuracy, avatar connections, teamwork, content knowledge, and application of concepts. Once they are developed, rubrics can be used by game masters to assess players and teams relatively quickly and many LMS programs have software options that can integrate the rubrics into the course which is available to students and easy for the instructor to score as they may just need to click a box and the program automatically calculates and reports the grades to players. However, the rubrics, while objective, can be seen as rigid and may not easily offer instructors a way to give extra points for creativity and extra effort. |

*(Continued)*

**Table 5.1 (Continued)**

| **Outcome Mapping** |
| --- |
| Outcome Mapping is an assessment method in which the game master recognizes players and teams as they achieve specific course-related learning objectives. In order for these to be effective, they must be closely aligned with the game round tasks. In a business course RPG game, student players may be asked to work as marketing teams developing a marketing plan to increase enrollment for a fictional university. The team goal is to use the marketing principles they learned about in the course to develop a plan for this client within the given budget and technology constraints. The plan would need them to identify prospective students, identify strategies to recruit the students and create a plan to effectively market to that population. For outcome mapping to be successful, the game designer would need to build in checkpoints in which players would be demonstrating the learning goals. The game master would be able to assess whether students met goals and offer constructive feedback if needed. The assessment does help to make the feedback more specific and targeted, but it does require extensive planning initially, and the feedback may be time consuming for the game master. |

demonstrate their knowledge and skills in real-time scenarios (Gallardo, 2020). Recording player responses and evaluating them using the rubric allows players and game masters to acknowledge areas of strength and identify opportunities for growth. In our games, we use rubrics for players to assess themselves after each round, and the game master reviews what the players think about their own assessments and offers feedback based on the game master's observation of the player during the game round. The points they earn on the rubric can potentially become their grade for participation in that game round. In games where we include a competition component, the points are recorded on a team leaderboard that is available and shared with the entire class. Student players earn points from their self-assessment, the game masters assessment and they are assigned a "secret mark" or peer from the game they use a similar rubric to assess their mark. The points on the leaderboard are cumulative and the winners are declared at the end of the game. Grade rubrics have enabled us to use a variety of assessments in the form of player self-assessment to reflect on their own gameplay, game master assessments and peer assessments to enable players to evaluate each other's contributions (Mrangu, 2022).

Unlike direct observation, which can be subjective and may not capture the full scope of a player's preparation, abilities, or contributions, rubrics provide a clear set of criteria against which players' performance can be measured. We have found using a more objective, transparent, and structured approach helps to motivate players to be prepared and actively engaged in the game rounds as well as making sure that all players are assessed on the same

**Table 5.2 Examples of Data Tracking, Outcome Mapping, and Feedback Loop Assessments**

**Data Tracking Assessment**

**Purpose:** Collects Performance Data
**Scenario:** Healthcare RPG—Diagnosing a Patient

| Player Name | Task Type | Time Spent (min) | Attempts Made | Collaboration Score (1–5) | Diagnosis Accuracy (Yes/No) | Points Earned |
|---|---|---|---|---|---|---|
| Avatar 1 | Research | 12 | 3 | 4 | Yes | 18/20 |
| Avatar 1 | Decision-Making | 8 | 2 | 4 | Yes | 16/20 |
| Avatar 1 | Collaboration | 5 | – | 3 | Yes | 14/20 |
| Avatar 2 | Research | 11 | 3 | 4 | Yes | 17/20 |
| Avatar 2 | Decision-Making | 8 | 1 | 4 | Yes | 15/20 |
| Avatar 2 | Collaboration | 5 | 3 | 2 | Yes | 16/20 |
| Avatar 3 | Research | 10 | 3 | 4 | Yes | 17/20 |
| Avatar 3 | Decision-Making | 6 | 1 | 4 | Yes | 11/20 |
| Avatar 3 | Collaboration | 5 | 4 | 3 | Yes | 12/20 |

## Outcome Mapping Assessment

**Purpose:** Evaluates Learning Objective Mastery
**Scenario:** Business Simulation RPG—Marketing Campaign Development

| Player Name | Objective | Task Description | Achievement Status | Evidence Provided | Points Earned |
|---|---|---|---|---|---|
| Avatar 1 | Audience Analysis | Target Audience Profile | Achieved | Yes | 20/20 |
| Avatar 1 | Strategy Development | Marketing Plan Development | Achieved | Yes | 18/20 |
| Avatar 1 | Message Clarity | Campaign Presentation | Not Achieved | No | 10/20 |
| Avatar 2 | Audience Analysis | Target Audience Profile | Achieved | Yes | 20/20 |
| Avatar 2 | Strategy Development | Marketing Plan Development | Achieved | Yes | 18/20 |
| Avatar 2 | Message Clarity | Campaign Presentation | Achieved | No | 15/20 |

*(Continued)*

## Table 5.2 (Continued)

### Feedback Loop Assessment

**Purpose:** Provides Structured, Specific Feedback
**Scenario:** Educational RPG—Lesson Plan Presentation

| Player Name | Feedback Type | Feedback Provided | Suggested Improvements | Response to Feedback | Points Earned |
|---|---|---|---|---|---|
| Avatar 1 | Presentation Clarity | Clear delivery, good visuals | Include Instructional Materials | Yes | 18/20 |
| Avatar 1 | Evidence of Preparation | Well-prepared content | Connect to developmental level of students | No | 14/20 |
| Avatar 1 | Collaboration with Team | Active engagement | Great Job Sharing Ideas | NA | 20/20 |
| Avatar 2 | Presentation Clarity | Clear delivery, good visuals | Justify your instructional decision-making. | Yes | 17/20 |
| Avatar 2 | Evidence of Preparation | Well-prepared content | Add in ways to include technology | Yes | 16/20 |
| Avatar 2 | Collaboration with Team | Engaged | Nice work, but share more with your group. You have good ideas | Yes | 15/20 |

standards, reducing biases and making evaluations more reliable (and easy) for players and game masters (Kelly, 2020). We also found that vaguely worded or open-ended self-assessments and peer reviews, while useful for encouraging reflection and collaboration, were more difficult to align with the educational objectives of the game. Creating rubrics specially aligned with the task analysis and expectations of the game rounds helped to address these issues by providing explicit guidelines required for individual and team for success. The rubrics helped us more clearly communicate to players what the specific skills or outcomes they should be able to demonstrate during the game round. A well-designed rubric (linked to content and examples from the round) can assist with game productivity and provide concrete feedback to players (Gallardo, 2020). If your LMS allows you to add rubrics with point levels and feedback descriptions to your assignments, it is also relatively easy for the game masters to review the player's reflection and offer specific and objective feedback by just clicking a box on the scoring rubric when grading. Rubrics can emphasize different aspects of gameplay, such as strategic planning, collaboration, or problem-solving (depending on the objectives of the game). By setting clear expectations and criteria, rubrics promote active participation, promote communication, and provide meaningful feedback that helps players understand their strengths and areas for improvement (Nawrin & Sadek, 2022). The structured approach supports progress and competition and encourages the accumulation of points and potential competition. Table 5.3 shares information related to the potential advantages of using RPGs to assess individual player and team progress in your RPG.

# How Do I Maintain Player Motivation?

## *Level II (Experienced—Intermediate Game Designers)*

Multiple types of motivation can occur in the teaching environment when engaged in RPGs: *extrinsic motivation* (i.e., motivation driven by external rewards such as badges, points, and leaderboards—tangible incentives); *intrinsic motivation* (i.e., motivation that is driven by personal interest, curiosity, or enjoyment of the activity—not an external tangible); *social/ collaborative motivation* (i.e., motivation due to group dynamics, teamwork and the desire to contribute to a shared goal or community); and *mastery/ skill-building motivation* (i.e., motivation driven by desire to improve individual

**Table 5.3 Potential Advantages of Rubrics to Assess Player and Team Progress in RPGs**

| Advantage | RPG Advantage Description |
|---|---|
| **Consistency** | Rubrics can help to provide structured, objective evaluation standards. Sharing rubrics with players before, during, and after the game adds a level of transparency to players so there is a clear understanding of what they need to do to be successful. |
| **Clarity of Expectations** | A clearly defined rubric can help to improve the RPG experience because players understand what they need to do to prepare for the game rounds and achieve tasks and advance through the game tasks. |
| **Feedback and Improvement** | Rubrics can offer players feedback about how they performed in the game, how accurately they may have applied course content along with feedback about what they may need to work on to meet learning objectives and complete game tasks. |
| **Adaptability** | Rubrics can be easily developed by many different tools to connect tightly to game round tasks. The rubrics can be easily adjusted by game designers or game masters as needed according to issues that may be encountered during before, during or after the game rounds. |
| **Enhanced Learning** | Rubrics can be effectively used to support active participation in game rounds and communication with others in the game if the player knows they will be assessed on how often and how well these interactions are demonstrated. |
| **Self and Peer Assessment** | Rubrics can be a useful way for players to assess their own progress, engagement and productivity in game rounds which will help them to identify ways to improve for the next round. They can also be used for peer reviews. |

skills or knowledge over time). Both traditional and RPG learning includes motivation types in some form (Torres-Toukoumidis et al., 2021). Traditional methods might include quizzes, group discussions, and reflective essays that promote extrinsic, social, and intrinsic motivation. In a RPG simulation, student players may assume avatar roles and earn points or badges for appropriately applying course content and helping a team meet a game learning objective. As a RPG designer, it is important to understand how the different motivators impact and play out differently than in the traditional classroom; specifically intrinsic and extrinsic motivators and student players.

The concept of player motivation and incentives has already been discussed in detail in Chapter 3. In this section, we will be looking at game design specific watch outs to keep in mind when designing RPGs which include intrinsic and extrinsic motivators (Prensky, 2002). When developing RPGs you must build your game by considering your student player's motivations and different ways in which this impacts and occurs in your game rounds. Intrinsic and extrinsic motivation co-exist within the RPG but need to be closely monitored and controlled to ensure player involvement. Intrinsic motivation comes from the enjoyment of the learning process within, creating a self-driven engagement with the RPG (Topîrceanu, 2017). Players become absorbed and motivated by the actual learning from RPG participation: immersive narratives, complex engaging challenges, collaborative problem-solving, and critical thinking opportunities with other players. By creating and building intrinsic motivation for the players within the game, they are more likely to transfer the skill and knowledge acquired to long-term, real-world academic and professional goals. Students who are intrinsically motivated, become invested in the RPG working to solve complex real word problems rather than the extrinsic motivators (e.g., points, badges, leaderboards) something more internally driven. Debating sustainable strategies, negotiating stakeholders' interest, and experiencing firsthand consequences of decisions made leads to sustained learning of class theoretical concepts (Campillo-Ferrer et al., 2020). *Soft skills* such as collaboration, negotiation, and adaptive problem-solving are enhanced. Role-Playing Games insights will have lasting practical value in academic learning and professional goals. But watch out! Intrinsic motivators can be a double-edged sword in RPG-based learning environments. For some players, intrinsic motivators encourage internal self-driven engagement; but remember that not every player may be drawn to the RPG scenario or thematic elements. Uneven student engagement across the class with players struggling to connect (i.e., development intrinsic motivation) may occur (Sabtu, 2023). Learning outcomes are better assessed through a combination of student self-reports and observable engagement. Overemphasizing intrinsic rewards may leave students who need external validation—such as grades, points, or certificates—feeling unmotivated. Conversely, relying too heavily on extrinsic rewards can shift the focus from meaningful learning to merely winning badges and certificates. Balancing this relationship of motivation is important (see Chapter 3 for more information). Used thoughtfully, extrinsic motivators can complement intrinsic motivation. However, avoid creating an overly competitive atmosphere that takes away from the game's educational goals. When players are more concerned with accumulating rewards over mastering RPG related course content, the intended learning outcomes may be compromised. Cultivating long-term strategic decision-making skills are replaced with quick "wins." The deeper understanding of course content is diminished. Game Designers must carefully manage extrinsic rewards to motivate learning without detracting from the core educational objectives of the RPG (Torres-Toukoumidis et al., 2021).

## Game Log

*This chapter focuses on how to keep players engaged in RPGs by proactively identifying and preventing some of the problems we discovered as game masters and GBL researchers related to student players and their motivation, engagement, and feedback systems. We elaborate on some of the intrinsic and extrinsic motivators for game designers to keep in mind including—intrinsic, extrinsic, social, and content mastery goals. The challenge for game designers is to design a game that compliments the class content without overwhelming the students or the instructor. As is the case with any educational activity, student motivation is closely linked with engagement. Our students may be motivated by personal interest or enjoyment, and they may also be motivated by extrinsic GBL rewards such as points, badges and leaderboards. Player motivation is central to engagement. Intrinsic motivation comes from personal interest and satisfaction as they contribute to their team, while extrinsic motivation relies on rewards like points, badges, and leaderboards. In this chapter we share suggestions for maximizing student engagement without letting the game mechanics distract from the RPG content-related purpose. We also elaborate more on effectively assessing players in an RPG. Assessing players and teams can be challenging because the game rounds are interactive, fast paced and the goals may be multifaceted. To address this, we share some information about varied RPG assessments such as data tracking, outcome mapping and feedback loops, but we suggest that keeping it simple with grade rubrics as they can be useful because they simplify assessment and provide clear expectations for players and are easy to use for game masters and/or instructors. Our goal is to emphasize that these tools are intended to prevent problems before they occur. By designing RPGs with clear expectations, appropriate motivators, and systems that actively monitor and support engagement, you can create RPGs that are enjoyable and effective.*

*Designing RPGs for higher education is a balancing act for all three components (i.e., the player/avatar, the game master, and game designer). Keeping players motivated and moving toward meeting game round tasks (and learning goals) is the primary concern. We found this is generally the case (even with games that are very imperfect). We also found that while most students embrace the RPG, others may not enjoy the experience or may lose sight of the goal and just participate for the points. We emphasize (again) about the importance of the game master to provide players with clear guidance, and help them to see how in-game decisions relate to real-world learning. Teamwork.... Have you ever been in a group project where one person takes over while others stay silent? The same dynamic can happen in RPGs. Unclear roles can leave some players hesitant to contribute, while dominant voices steer the discussion and decisions. When designers listen and act to address student input, RPGs are improved. Adjusting mechanics, changing difficulty levels, and refining scenarios keeps the experience relevant and challenging. In the next chapter, we will talk more about how implementing RPGs into your classes can potentially benefit your students and your program. We will also share insights into the many new AI and technology tools you might want to consider using when developing your new RPG (we sure wish those resources had been around when we developed our games)!*

# 6 AI, Social Media, and the Future of RPGs in Higher Education

## Game Master's Prelude

*Writing this final chapter was harder than I expected. I thought that summarizing the advantages of RPGs, offering last-minute advice, and sharing ideas about the future of gamification in higher education would be straightforward. But as I started researching information for the chapter and writing about what I have learned from the process and how it has changed my perceptions and instructional decision-making in my own practice, I realized how much the experience has meant to me. Teaching has always been my passion. I loved teaching my students in the K-12 settings, and I am still honored to have the opportunity to influence teacher educators in the higher education setting. I've never wanted to do anything else. My years as a teacher in K-12 settings taught me that good teaching isn't about mastering every subject—it's about understanding the content you are teaching from the student's perspective—knowing how students think, what they bring to the table developmentally and intellectually, and how to make learning meaningful and relevant to them. In my years covering classes for other teachers, I have been asked to teach content I had little or no expertise in. I've taught advanced math I did not understand and French classes when I could only remember about five key vocabulary words from high school. Yet, I found that if I connected with students, recognized their needs, and showed them how the material mattered in their own lives, they would always find a way to engage and succeed.*

*Connecting content with student needs is why I believe RPGs are a perfect fit for higher education—and yes, K-12 too (but that's probably a topic for a different book). Role-Playing Games can create opportunities for every learner to engage, collaborate, and apply real-world skills in ways that feel both personal and relevant. It's hard to believe I only started using RPGs in my classes three years ago because they've become a cornerstone of my teaching. In our program, we run about twenty-four game rounds a year in eight courses. I can honestly say that by the time players share reflections in the final round of the game, I'm amazed* at how impactful the experience is for students. As an instructor, it did take some time to create the first game, but it was very easy to reuse the game elements, copy them into other classes, and adapt the scenarios according to different learning objectives for other classes. As I said earlier, I've been researching and learning about AI tools and exploring how they can help with game development and improvements to prepare for writing this chapter. The possibilities are exciting (and, yes, overwhelming). Learning new technology can feel like an extra cognitive load that many instructors (including me) may think they don't have time for, but taking the time to learn things now can potentially save you time in the future. However, my advice is to take it slowly and stay open to new ideas. Maintaining an open mindset is what we ask of our students, and we should model this open mindset and willingness to learn new things to meet the changing needs of our students. The world is constantly changing and unpredictable, and it's our responsibility in higher education to help our learners develop the skills they need related to what we are teaching. After all, we are not in this profession because we are hoping to get rich (I made more as a K-12 teacher than a professor). My students are online from all over the world and in different time zones. On some days our game rounds start about the time I am typically asleep, but I always leave the game rounds feeling rejuvenated and excited about the game because I can see the changes in my student players as they apply what they are learning in the course and engage with their teams—their energy and enthusiasm is contagious. This chapter's goal is to inform and inspire you to consider using gamification in your program—whether you're a new game designer or a seasoned gamer looking for fresh ideas. I'll share what I've learned about marketing, social media, AI resources, and how to potentially use RPGs to make courses and programs more effective.

## What Are the Potential Ethical Considerations of RPGs?

### *Level I (Novice Game Designers)*

Game designers and game masters must be cognizant of potential ethical challenges related to RPGs, and perhaps the most important is student privacy. As you develop your game, be mindful as to whether your game tasks include collecting and storing data related to student progress, interactions, and assessment (Thorpe & Roper, 2019). The game master might collect demographic data when assigning avatars with backstories and experiences that are different from the student player. For example, in my games, I have students complete a game survey the first week of class related to the days and times they are available, their time zone, their primary professional roles, and any previous avatar experiences they have had with the games. I reuse the basic avatars in different classes, but the avatars have new tasks related to the course content and the game settings are different. I try to pair students with avatar characters that are different from their own so they can experience the game challenges from another perspective. While I encourage student players to remain in character, it is possible that during the game, players share personal experiences related to their profession, region, family, finances, or other sensitive topics, raising concerns about data security and confidentiality. *The Family Educational Rights and Privacy Act (FERPA)* includes mandated practices for maintaining data protection related to student records. Role-Playing Games designers must protect student privacy. Data collection should include only game-related information. Using avatar personalities can help safeguard student identities. Only authorized instructors or designated facilitators, should have access to student assessment data, and information should be securely stored on password-protected, institution-approved, and secured devices and platforms. In my games, the assessments are uploaded and archived into the course record (Thorpe & Roper, 2019). If reflections or student experiences are shared for marketing or research purposes, responses should be anonymized, and consent must be obtained. Anonymizing data, storing it securely, and adhering to relevant privacy regulations are important responsibilities. Future game designers must ensure the game set up, tasks, and data generated during play comply with FERPA regulations. RPGs may involve students sharing personal reflections or engaging in collaborative tasks where they interact with peers. The interactions can sometimes lead to sensitive or confidential information disclosed intentionally or unintentionally (Blunn, 2022). Table 6.1 shares some potential ethical concerns related to FERPA that game designers and game masters should be mindful of when creating and facilitating RPG rounds.

## Can RPGs Make Online Courses More Relevant?

### *Level II (Experienced—Intermediate Game Designers)*

As noted in Chapter 1, there is a growing demand for online course options (especially at the graduate level) because adult learners are often managing multiple responsibilities. In response, more IHEs are offering online learning options (Alexander, 2020; Ambrose & Wankel, 2020). One of the challenges

## Table 6.1 Potential Ethical Concerns in RPGs—What Not to Do

| Ethical Concern | What NOT to Do |
| --- | --- |
| Exploiting sensitive topics | When developing your RPG round, consider the dilemma from your student player's perspective. Avoid using real-world trauma, discrimination, or abuse as in your scenario without clear educational intent. Consider the potential impact of participating in an RPG related to abuse if one of the student players has a similar experience. |
| Bias in character roles | When developing your RPG avatar characters, avoid potentially reinforcing harmful stereotypes as those might be distracting to players. |
| Excessive competition | Although a little competition in an RPG can make the game more engaging and exciting for players. Make sure the purpose of the game is not focused on individual competition as that might impact collaboration and team progress. Celebrate team accomplishments and excellent examples of content application when opportunities arise. Be generous with your praise and encouragement. |
| Neglecting player agency | When developing RPGs, integrate many opportunities for student players to think critically about the situation and connect what they are learning to a variety of potential decisions and solutions. Avoid limiting choices to a small set of predetermined outcomes. |
| Inadequate support for players | When you create your RPG, avoid removing yourself from the game and leaving it all up to the players to get things done. While they are adults, the RPG is stronger if the students feel supported and their efforts recognized by the game master (instructor). Be sure your players have the support they need to complete challenging tasks, find the needed supports, and be ready to get involved to redirect and motivate them when needed. |
| Failure to provide feedback | Active game round monitoring is important for many reasons, but perhaps the most important is to keep the game rounds moving forward in a positive direction. Be sure to develop RPGs in which the game master has a clear role and knows how and when to step into the game and offer players or teams constructive feedback. |

*(Continued)*

**Table 6.1 (Continued)**

| Ethical Concern | What NOT to Do |
|---|---|
| Ignoring diverse perspectives | Remember that the goal of GBL is to give players an opportunity to apply new learning in real-world scenarios but also to consider ways to address a problem from a different perspective. Make the most of opportunities to reinforce the idea that the different knowledge, skills, and experiences of the team make the team stronger and more capable of solving the challenges in the game (and in life). |
| Infringing on privacy | The most important potential ethical concern in RPGs is to respect player privacy. Do not require or even encourage student players to disclose personal or sensitive information about themselves, their families, their businesses, financial information, political affiliations, and so on. Be sure to monitor the game rounds and immediately offer feedback if this starts to happen. Remind the team to stay in character and focus on the team agenda and game tasks. |

of online learning is maintaining meaningful collaborative opportunities to engage with peers since students are not physically present; promoting collaboration and critical problem-solving when applying new learning can be difficult (Chamberlin et al., 2023; Franco & DeLuca, 2019). Incorporating GBL experiences into your course can help you prioritize engaging and relevant learning experiences that align with your student's goals and real-world applications (Halabieh et al., 2022; Hoque et al., 2023). Throughout this book, we have reinforced the potential for RPGs to motivate and inspire your students by tapping into their personal goals, competitive nature while simultaneously enhancing collaborative and problem-solving skills with real-world, relevant tasks (Irwanto et al., 2023; Rivera & Garden, 2021). One of the most exciting aspects of the game from an instructor's perspective is seeing a sense of purpose an RPG round—that often starts out with students being nervous but eventually evolves taps intrinsic motivation, as students feel personally invested in their avatar's progress and the outcomes of their collaborative efforts (Saxena & Mishra, 2021). Often, in the final round of a game, my students express a desire to "find out what happened next?" However, it is important to make sure the game is engaging but not overwhelming, tasks must be individualized so each player's contribution is required and valued, competitive without hampering collaboration and the assessment methods must be able to objectively measure all these aspects of the game . . . (sounds easy, right)?

As a game designer, you can accomplish these tasks in many ways such as by integrating mechanics that reward personal contributions and team-based problem-solving. Fortunately, you do not really have to make sure all these elements are present, connected, and working effectively when you create your first game (Kim & Maloney, 2020).

## Can RPGs Help Students Adapt to Changing Policies and Workforce Demands?

### *Level II (Experienced—Intermediate Game Designers)*

As a current or future game designer in higher education, the tools and strategies you implement will shape the way players—your students—engage with content, collaborate with peers, and interact with others. Teaching content while simultaneously reinforcing the benefits of actively listening, considering other perspectives, shared decision-making, and effective, productive communication skills can potentially be as valuable for students to learn as the curriculum you teach. The key is the game designer's thorough knowledge of their curriculum and how it connects to real-world situations (Chamberlin et al., 2023). Your expertise in conjunction with your knowledge of your student's field-related needs can help to ensure that game's tasks and scenarios are tightly linked to what students will encounter in their professional lives. Adult learners often bring previous real-world experience to the table, and they want to see how what they are learning applies to their future careers. When students understand that the game tasks reflect real-life situations, they are much more likely to engage deeply with the content. Players recognize the game is a classroom activity as well as a way to prepare for their careers (Campillo-Ferrer et al., 2020). An obvious benefit of online learning is the flexibility for students in different time zones with varied schedules, but online learning can also create barriers due to the lack of face-to-face interaction. Discussions in game environments can offer student players the opportunity to actively engage with the content, interact with their peers on the team, ask questions, and minimize the isolation (transactional distance) students often report (Shoenberger, 2024). Think about all the potential benefits of giving your students an opportunity to step into roles that might mirror skills needed in their current or future careers. Your instruction will go beyond simply learning the material as your players' experiences align with current industry standards and contemporary needs (Campillo-Ferrer et al., 2020). The shift to online courses can also impact job satisfaction and meaningful connections for instructors. Transactional distance creates challenges for instructors as well as they may become more focused on the administrative and research demands of their role and actually start to think they have little time to connect personally with students. Unfortunately, contemporary online instructors may believe their primary responsibilities focus on course setup, designing instruction, posting announcements, and grading assignments, which can limit opportunities for direct, personal engagement with students (Mosquera et al., 2022). RPGs can make learning activities more enjoyable for instructors as they see the players apply their own experiences and content-related skills in creative, interesting, and often unexpected ways through game rounds. Game masters have the opportunity to manipulate the game and redirect players as they work through their round tasks. The game can help to make your course more effective as instructors who also interact with players in game rounds better understand their students' interests, strengths, and needs in relation to real-world applications of the course content.

Instructors who are not actively involved in the practice of their field may be surprised at how much priorities and practices have evolved. Role-Playing Games can offer instructors an opportunity to stay connected with the latest research as well as with the real-world relevance of what they are teaching. Higher education is facing a growing gap between what is being taught and the rapidly changing challenges of an unpredictable future. Due to recent changes in higher education policy, funding and workforce reductions, your students may be having different college experiences than the students you had in mind when you designed your course and curriculum. Institutions are beginning to think about the impact that changes in resources and the support students receive might have on learning. This is a good time to reflect on your course design and teaching strategies to help students meet these new challenges. Many borrowers now face higher repayments, especially with restrictions on income-driven repayment plans and public service loan forgiveness programs may inhibit our student's enrollment and make the competition among programs more important. The changes reinforce the need for IHEs to adapt and consider more innovative approaches to curriculum design, research priorities, and support services (Salman et al., 2024).

RPGs can become an effective assessment tool for instructors, offering our learners the opportunity to observe firsthand how players creatively work toward shared goals, which reinforces the meaningfulness of the content. Each game round allows instructors who simultaneously play the role of game master to identify whether content adjustments are needed, within the game and the classroom, to better align with the current needs related to the curriculum as well as the industry or related field. We must shift from teaching based on our past experiences to developing the knowledge, skills, and capacities needed for whatever the future may hold for our students. Moving out of your comfort zone and being open to trying something new can be a powerful way to keep your teaching relevant and forward thinking (Ramic-Brkic & Balik, 2023). As educators and game designers, we have the opportunity to shape the future and help educate our student citizens and help them to apply new content and be able to distinguish between reliable and unreliable sources, recognize logical fallacies, and make informed, logical decisions. We have the ability to create experiences that will motivate and support the next generation of thinkers, problem-solvers, and leaders. The future of education must be interactive, collaborative, and engaging, and RPGs can help make that happen (Adare-Tasiwoopa ápi & Silva, 2024).

# How Can RPGs Build Content-Relevant Communication Skills?

## *Level II (Experienced—Intermediate Game Designers)*

Throughout this book, we have emphasized the social learning aspects of RPGs—such as player collaboration, problem-solving, and competition—as powerful tools for student engagement (Campillo-Ferrer et al., 2020). Digital literacy skills are an important aspect of our student's personal and professional lives as they are often required to generate, review, and respond to multiple emails, digital calendars and participate in varied discussion forums, share live documents in cloud spaces, collaborate on projects, and attend virtual meetings. Digital communication is connected to how our students learn and interact with the world. As instructors we can teach, reinforce and promote these skills as they are related to academic and professional success (Kahn et al., 2022). Direct instruction of professional *code-switching* refers to the ability to know when and how to adapt one's language, tone, and communication style based on the setting, audience, and purpose. Making our learners aware of this potentially strategic tool can help them develop more effective communication skills in different professional and academic environments (Chui et al., 2016). RPGs can help our students recognize when it is appropriate to use formal, structured and more academic language (e.g., professional emails, presentations, committee meetings) while also being able to shift to more conversational, collaborative language when appropriate when they are interacting with people they know well (e.g., team problem-solving discussions, networking events). Contemporary instructors should not assume their students recognize the expectations of different communication settings (Albahoth et al., 2024). Integrating Game Rules (or meeting norms) into the agenda for each round and reviewing those norms prior to the game rounds starting is one way to emphasize the need for players to use the soft skills needed to maximize collaboration and productivity as they work through tasks (Dinh et al., 2021). Your RPGs can provide your students with opportunities to practice situational awareness and improve their literal and digital literary skills and enhance their ability to switch between professional, academic, and casual communication styles. Understanding the norms and expectations of each digital platform is important because each of them have unique communication norms and social rules. Consider taking advantage of making communication expectations more clear for your learner by pointing out that communication expectations vary according to purpose and audience in academic and professional settings (e.g., professional emails should have a clear subject, a polite greeting, and a well-organized message). On the other hand, discussion forums in LMS platforms like Canvas or Blackboard work best when responses are structured and add to the conversation in a meaningful way. Instructors should not assume that students are automatically aware of these differences and RPGs can help instructors to model and provide guidance to ensure effective and appropriate interactions. When working in RPG teams, players might be tasked with using a variety of collaborative tools such as Google Docs, which allows real-time document editing, Microsoft Teams, which integrates chat, file sharing, and video conferencing, and Slack, which organizes team communication through channels and direct messaging. Again, do not assume all students understand how to use these tools and recognize commonly understood communication expectations. Participating in virtual meetings through Zoom or Google Meets requires basic understanding of managing audio and video settings, using chat functions effectively, and engaging professionally with others. The expectations between platforms may be different from what your learners are used to using so scaffold support for these learners through the use of short video demonstrations of how to use the program (Kahn et al., 2022). Instructors can record themselves via Zoom as they share screens and demonstrate the technology or link to a Youtube or other platform related technology. You can link the resources to the game setup or game round descriptions (Spante et al., 2018).

## How Can Social Media Integration Strengthen My Program?

### Level II (Experienced—Intermediate Game Designers)

Social media plays a major role in how people interact, with over 5.22 billion users worldwide (DataReportal, 2024). The majority of social media users fall within the eighteen to thirty-four age range, which overlaps significantly with the age of most college students, typically ranging from eighteen to twenty-five years old (National Center for Education Statistics, 2023). Integrating social media into GBL can further enhance digital and social learning and help to keep students engaged and connected. Including social media in the RPG process can offer players more opportunities for collaboration, real-world skill building, and promote your course or program to a wider audience (Rennie & Morrison, 2013). The role of social media has become more important in IHEs in relation to student engagement and recruitment. Role-Playing Games scenarios can take advantage of this trend by including social media elements into post-round reflections and encouraging your learners to share and build on what they learned in the game by engaging in professional discussions, building networks, and staying connected to the latest research and resources in their field. Social media can be used to strengthen communication between students and institutions. Role-Playing Games which integrate social media aspects can help students to connect academic learning with digital literacy skills. By sharing their experiences and interacting on social media, they can also build digital literacy and real-world communication skills. RPG assignments can be adjusted to include content-related reflection and discussion on social platforms, allowing students to share their experiences and engage with professionals. The visibility can benefit students and improve your institution's credibility and presence (Datsenko et al., 2020). An active social media presence can help your institution be more trustworthy and engaging to prospective students. Encouraging your players to share their learning experiences and growth through social media can help your organization to be more competitive in recruiting students. By designing RPG experiences that integrate reflection, networking, and knowledge-sharing on social media, game designers can create meaningful, engaging learning experiences that benefit students and institutions (Datsenko et al., 2020). When you bring social media into your RPG scenarios, players can learn how to communicate ideas effectively, market concepts to an audience, and engage with digital communities in meaningful ways (Cordero-Gutiérrez & Lahuerta-Otero, 2020). Teaching and reinforcing the power of social media and the need for digital professionalism can help RPG players better understand how these tools can be used to influence how their avatars and the fictional companies are represented and perceived by others. Integrating these skills into game scenarios can potentially improve the game experience. For example, if a team scenario required players to review and respond to a series of professional emails, collaborate on shared documents, to troubleshoot and respond to digital miscommunications, players develop meaningful, real-world skills (Cordero-Gutiérrez & Lahuerta-Otero, 2020). A School Leadership Team (school administrators, teachers, and public relations staff) or hospital public relations teams (administrators, investors, lawyers, employees, etc.) might be asked to resolve a situation where a misleading social media post has spread false information about a new policy causing concern in the community. The RPG team must identify the misinformation, use new content learning to collaboratively assess the misinformation, construct a professional response, and effectively use social media communication and other digital literacy platforms to re-establish trust with the school community. In a business or marketing strategy RPG, students can create and execute social media campaigns as part of their game objectives. The team might develop promotional content, design marketing strategies, or simulate the launch of a new initiative within the game world. Encouraging students to reflect on their role-playing experiences through social media can also enhance their learning. In all of these RPG examples, players must apply new content learning, critical thinking, digital literacy, and problem-solving skills to analyze, problem solve, and collaborate to achieve a common goal (Zhan et al., 2024). Integrating real-world social media challenges into RPG scenarios can potentially help strengthen each player's ability to engage in effective, ethical, and strategic digital communication (Mujallid, 2024).

Post-game round reflections can promote individual assessment of skills and team-based thinking and reasoning and simultaneously provide instructors with insight into the impact of each game round. By analyzing these reflections, instructors can identify trends, and make adjustments to the game as it evolves to better meet the changing needs of your players. Another potential benefit is the ability to highlight and reinforce player and team reflections that may demonstrate exceptional insight, critical thinking about the usefulness of the experience in relation to the curriculum. One of the first post-game (final-round) discussions included a round-robin type sharing of their thoughts with other players. One of my students started her response with, "I was thinking about Bloom's Taxonomy, and I believe this game represents the highest level because we are creating." Others talked about the prep required for play, how nervous and impressed they were with other avatars, how meaningful it was to consider the problem from a different perspective and how realistic the scenario was as "Some players acted like what is common in these meetings in real life—they either really didn't care or they were outstanding actors." As an instructor, I was totally surprised by the profound impact of my very imperfect game on my student players. I was so glad that I had decided to record the rounds for players to reflect on later—also keeps players more engaged during the rounds so they do not feel as if they need to take notes or remember what they did or others said. Recording the sessions also gave me the opportunity to identify potentially strong candidates to share their experiences with future cohorts or on professional platforms. However, it is also important for instructors to be sure that any student participation through social media, marketing campaigns, and so on, fully complies with Family Educational Rights and Privacy Act (FERPA) and institutional policies. Students who volunteer to share their insights must do so with appropriate permissions and a clear understanding of how their contributions will be used. To maintain ethical standards and avoid any perception of quid pro quo, these opportunities should be offered only after the course has ended and students must know that participation is voluntary and unrelated to course outcomes (Datsenko et al., 2020).

Platforms such as ResearchGate can provide players with opportunities to ask questions, connect with researchers, and distinguish reliable information from misinformation (Datsenko et al., 2020). As part of the post-round activity or reflection assignment, students might be asked to create a LinkedIn or ResearchGate account to research given tasks, ask questions of experts, share their educational progress, professional growth, and ongoing training efforts. These social media platforms can help your learners to showcase their learning experiences, connect with industry professionals, potentially find or supplement their employment and build professional networks. A positive student post sharing the benefits of RPG learning in your class—such as handling misinformation, crisis communication, experiential learning, and real-world relevance—can promote your institution's brand awareness or spark the interest of prospective students (Komljenovic, 2018). To maintain privacy, our students must be directed to share general insights rather than specific game details that could identify classmates or internal course discussions (US Department of Education, 1974). Facebook, Twitter (X), and Instagram are also potentially valuable platforms which might be used by players to engage in real-world, professional interactions and conversations. Students and faculty can participate in relevant discussions by using hashtags associated with digital literacy, education, healthcare, or marketing, depending on the game's focus. For more in-depth reflections, players might use institution-hosted social media blogs or department-run social media accounts, such as Facebook, Instagram, or Twitter, to share their experiences. Asking RPG players to share their experiences on social media can help to establish a sense of identity tied to your program or *brand loyalty* which can be an effective marketing strategy that takes advantage of the "low hanging fruit" of satisfied RPG players to spread the word and reinforce the value of your program which can in turn motivate others to trust and consider your program. When current students and alumni consistently highlight the impact of RPGs, they can attract new students, strengthen alumni connections, and improve your program's reputation (Kaushal & Ali, 2020).

When our students share how RPGs' game experiences have helped with their personal and professional growth, they can potentially attract future students through the consumer marketing funnel. The Marketing funnel is a foundational concept in marketing which begins with brand awareness (Sams et al., 2023). When one of your learners shares their positive experiences with their networks or on your IHE social media channels, potential students might become interested and start learning more about your program. Over time, the potential student (or lead) may progress through a series of stages in which they consider your program and decide whether it is aligned with their own goals. The hope of course is that social media engagement and links to your IHE webpages and resources may help guide potential students through a consumer decision-making process in which they eventually choose to apply for and enroll in your program. When RPG gamers share their stories, they aren't just endorsing your program; they're inviting others to become part of something meaningful (Santini et al., 2021). Instructors must keep in mind that while RPGs can be effective tools for attracting prospective students, work collaboratively with your colleagues to be sure all shared content complies with FERPA and protects student privacy (Staudt Willet, 2024). The process does not necessarily have to be very difficult. I reached out to our marketing team and they gave me a release form to have my students sign if their materials were used on the website or for marketing purposes. The process was easier for students who wanted to share their experiences on social media. Table 6.2 provides an overview of potential ways game designers may consider how social media applications might enhance the RPG experience for their student players and/or assist with program marketing and brand awareness to attract new students.

## What If I Design a Game for Others to Manage?

### Level I (Novice Game Designers)

While the significance of the game designer and the game master was discussed in Chapter 3, it is important to emphasize the potential impact this relationship may have as the game evolves. The ideal situation would be if the course instructor was responsible for designing the course content so they would also be the game designer and the game master when game rounds were played. If this is the case, the game master will likely feel comfortable adjusting the game if any unexpected or unclarified concerns arise in the game (Fraguas-Sánchez et al., 2022). In this instance, the game designer (course author) is essentially writing the lesson plan for the game round and because they wrote the plan, they know the learning goals and how the goals are aligned with the relevant curriculum standards and student learning needs. The game master is likely to be much more comfortable adjusting instruction in real time just as a traditional classroom teacher who planned their own lesson would feel if they had to adjust instruction because of an unexpected turn of events such as recognizing students did not have the expected and required prior knowledge needed for the lesson. The

### Table 6.2 Social Media Tools for RPG Games

| **Discord https://discord.com/** |
| --- |
| Discord is a social media platform that offers voice, video, and text chat that game designers can potentially integrate into RPG games before, during and after game rounds. Discord's users are typically in their mid 20s–30s, and this is a popular application in the gaming community who are interested in music, art, and programming. Discord can be used to communicate for team members to communicate prior to game rounds, and it can also be used as a post-game debriefing platform. The social media tool can be effective to promote collaboration and team-building and can also help to improve institutional branding when the content is shared with or read by prospective students. However, there are some potential FERPA concerns that game designers should be aware of such as the potential for unauthorized sharing of student data, so it is recommended that instructors provide student players with clear guidelines for acceptable use. |
| **Facebook Groups https://www.facebook.com/groups/** |
| Facebook Groups are a social media platform in which users with shared interests connect over shared interests. The demographics of Facebook users include about 25% of users in the 25–35 age range, about 20% in the 18–34 age range and about 20% in the 34–44 age range so this platform can potentially target adult learners with shared interests in your content area or RPG tasks. Role-Playing Games designers may want to use this platform for students to share their game experiences after rounds. Students may also be asked to share their experiences on the department pages to showcase the innovative and immersive learning opportunities in your organization. Facebook Group posts from your RPG players may help to improve institutional branding when the content is shared with or read by prospective students. However, there are some potential FERPA concerns that game designers should be aware of such as the potential for unauthorized sharing of student data so it is recommended that instructors provide student players with clear guidelines for acceptable use. |
| **Instagram https://www.instagram.com/** |
| Instagram is a social media platform in which your players might want to share photos and videos of themselves as they prepare for or debrief after game rounds. Instagram users are typically between 18–34 years old so they are a prime target of potential students who may be interested in learning about how your program creatively engages and supports students and helps them to develop useful, real-life skills. Instagram posts from your RPG players may help to improve institutional branding when the content is shared with or read by prospective students. In addition, there are some potential FERPA concerns that game designers should be aware of such as the potential for unauthorized sharing of student data so it is recommended that instructors provide student players with clear guidelines for acceptable use. |

*(Continued)*

**Table 6.2 (Continued)**

| Twitter https://twitter.com/ |
|---|
| Twitter (rebranded as X) is another popular social media tool that you may be able to integrate into your RPG experience. Users are typically in the 18–34 age range, and they share short messages, or tweets with others about different topics of interest. The tool can be used to motivate your players as they share experiences with the game to future potential students. However, the messages are typically short and limit what can be shared and the content does not normally last for very long. While X posts from your RPG players may help to improve institutional branding when the content is shared with or read by prospective students, there are some potential FERPA concerns that game designers should be aware of such as the potential for unauthorized sharing of student data so it is recommended that instructors provide student players with clear guidelines for acceptable use. |
| **LinkedIn https://www.linkedin.com/** |
| LinkedIn is a social media platform for professional networking that can connect your students to others with similar interests. LinkedIn members are typically between the ages of 25 and 35 years and can use the tool to share information about their positive experiences in your course, with your school, and so on, with their networks. They may even share game badges and achievements with their networks. LinkedIn posts from your RPG players may help to improve institutional branding when the content is shared with or read by prospective students. However, there are some potential FERPA concerns that game designers should be aware of such as the potential for unauthorized sharing of student data so it is recommended that instructors provide student players with clear guidelines for acceptable use. |

instructor would likely be able to seamlessly recalibrate lesson activities, offer additional needed insight and guidance and keep students moving forward toward meeting learning goals. However, if the instructor is expected to teach a lesson that they did not author, they might not see the connections and rationale behind the lesson components and subsequently struggle to make real-time, meaningful adjustments to keep the learners on pace with meeting the learning goals.

As a teacher education professor, one challenge I have noted for my learners as contemporary educators is that often, in K-12 settings, there has been a move toward scripted teaching, pacing guides, and duplicating courses. The issue is also prevalent in higher education, particularly in online courses as many LMSs can replicate previous classes that may have been designed by someone else which can leave instructors—especially adjunct faculty—feeling disconnected from the course content (Mackh, 2018). Instructors tasked with teaching someone else's lessons or courses may not know how (or be permitted) to modify the content according to the needs of students or they may feel they lack the authority to make such changes. While pre-developed lesson resources help ensure what is being taught is in alignment with curriculum standards and timely instruction, challenges may occur when you are asked to teach or facilitate an activity you did not design. Without direct involvement in the planning process, facilitators may not fully understand the rationale and decision-making of the instructional designer. Therefore, the connection to curriculum or industry standards, link to developmental needs of the learners, as well as the potential challenges and benefits of how task completion is linked to the short- and long-term "soft skills" related to real-life simulations may not be clear (Ashcroft & Foreman-Peck, 2013). Similarly, if the game master is not the Game Designer, they may struggle to fully grasp how the game rounds connect to the content scenario, which could impact gameplay flow and learning objectives (Tran & O'Connor, 2024). When faced with unexpected challenges or a need for modification uninformed facilitators may struggle to adapt the game tasks or clarify unintended obstacles which could potentially hinder player engagement and team success (Narayanan et al., 2023). As a game designer, consider both the varied needs and experiences of both the players and the game master when you design your game. Take the time to clearly task analyze game instructions and tasks to minimize the potential for misunderstanding (even if it seems like your players should already know what you are talking about and/or be able to do). Also keep in mind that a game designer may be a content expert but might not be fully up to date with current industry standards or player needs. A well-designed game should not be static; instead, it should be flexible and adaptable, allowing for adjustments that promote engagement and better align with student needs. An effective game evolves over time, ensuring a more relevant and impactful learning experience (Danaei, 2019).

## How Can Experience and Knowledge of Students Improve My RPG?

### *Level I (Novice Game Designers)*

Game design can feel complex and overwhelming initially—for both the designer and the players. That is why this book encourages starting with a simple scenario and gradually building the game as needed to address the course constructs and player needs. The stages of game development are broken down into manageable steps, making the process less intimidating. Game designers must remember that people tend to prefer familiar activities, and the same is true for players. Introduce the game gradually, creating a comfortable space and offering the human and digital resources players need to feel supported in taking risks. Find ways to help your students to understand that the game master will be there to guide them through the game tasks and expectations. Ensure game rounds are well-structured and make the first experience engaging and easy, setting the stage for a successful introduction. Your goal is to create an experience that motivates and challenges students without intimidating them. The game must be designed so every player is able to engage fully with the game. So, how do you achieve that delicate balance? An effective game designer must tap into what you know about your students and the typical curriculum challenges what typically interests them, and where they might struggle with application of content. Some players may have a lot of prior knowledge in the field, while others might be new to the subject. Players should be challenged and not overwhelmed (Leaning, 2015). Another important factor is understanding the struggles and gaps in content knowledge that students may have. Game designers need to know what concepts are likely to confuse students or what areas they tend to struggle with. If a group of students is having difficulty with a certain concept, the game designer can create a scenario that allows them to practice that specific skill. The designer can break down complex tasks into smaller, more manageable steps. The game designer and the game master play a key role in the effectiveness of an RPG game (Majuri et al., 2018). The game designer focuses on the content, task analysis, resources, assessment methods, and alignment with course objectives. The game master is responsible for ensuring players understand what they need to do through each of their tasks and helping to facilitate the team through the game tasks before, during, and after each round. The game master must know the structure, the objectives, and how to help students overcome obstacles during gameplay (Khair, 2022). The game master may be tasked with setting up the teams, assigning team roles, synchronizing student schedules to coordinate periodic synchronous game rounds, and coordinating communication with players via course announcements, calendar invites, and so on. The game designer might want to conduct a practice or beta test or practice round of the game after it has been developed, running through the game themselves to task analyze and document each needed step of the process. The beta test can help you to identify potential obstacles players or teams may experience in the game and prepare for them (Sari et al., 2021).

# How Can AI Help with RPG Game Development?

## *Level I (Novice Game Designers)*

As I mentioned at the beginning of the chapter, I researched several new AI applications to prepare for writing this section that can potentially simplify the game development process by helping you brainstorm and organize ideas, task analyze game mechanics, and generate or refine RPG scenarios. I sure wish I had access to tools like ChatGPT, Gemini, or M360Co-Pilot when I initially drafted my game scenarios. I used this tool recently to revise the game round scripts for my players. I also learned about some AI mind-mapping tools (e.g., *Miro* or *MindMeister*) that can generate visual representations of RPG game rounds. I found the Text-based AI programs (like *Claude* or GPT-based apps) can help game designers to task analyze and revise complex instructions for clarity from the novice game player's perspective. Remember that your players and/or your game master will not have the innate knowledge of the RPGs purpose and progression as the Game Designer. So, using these tools can help you to be sure your game expectations are clearly and objectively described for new game players to maximize the potential for success. Keeping this in mind is even more important if your RPG game includes asynchronous team activities and deadlines. As your game evolves, new challenges and refinements will naturally emerge—add these updates to your game master manual to be sure the game master understands the reasoning, thinking, and decision-making behind the game tasks so they can effectively assist players (Stampfl et al., 2024). Consider using collaborative digital platforms like *Notion, Google Docs, or Confluence* to maintain an easily accessible game master manual. You may want to store the game master manual in an instructor-only digital folder in your LMS to be sure your game master has access. Be sure to include details such as the game's purpose, timeline, implementation steps, points of emphasis, technology integration, troubleshooting guidance, and how to request assistance when needed. AI speech-to-text applications (e.g., Otter.ai) can help document real-time feedback from playtesting sessions, ensuring continuous improvement (French et al., 2023). A well-written game master manual is needed to ensure a smooth game experience. The manual must provide clear, concise instructions for leading the game and managing any challenges that arise, with specific tasks outlined for each round (Manzano-León et al., 2021). To make this process less demanding for game designers, technology can be a valuable tool. For example, AI tools can help generate initial drafts of your game master or automate repetitive tasks like step-by-step instructions and troubleshooting guides. Use the AI chatbots as writing partners and idea generators. Remember that the AI tools can help you, but they are not sentient. The AI resource does not know your learners, your thinking and reasoning behind your decision-making or the potential knowledge gaps of your learners. So, go back and forth with the bot and use what you think is useful from the ideas generated when writing the game master manual. Using platforms like Google Docs, Microsoft Teams, or Outlook shared folders can make it easier to update the manual in real-time as multiple contributors work on drafting and revising the manual simultaneously to make sure it is an up-to-date resource. Game designers might also use AI to run test rounds of the game, helping identify potential issues in a mini beta test. For technology-heavy aspects of the game, embedding instructional videos or automated tutorials directly into the manual can reduce the need for long written explanations and make it easier for game masters to use any digital resources or appropriate AI applications to facilitate the game as it evolves (French et al., 2023). By incorporating these tools, game designers can create a game master manual that is efficient and free up time to focus on refining the content while ensuring the game's operations are clearly defined and easy to follow. The designer should be ready to assist the game master or communicate with the game master to make sure they know how to adapt the game based on player feedback and game round participation (Toda et al., 2023). If students express confusion or frustration during the game, the game master can adjust the pace or provide more support. The goal is to keep students engaged and learning while ensuring that the game remains challenging and enjoyable. Game master interactions with players throughout the game can enhance an individual player's growth as well as a team's collective achievements, as players recognize how their contributions and collaboration lead to successful outcomes (Dorożyński & Dorożyńska, 2022).

Designing RPGs for higher education might feel intimidating at first. Creating a meaningful and engaging game scenario that aligns with your content goals can seem overwhelming, especially if you are unfamiliar with game design or technology. I encourage you to trust what you know about the relevance of your content and connection to real-world challenges when you determine your short and long-term game objectives. I also suggest you consider exploring some of the amazing resources that our students have available to them (e.g., AI applications) when developing your game round tasks. Integrating AI into your game can make the game development and application process easier and more enjoyable (French et al., 2023). As I previously stated, imagine the AI chatbot as a thinking partner "assistant" who helps you brainstorm plot twists, generate character backstories, and even generate and refine dialogue examples. What may seem complex at the start can be manageable, even exciting, once you break it down into smaller steps (Stampfl et al., 2024). Table 6.3 provides AI applications new game designers to keep in mind when developing and implementing RPGs in higher education, helping instructors and designers navigate these ethical concerns. Also remember that you do not need to feel as if you need to have a perfect game. If your RPG has players negotiating a deal, AI might be able to help generate realistic outlines of tasks using industry-specific language while simultaneously including Belbin's Team Roles and specific content standards (Stampfl et al., 2024). AI-generated content might be able to save you time and offer fresh perspectives and/or help you consider ideas or perspectives you may not have initially considered. *Twine* is a free program that game designers can use to create interactive RPGs with branching scenarios to use with game rounds (French et al., 2023). After creating your initial game design and game rounds, you might use AI to generate plot choices and pathways for your players with interactive variables, unexpected (content-relevant) conditions, and systems to track individual team and player choices (Stornaiuolo et al., 2024). *Goblin Tools*, a set of game design and quest creation tools, is one of the foundational resources that new designers might explore. AI-powered visual generators such as *DALL-E* and *Artbreeder* can be used to develop visual aspects of the RPG. Game designers can use these AI tools to create unique game content visuals and incentives. Rewardful is another AI program that can help you create digital RPG rewards. SurveyMonkey AI is a tool you might want to use to offer an analysis of player behavior and performance. However, I encourage you to use your own judgement when selecting game elements because the goal should be for the game to complement your instruction, not overwhelm or take over your course (AlSagri & Sohail, 2024). Table 6.3 shares some examples of AI tools game designers may want to consider related to generating the game task narratives as well as brainstorming potential team collaboration opportunities in their RPGs.

**Table 6.3 AI Tools for Narrative Generation and Collaboration**

| AI Dungeon https://aidungeon.io |
|---|
| AI Dungeon is a text-based AI tool that game designers can use to help develop RPG game round tasks (storylines, descriptions) by brainstorming with the chat bot to develop interesting, realistic avatars with characteristics similar to that of a real team. You can also use the program to help you generate game tasks (quests) and potential example dialogues. The program is free and easy to use and can help you create an immersive RPG experience. The program offers game designers an opportunity to simulate player interactions to test the game round experiences and make potential adjustments prior to implementing the game in your course. However, the customization options are limited and the quality of the program output is linked to the text input and knowledge expertise of the game designer. |
| **Arcweave https://arcweave.com** |
| Arcweave is an AI tool that RPG game designers may want to use to develop an interactive RPG using visuals (fancy game flowchart). The program can help you integrate branching scenarios into your game (game changes based on player decision-making) so your players experience the benefits (and consequences) of their choices right away. The program offers players opportunities for real-time collaboration in the virtual game world as they work with their team toward meeting game round objectives. The program is not free, and the skill level needed to develop the program is designated as "intermediate." |
| **ChatGPT https://openai.com**<br>**Gemini https://gemini.google.com**<br>**M360CoPilot https://copilot.microsoft.com** |
| All of these generative AI programs provide users with an AI-powered chatbot-like conversational program that RPG game designers can use to share and brainstorm ideas for game round objectives, goals, and tasks. You can upload your syllabus and course calendar and existing assignments and ask for ideas about when and how often game rounds might be appropriate for your course. Game designers can use the chatbot to help with task analysis of game tasks considering time constraints and content knowledge. You can use it for ideas about avatar development and creating badges, and so on. The basic program is free and relatively easy to use, and game designers will get better at prompting as they exchange ideas with and request revisions based on yours and your player's needs. Access to the more advanced tools is a subscription, and you do need at least intermediate skill level with technology to use the platform effectively (but it is not hard to learn). |
| **CharacterGPT https://arxiv.org/abs/2405.19778** |
| CharacterGPT is an AI program that RPG game designers may want to use to create and interact with virtual characters that have distinct personalities, appearances, and voices. The program can create AI characters from text descriptions with background stories, personalities, intelligence, behavior, and voice. The program actually has MANY potential uses and it is free (at this time). CharacterGPT seems user-friendly but intermediate to advanced technology knowledge may be needed because the user may need to have at least a basic understanding of blockchain and ALI Utility Tokens. |

# What Are GPTs and How Can They Help Me Build an RPG?

## Level II (Experienced—Intermediate Game Designers)

I learned about *GPTs* recently, and I wanted to be sure to mention them in this section on how AI might help game designers. Generative Pretrained Transformers are AI models that can be used to help you create content-related text for your game rounds and build interactive game tasks in each of your game rounds. Because RPGs are all about collaboration and problem-solving, the tools can create game scenarios where players assume avatar roles and work together to achieve a common goal (Yang et al., 2024). By asking the GPTs to incorporate Belbin's Team Roles into your avatar bios, you can help to make sure each player can bring a unique skill set to the group and improve the likelihood that your team players represent typical personality types and varied experiences often found in real-world teams. As a game designer and content expert, you can interact with the AI chatbots and ask them to help you to develop a realistic, content-related scenario which would require players to work cooperatively with team members to resolve a problem. In a Hospitality RPG, the game might focus on a crisis at a luxury resort where a VIP guest has filed a major complaint with headquarters related to local DEI restrictions. The team must resolve the issue while balancing customer satisfaction, company policy, and the company's reputation. In a Marketing course RPG, a university marketing team might be tasked with creating an effective enrollment campaign which requires them to analyze data, marketing tools and strategize ways to attract more students. In a Healthcare RPG, student players might take on the roles of doctors, nurses, and administrators facing an ethical dilemma about a patient's DNR and treatment plan.

Full disclosure here, I have not used any of these applications in my own games, but I have watched several videos over the past few weeks that helped me to recognize the amazing potential resources for future RPG game designers. Many of these tools are often used with digital RPG game development, but they can be used with traditional RPGs as well. The interactive nature of tools may help with developing or enhancing asynchronous game rounds. One very impressive-looking game resource I learned about was the AI application *Arcweave* which is similar to a digital whiteboard with interesting and creative backgrounds and wonderful visual options that game designers can use to plan and organize your game rounds as you develop an easy-to-follow and attractive visual flowchart and communicate the specific tasks and objectives for teams. *Arcweave* can be used to map out the narrative and identify decision points where the team's choices impact the game's outcome (Nowak et al., 2023). *GENEVA* is another AI tool that is often used for video games but you can use to create effective branching storylines where player choices impact game events and the tools can be used to help your student players understand how their choices are related to consequences, encouraging them to think critically about trade-offs and strategy (Geneva, 2023). For example, in a Marketing RPG, the team's decision to focus their budget on social media ads instead of on-campus events could result in higher engagement but fewer long-term enrollments. In a Healthcare RPG, an early choice to pursue aggressive treatment might improve patient outcomes but could also strain hospital resources, forcing the team to justify their decision in later rounds (CharacterGPT, 2024). *CharacterGPT* can be used to create or refine avatars with unique (and potentially fun) personalities, backgrounds, and expertise. A front desk avatar in a Hospitality RPG might be helpful or rude depending on how the players interact with them. An admissions officer in a Marketing RPG might challenge the team to justify their advertising choices (Calypso, 2023). *Unity* is another advanced RPG game engine that helps designers create RPGs by providing digital resources you can use to build settings, animate player avatar characters, and add game scenery, develop quests, player challenges, generate dialogue, and develop multiplayer features (Zhang et al., 2024).

While all these resources are exciting and new programs are being developed all the time, I encourage you again to remember that throughout your RPG, applying new learning should be the primary goal for players to experience individually as well as part of a team. Each round should align with specific learning objectives, ensuring that students are applying their knowledge in a meaningful way. Remember to keep it simple at first. You may use ChatGPT to generate ideas and structure the story before incorporating more advanced tools as you feel comfortable expanding your game. Table 6.4 offers game designers information about potential AI tools they might want to consider to develop RPG visuals and audio game components.

The best way to learn is by jumping in, experimenting, and seeing how these tools can bring your game to life. While there may be a learning curve at the start, once you become familiar with AI programs, you will find creating and refining narratives becomes easier as each future RPG will take less time due to your familiarity with the process. While AI-generated content is a

### Table 6.4  AI Tools for Visual and Audio Design

| |
|---|
| **Artbreeder https://artbreeder.com** |
| Artbreeder is a simple and fun AI website creator that game designers can use to create pictures to use in your game by mixing other pictures together. The program is free (limited access) and can be used to design characters for your digital RPG. The program is easy to use because it's just sliding bars and creates unique images by mixing or "breeding" different pictures together. It may be a useful program for RPG game designers who want to quickly create a character portrait or abstract art for your game. |
| **Canva https://canva.com** |
| Canva is another AI tool that new game designers may want to use that is easy and free (limited access). The Canva program can be used to create posters, character sheets, game maps, and social media posts to promote your RPG. The program has lots of templates you can start with so you do not necessarily need to be very techno savvy to create an attractive and professional looking resource. |
| **DALL-E https://openai.com/dall-e** |
| DALL-E is an AI tool that new game designers may want to consider when creating visuals for your RPG game. DALL-E uses AI to create images based on what you are describing as your setting such as, if you need a classroom setting, you could type a prompt like "modern classroom with desks and a whiteboard, students listening to a teacher." You can use the program to generate character avatars as well with your description such as "Middle school student with glasses and a backpack, smiling." To design maps or layouts for exploration, you can describe scenes like "Floor plan of a high school with hallways, classrooms, and a cafeteria." Again, the program is free (limited access). |
| **InVideo https://invideo.io** |
| InVideo is an AI tool that is free (limited use) and easy to use if you want to make videos for your RPG including trailers, animated scenes, promotional videos, or cutscenes to make your game more engaging. The program has several templates to consider so you do not need to start from scratch and it is easy to add or edit the text animations (really, no video editing experience needed). |
| **PlayHT https://play.ht** |
| PlayHT is an AI tool that you may want to use in your RPG if you need to convert written words into realistic voices. The program is free (limited access). Again, the program is pretty easy to use, you just type what you want your character to say, choose a voice, and it reads it out loud. PlayHT is great for RPGs where you want to add voice acting to your characters or have narrators tell parts of your story. |

great starting point, you must edit and refine it to ensure it aligns with your learning objectives. Artificial intelligence can enhance the design process, but the game designer must create the connections that will resonate with your players (AlSagri & Sohail, 2024). Table 6.5 shares some examples of AI tools game designers may want to consider related to RPG player feedback and considerations to maximize the potential for a positive game experience for all your student players.

### Table 6.5 AI Tools for Accessibility, Feedback, and Multilingual Support

| Diffit https://diffit.io |
| --- |
| Diffit is a free (limited access) for teachers AI program that is not actually a game design tool, but it does have some features that may help game designers to make their games be more accessible to game players with unique needs (visual or hearing impairment, language learners and players who might benefit from a simplified version of text materials or directions). The program can be used by game designers to by simplifying complex narratives or translate content into different languages or generate materials teams may need to complete tasks. The program is easy to use and can generate materials based on your text-based prompts or you can link articles, videos, chapters, and so on to generate creative materials in PDF or electronic formats. |
| **Goblin Tools https://goblin.tools** |
| Goblin Tools is another free (limited access) suite of AI tools that can help game designers. The Magic ToDo tool can help by task analyzing procedures into specific, manageable steps, and you can choose how "spicy" or how much help you need with your analysis and explanations. The Estimator tool can be used to consider how long it might take to complete the tasks identified in the ToDo list. The Formalizer tool can help you generate avatar character text responses that would match the tone of the character based on the biographical description and potentially estimate how long it should take to complete the task and assist with task management and communication. Again, this tool is not designed specifically for RPG game design, but the program does have some potentially useful features. |
| **Google Translate https://translate.google.com** |
| Google Translate is a free tool that game designers can use when needed as a translator as it can translate (text, speech, and images) in over 100 languages and it has the ability to translate from text. Unfortunately, the accuracy of the translations is not consistent so if you can, have the translations reviewed by a native speaker or translator. |
| **Survey Monkey AI https://surveymonkey.com** |
| Survey Monkey AI is a free (limited access) tool that game designers can use to create, distribute, and analyze surveys from your players to gather feedback you can use to identify problems and make needed changes to your RPG. The surveys are easy to use (really) and distribute. The analytics tools can help game designers see trends and areas for improvement based on player feedback. |

# What Is Overgamification and How Can I Avoid It?

## *Level II (Experienced—Intermediate Game Designers)*

While connecting with their avatar is important, the game master must facilitate the round so the players are a positive and productive part of the team. Game masters must work with players before, during and after the round to keep the team focused and prevent them from going off on avatar tangents which can delay team progress (but be very amusing). Game Designers can help to keep this from happening by outlining clear agendas with proposed time constraints and readily available resources. Making sure the players understand the game objective and how they will be assessed is also important. A well-structured game balances creativity with purpose to maximize the potential that the RPG game activities promote team problem-solving rather than distracting from it (Hung, 2017). Game designers and game masters must be careful not to let the engaging or competitive nature of the game become the focus. After all, the goal is to apply content, develop skills, and emerge a more informed learner vs accumulating points, badges and/or "winning" the game. Again, the game designer's content expertise and knowledge of player needs is very important, in creating a game that promotes meaningful learning. Now that I have shared numerous potential game resources you may consider when developing or refining your game, I want to caution you about the potential disadvantages of overusing game tools. *Overgamification* can happen with excessive applications of game elements which can adversely impact the learning experience of your student players because they do not recognize the game tasks as being meaningful and significantly connected to their learning and personal goals. AI resources must not overwhelm players with leaderboards and rewards to the point where the rewards do not feel genuine. When this happens, the game can become more frustrating than engaging. When using AI resources, remember that your goal is to support players through the game tasks rather than to control the experience. Another challenge of *overgamification* is the risk of creating a competition that alienates some players. When creating game tasks, be cognizant about whether the prior knowledge of students may give them an advantage (another reason to consider assigning avatars with different backgrounds and experiences rather than allowing students to choose an avatar). One way to minimize this potential is for game designers to be sure the RPG scenario for each round does not rely on expertise and/or experiences that are not part of the course content (Castillo-Parra et al., 2022). Assigning avatars with varied backgrounds, experiences, and knowledge levels is important, and be sure the round tasks encourage players to stay in character and work through tasks from their avatar's perspective rather than relying on their own skills and experiences. The practical application of new academic content knowledge should be all that is required for teams to complete their tasks (Thorpe & Roper, 2019). Since RPGs involve group decision-making, disagreements are bound to happen. Without clear expectations, conflicts can derail the game instead of pushing players to think critically. Setting up simple collaboration rules related to group decision-making roles, voting, the need to find consensus is how the game master can keep the game running smoothly. The game master must ensure the team knows the key milestones they need to demonstrated to be successful. When players understand what is expected of them as a group, they are more likely to stay on track and apply what they are learning (Dorożyński & Dorożyńska, 2022).

## Game Log

*If you're a novice or advanced game designer interested in developing or refining an RPG that helps your students to be more prepared for real-world challenges associated with your class content, this chapter is for you. We emphasize the need for game designers to be respectful of student privacy and the potential ethical considerations of RPGs. We discussed how RPGs can enhance IHE programs by making learning more engaging, collaborative, and, most importantly, relevant. The hope was to share information about the many available resources which may help you to develop, refine, or copy an RPG that makes sense for your program and student players. Taking into consideration the numerous potential changes in higher education programming related to the political agendas of politicians, in conjunction with potential limited access to financial aid—it is clear we may not be able to continue to do what we have always done. Higher education professionals must remember that they may need to compete for future students, and they must keep the needs of contemporary adult learners in mind when planning and designing instructional activities. Role-Playing Games can help to address the needs of adult learners by offering them learning experiences that align with their career goals and give them skills they can use right away. By designing RPG content-related challenges that mirror industry-specific challenges, we can help students apply what they are learning in ways that feel meaningful. We discussed communication and collaboration and their importance when the person who creates the game is not the same person facilitating the game. We talked about weaving social media into RPGs to give students meaningful practice in digital communication and professional networking as well as keeping connected to current research and trends in the field. We reviewed a selection of AI applications to assist you in your game design process whether it is brainstorming scenarios, game mechanics, tasks, or avatar bios. The chapter and the book end where they began. The point of an RPG is not to win the game, but to play the game in a way that keeps every design decision relevant to your content and learning goals. It is your turn now! Create your own RPG. Stretch the boundaries of what teaching and learning can be when play, creativity, and purpose combine!!*

# Glossary of Terms

**Achievements** (similar to *skill badges*) are another advanced reward you can integrate into your RPG to reinforce players and promote social interaction.

**Arcweave** is similar to a digital whiteboard with cool backgrounds and wonderful visual options that game designers can use to plan and organize your game rounds as you develop an easy-to-follow and attractive visual flowchart and communicate the specific tasks and objectives for teams.

**Artificial intelligence (AI)** in relation to RPG development refers to the use of computer software programs to mimic human intelligence to enhance game design, personalization, NPC interactions, and automated assessments to improve player experiences and provide targeted feedback.

**Augmented reality (AR)** in relation to RPG development is the technology that overlays digital content onto the real world. AR can create immersive learning environments for players to interact with virtual characters, and so on, in real-world settings.

**Belbin's team roles** focus on nine behaviors of effective teams. For RPG game designers, beginning with a model like Belbin's can offer advantages when building game avatars and scenarios.

**Beta testing** in reference to RPGs is a practice test or run of your new game before you integrate it into your course. Beta testing allows a group of players (who were not involved in the initial game design) to play the game, work through the tasks and provide valuable feedback related to potential areas for improvement.

**Bleed** can happen if an avatar player's personal experiences and emotions are triggered during the game activities. When this happens, the student player may feel personally attacked or defensive. The tension in the game round can escalate, and schisms may occur.

**Brainstorming protocols** into an RPG game round can be used to guide players in generating and refining ideas that may contribute to the team tasks.

**Brand loyalty** is a satisfied student customer's ongoing preference for an institution, driven by positive experiences, satisfaction, and trust. IHEs can motivate RPG student players to support marketing by enhancing engagement, creating memorable learning experiences, and encouraging them to share their positive experiences with others.

**Character-based RPGs** can be used by game designers to encourage students to assume an avatar character's bio as they progress through an RPG, promoting empathy and understanding by placing them in different roles.

**CharacterGPT** can be used to create or refine avatars with unique (and potentially fun) personalities, backgrounds, and expertise.

**ChatGPT** is an AI program that game designers may consider using when developing avatar characters, generating ideas for game rounds, agendas, and so on.

**Collaborative RPGs** include the need for effective communication and teamwork skills in the game. Student players in these RPGs must actively listen to and consider input from their team members to achieve shared goals. The previously described RPGs give game designers the option of focusing on individual player decision-making and contributions, but Collaborative RPGs are team focused and can be used to reinforce communication, cooperation, team productivity, and achievement of common goals.

**Course instructor** in higher education is the educator responsible for delivering content, assessing student performance, and facilitating learning within the course.

**Critical decision round** is the recommended third round in a game, and the focus of the game tasks may be to build on the team insights gained from the previous round, and teams are potentially asked to complete and report on their final game round tasks.

**Cross mechanic RPGs** can integrate immersive and non-immersive game elements into an RPG because they can help to make the game engaging and also assist with structure and clear pathways to achieving measurable learning objectives.

**DALL-E** and **Artbreeder** can be used to develop visual aspects of the RPG. Game designers can use these AI tools to create unique game content visuals and incentives. Rewardful is another AI program that can help you create digital RPG rewards.

**Data tracking** is all about gathering useful information (e.g., time on tasks, decisions made, contributions to the team, connections with their avatar, etc.).

**Decision fatigue** may occur if students are assigned avatars for which they did not have essential background knowledge. These students did not feel well equipped with knowledge needed for success.

**Decision-making model** (often in the form of a flowchart or other visual diagram) can give teams a specific, structured problem-solving strategy to help guide players through the round decision-making and task completion. The resources (which can be integrated into the game resources) can help student players to stay focused and more carefully analyze their choices and make decisions.

**Design flaws** in relation to RPGs are unexpected game design problems that might occur when expectations and deadlines are unclear.

**Extrinsic motivation** in relation to RPGs is about player motivation driven by external rewards such as badges, points, and leaderboards or tangible incentives.

**Feedback loops** are potential RPG assessment methods that can be used to offer your student players regular updates on their progress. To build effective feedback loops, you need to decide when players will receive feedback, whether it's immediate after tasks or at the end of missions. Encouraging players to assess their own progress and incorporating peer feedback when relevant provides even more insight especially if you keep a record of feedback and improvements over time.

**Game collapse** in relation to RPGs can occur when players are confused about what they should be doing individually to promote the team progress or when players feel frustrated, and distracted by disjointed game mechanics rather than feeling supported and motivated to continue.

**Game designer** or person responsible for creating the game is to align the game objectives with course objectives.

**Game elements** are the components that make up the game to create the overall experience.

**Game frame** is a detailed scenario that includes the narrative, the rules teams will follow, expectations of players, and the challenges players will address as they progress through the game.

**Game master** in relation to RPGs sets up the game, facilitates the rounds, guides the team, and supports the players during the game to ensure the game runs smoothly.

**Game mechanics** are the rules and systems that guide player interactions, create challenges, and help teams achieve long- and short-term learning goals and milestones.

**Game play** refers to the act of playing games to engage players in games to facilitate learning.

**Game rRestart** can occur if the team members are so far off track of meeting objectives that they cannot realistically complete the tasks within the given timeframe. The game master must direct the game to restart the game from a given point.

**Game tasks** (steps or activities) that your player teams must complete to achieve the STG.

**Game theory** is related to understanding how people make decisions when their choices affect others. Game theory considers how conflicts and cooperation can be analyzed and has been useful in many real-world situations such as designing auction systems and guiding economic negotiations.

**Game-based learning** is when game-like elements or tasks are integrated into educational activities to improve student engagement and promote student achievement.

**Gamification** noted in the literature is the integration of game design elements and mechanics into non-game environments.

**Gamification strategies** is the specific plan of how to incorporate elements (e.g., points, badges, or leaderboards) into the game you are creating to make the overall experience more successful.

**GENEVA** is an AI tool that is often used for video games, but you can use to create effective branching storylines where player choices impact game events and the tools can be used to help your student players understand how their choices are related to consequences, encouraging them to think critically about trade-offs and strategy.

**Goblin tools**, a set of game design and quest creation tools, is one of the foundational resources that new designers might explore.

**GPTs** are AI models that can be used to help you create content related to text for your game rounds and build interactive game tasks in each of your game rounds. Because RPGs are all about collaboration and problem-solving, the tools can create game scenarios where players assume avatar roles and work together to achieve a common goal.

**Grade rubrics** can offer a more systematic and transparent way to evaluate performance in RPGs.

**Immediate feedback** and opportunities for reflective learning play an important role in RPG design and implementation.

**Immersive game mechanics** are useful if you want your student players to feel as if they are really involved in the game and their interactions and decisions in the game are important. Student players become invested in the game tasks as they are drawn into the game round because they are considering a different perspective and developing meaningful skills.

**Institutions of Higher Education** (IHE)

**Intrinsic motivation** in RPG refers to player motivation driven by personal interest, curiosity, or enjoyment of the activity.

**Introduction and role immersion (Round 1):** This RPG round is described as a potential first game round in which the focus is to introduce players to the game and ask them to review their assigned avatar's bios, motivations, and potential contributions and biases in relation to the overall game activities.

**Leaderboards** can be used in RPGs with a competitive element to offer a visual of individual and team performance by displaying rankings based on earned points.

**Learning management systems** (LMS) in higher education refer to the software program used by the instructor to create, deliver, and manage educational courses.

**Leveling up** refers to the process by which players gain experience points to advance to higher skill levels. The progression (moving from novice to expert or beginner to advanced) is motivating for student players.

**Levels** are another important mechanic commonly used in RPGs, as they can represent progression in the game.

**Lewin's Change Theory** in RPG design involves Unfreeze (challenging traditional teaching), Change (introducing RPG mechanics for learning), and Refreeze (integrating successful RPG elements as standard educational practices).

**Long-term game goals** in an RPG setting represent the broader big picture goals that players work toward over the entire course of the game or several rounds.

**Long-term milestones** involve broader objectives which may be developed throughout the game and often highlight the importance of collaboration and different viewpoints in solving intricate issues. By clearly defining and consistently reinforcing milestones and their relevance you can help to make sure your game remains purpose driven.

**Mastery/skill-building motivation** in RPGs refers to player motivations by desire to improve individual skills or knowledge over time. Both traditional and RPG learning includes motivation types in some form.

**Meeting agendas** in RPGs are important for clarifying what is expected of individual players and teams during each game round. The agendas should indicate when players need to participate and what information they need to be able to share with the team when they are scheduled to participate.

**Microsoft teams** is a collaboration tool that might be used in RPGs for video calls, chat, and file sharing, supporting game round sessions, team communication, and resource sharing.

**Milestones** are key goals or achievements that guide players through the game and measure progress. The milestones can be categorized into two primary types: short-term and long-term.

**Mission** in RPGs usually includes a content-related team challenge or task to complete.

**Non-immersive game mechanics** are related to measuring student player progress toward learning milestones in the game and providing players with meaningful feedback to help them to recognize their strengths and opportunities for growth.

**Observation logs** can be used to record how often players collaborated, methods of communication, and any moments of confusion or difficulty.

**Opportunities for advanced learning** can help RPG game designers provide rewards to players with challenging tasks and specialized content that support academic and career goals. Providing opportunities for advanced learning, such as skills workshops, can enhance your student player's curriculum knowledge and help them to connect what they are learning with practical application to reinforce the importance of continuous learning and skill development.

**Outcome mapping** is another potential RPG assessment tool used to assess whether student players are achieving their learning objectives.

**Overgamification** can happen with excessive applications of game elements which can adversely impact the learning experience of your student players because they do not recognize the game tasks as being meaningful and significantly connected to their learning and personal goals.

**Point system** in an RPG is often a foundational game mechanic that provides students with a clear and quantifiable method for tracking their progress in completing tasks, mastering skills, or achieving specific objectives. Accumulated points (grades) allow students to see their subject matter mastery over time.

**Problem-based learning RPGs** require student players to resolve authentic, content-related real-world challenges. The game tasks might require students to research, ask questions and identify multiple potential solutions. Problem-based learning RPGs focus on the critical thinking and task analysis needed to find realistic and appropriate solutions.

**Quests** in an RPG often integrate a series of smaller, scaffolded tasks leading to a larger content-related goal.

**Real-time team activities** in an RPG allow the game master to strategically assign avatar roles based on a student player's strengths while simultaneously helping players to understand how the game will also provide them with opportunities for growth.

**Reflection round:** The most important reason is because asking your players to reflect on and consider their game experiences in relationship to what they learned about applying content in real life, working as part of a team, and considering a given conflict or problem from a different perspective can deepen the experience for your students who may not otherwise make the time to think about what they learned from the experience.

**Role authority** in RPGs can impact how players interact, make decisions, and solve problems throughout the game. Role authority is related to how power is distributed among player avatars and how that impacts team engagement.

**Role conflict** in an RPG can happen; role conflict can arise when a player's assigned avatar or role within an academic game round doesn't align with their expectations, if a player considers themselves as a strategist or analyst but they are assuming a role requiring them to be a persuasive communicator.

**Role immersion** in an RPG happens when players embrace and feel comfortable assuming their character's role as they interact with other players, share ideas (experiences, biases, etc.), make choices in the game according to their avatar's perspective, and respond to other players as if they are really in the game setting (Dymek & Zackariasson, 2016).

**Role-playing games** (RPGs) represent a specialized form of GBL where participants assume character roles and make decisions that intricately shape the game's narrative.

**Round-Robin brainstorming** strategy is commonly used in RPGs as each player takes turns sharing information relevant to the task and suggesting ideas. All of the avatar perspectives are considered using this strategy, and a variety of ideas are considered and shared (Parshuram & Ramesh, 2020; Plass et al., 2020).

**Scenario-based RPGs** immerse students in specific contexts, allowing them to explore complex situations and decision-making processes.

**Serious games** were designed to teach specific skills or concepts and were used for training, simulation, and educational purposes.

**Short-term goals (SGT)** in an RPG scenario function like quests or missions. Specific and immediate, these objectives are meant to be completed within a single game round or session.

**Short-term milestones** are content-specific goals players should be able to demonstrate within a single game round. A short-term milestone might require players to use their assigned roles to introduce themselves and discuss an issue related to the content.

**Shout-outs** (verbal acknowledgments of a player's contributions or achievements) and leaderboards, which display rankings based on points earned and accomplishments achieved.

**Simulation RPGs** are considered immersive because the student players have an opportunity to connect theory to life as they are faced with a realistic, content-relevant scenario, and they have to consider varied factors and make important decisions which enable them to apply what they have learned in the course and recognize the potential benefits and consequences of their choices.

**Social or collaborative motivation** in an RPG refers to player motivation due to group dynamics, teamwork, and the desire to contribute to a shared goal or community.

**Soft skills** in an RPG references interpersonal and professional social communication skills such as collaboration, negotiation, and adaptive problem-solving are enhanced. Role-Playing Games insights will have lasting practical value in academic learning and professional goals.

**Special roles** are potential forms of recognition in an RPG in which players may be designated as leaders, strategists, or experts in specific areas.

**Status achievements** are game (and content-related) milestones that your players can potentially work toward during the RPG rounds (tasks, skills, or experiences that players have not yet completed or mastered) to motivate players to explore different parts of the game.

**Strategic quest challenge** is the second RPG round suggested in which the focus may be on asking student players to also consider what they have learned in the course so far and to appropriately help the team apply what they are learning to complete given task(s). The focus is on strategic decision-making and the practical use of theoretical knowledge from the class.

**Structured frameworks** in an RPG can offer players clear guidelines and processes that can help them with decision-making and generating ideas.

**SurveyMonkey** is an AI tool game designers might want to use to offer an analysis of player behavior and performance.

**SWOT analysis model** is a more specific decision-making model that can help teams identify and consider relevant internal and external factors that the team should consider in relation to the team's goals as they carefully consider potential decisions and mutually agree on a consensus.

**Task analysis** in relation to RPG development involves breaking down the various activities and skills required of novice players to effectively complete given tasks in the game rounds.

**Taxonomy of Gamification Elements for Educational Environments (TGEEE)** can be a valuable resource for new game designers. The comprehensive framework can assist game designers in choosing and developing RPGs appropriate for their learners.

**Team norms** in relation to RPGs are mutually agreed upon respectful interactions, and incorporating debriefs can help to prevent or minimize team conflicts before they disrupt the learning process.

**Team theory principles** in relation to RPG development can help game designers better understand how groups work effectively together. Applying these principles in RPGs can potentially assist with player collaboration and productivity.

**The Family Educational Rights and Privacy Act (FERPA)** includes mandated practices for maintaining data protection related to student records. Role-Playing Games designers must protect student privacy.

**Transferable skills** in relation to RPGs are competencies and abilities that individuals can apply across different roles, industries, and situations and can include critical thinking, problem-solving, communication, teamwork, adaptability, and leadership.

**Tuckman's stages of group development** in relation to RPGs can help game designers better understand how teams evolve through forming, storming, norming, and performing stages.

**Twine** is a free program that game designers can use to create interactive RPGs with branching scenarios to use in game rounds.

**Unity** is another advanced RPG game engine that helps designers create RPGs by providing digital resources you can use to build settings, animate player avatar characters, and develop quests.

**Virtual reality (VR)** is a computer-generated simulation of a 3D environment. In RPGs, VR can create immersive learning scenarios where student players practice skills, collaborate, and solve problems.

**Vital rewards** can be used to improve player motivation in RPGs. Examples of vital rewards that can be integrated into your RPG are status achievements during collaborative projects.

**Zoom** is a video conferencing software. In RPGs, Zoom can be used for game round sessions, team discussions, role-play activities, and real-time feedback.

# References

Abdool, A., Ringis, D., Maharajh, A., Sirju, L., & Abdool, H. (2017). DataRPG: Improving student motivation in data science through gaming elements. In *Frontiers in Education Conference* (pp. 1–7). IEEE. https://doi.org/10.1109/FIE.2017.8190490.

Adare-Tasiwoopa ápi, S., & Silva, N. (2024). *Gamification in higher education: A how-to instructional guide*. Routledge.

Ajisoko, P. (2020). The use of Duolingo apps to improve English vocabulary learning. *International Journal of Emerging Technologies in Learning (iJET), 15*(7), 149–55. https://doi.org/10.3991/ijet.v15i07.13229.

Akhilesh, K. B. (2014). Interpersonal relationships, teams, and team building. In *R&D Management*. Springer. https://doi.org/10.1007/978-81-322-1946-0_12.

Albahoth, Z. M., Jabar, M. B. A., & Jalis, F. M. B. M. (2024). A systematic review of the literature on code-switching and a discussion on future directions. *International Journal of Academic Research in Business and Social Sciences, 14*(2), 61–80. http://dx.doi.org/10.6007/IJARBSS/v14-i2/20452.

Alexander, B. (2020). *Academia next: The futures of higher education*. Johns Hopkins University Press.

Al Ghamdi, A. (2017). Influence of lecturer immediacy on students' learning outcomes: Evidence from a distance education program at a university in Saudi Arabia. *International Journal of Information and Education Technology, 7*(1), 35. https://doi.org/10.18178/ijiet.2017.7.1.838.

Alismail, H. A., & McGuire, P. (2015). 21st century standards and curriculum: Current research and practice. *Journal of Education and Practice, 6*(6), 150–4.

AlSagri, H. S., & Sohail, S. S. (2024). Evaluating the role of artificial intelligence in sustainable development goals with an emphasis on "quality education". *Discover Sustainability, 5*(1), 1–26. https://doi.org/10.1007/s43621-024-00682-9.

Ambrose, S. A., & Wankel, L. A. (2020). *Higher education's road to relevance: Navigating complexity*. John Wiley & Sons.

Anagnostopoulou, E. (2023). Digital role-playing games as a novel approach to learning mathematics: A quantitative analysis. *Proceedings of the 17th European*

Conference on Games Based Learning / PhD Papers, 17(1). University of Sussex. https://doi.org/10.34190/ecgbl.17.1.1912.

Anderson, L. W., & Krathwohl, D. R. (Eds.). (2020). *A taxonomy for learning, teaching, and assessing: A revision of Bloom's taxonomy of educational objectives*. Longman. https://doi.org/10.5430/jct.v13n4p173.

Ajmal, M. M., Khan, M., Shad, M. K., AlKatheeri, H., & Jabeen, F. (2022). Socio-economic and technological new normal in supply chain management: Lessons from COVID-19 pandemic. *The International Journal of Logistics Management, 33*(4), 1474–99. https://doi.org/10.1108/IJLM-04-2021-0220.

Aranzabal, A., Epelde, E., & Artetxe, M. (2022). Team formation on the basis of Belbin's roles to enhance students' performance in project based learning. *Education for Chemical Engineers, 38*, 22–37. https://doi.org/10.1016/j.ece.2021.09.001.

Aritzeta, A., Swailes, S., & Senior, B. (2007). Belbin's team role model: Development, validity and applications for team building. *Journal of Management Studies, 44*(1), 96–118. https://doi.org/10.1111/j.1467-6486.2007.00666.x.

Aronson, B. (2020, March 30). How to succeed in online classes during the COVID-19 pandemic. https://inchemistry.acs.org/content/inchemistry/en/college-life/transitioning-to-online-classes.html.

Ashcroft, K., & Foreman-Peck, L. (2013). *Managing teaching and learning in further and higher education*. Routledge.

Barron, E. N. (2024). *Game theory: An introduction*. John Wiley & Sons.

Belbin, M. (2010). *Management teams: Why they succeed or fail*. Elsevier Science & Technology Books.

Belbin, R. M., & Brown, V. (2022). *Team roles at work*. Routledge.

Bhattacharya, T. (2023). Traditional children's games in India: Unlearning the attributes of subordination. In T. Chataika & D. Goodley (Eds.), *Handbook of Postcolonial Disability Studies*. Routledge.

Bell, K. (2018). *Game on!: Gamification, gameful design, and the rise of the gamer educator*. Johns Hopkins University Press.

Best, B., & Conceição, S. C. O. (2017). Transactional distance dialogic interactions and student satisfaction in a multi-institutional blended learning environment. *European Journal of Open, Distance and E-Learning, 20*(1), 139–53. https://doi.org/10.1515/eurodl-2017-0009.

Björk, S., & Zagal, J. P. (2018). Game design and role-playing games. In J. P. Zagal & S. Björk (Eds.), *Role-playing game studies* (pp. 323–36). Routledge.

Bledsoe, T. S., & Simmerok, B. D. (2013). A multimedia-rich platform to enhance student engagement and learning in an online environment. *Online Learning Journal, 17*(4), 1–10. https://doi.org/10.24059/olj.v17i4.398.

Blunn, M. (2022). Strategic risk management and game developers' ethical practices in design [Doctoral dissertation, Capella University]. ProQuest Dissertations & Theses Global.

Bolton, G. E. (2002). Game theory's role in role-playing. *International Journal of Forecasting, 18*(3), 353–8. https://doi.org/10.1016/S0169-2070(02)00027-4.

Bonnardel, N., & Pichot, N. (2020). Enhancing collaborative creativity with virtual dynamic personas. *Applied Ergonomics*, 82, 102949. https://doi.org/10.1016/j.apergo.2019.102949

Bowman, S. L. (2010). *The functions of role-playing games: How participants create community, solve problems, and explore identity*. McFarland & Company.

Bowman, S. L. (2023). Social conflict in role-playing communities: An exploratory qualitative study. *International Journal of Role-Playing, 4*, 4–25. https://doi.org/10.33063/ijrp.vi4.183.

Bowman, S. L., & Schrier, K. (2018). Players and their characters in role-playing games. In *Role-Playing Game Studies* (pp. 395–410). Routledge.

Bradley, H. E. (1860). *The checkered game of life*. Springfield, MA: Milton Bradley Company.

Branch, K. C. (2022). *A qualitative case study of health-related baccalaureate and graduate web-based simulated clinical learning platforms*. Western Michigan University.

Bryan, T. K., Lutte, R., Lee, J., O'Neil, P., Maher, C. S., & Hoflund, A. B. (2018). When do online education technologies enhance student engagement? A case of distance education at University of Nebraska at Omaha. *Journal of Public Affairs Education, 24*(2), 255–73. https://doi.org/10.1080/15236803.2018.1429817.

Cabellos, B., Pozo, J. I., Marín-Rubio, K., & Sánchez, D. L. (2022). Do pro-social video games promote moral activity?: An analysis of user reviews of Papers, Please. *Education and Information Technologies, 27*(8), 11411–42. https://doi.org/10.1007/s10639-022-11072-x.

CALYPSO. (2023). LLMs as Dungeon Masters' assistants. *arXiv*. https://arxiv.org/abs/2308.07540.

Calvet, L., Bourdin, P., & Prados, F. (2019). Immersive technologies in higher education: Applications, challenges, and good practices. In *Proceedings of the 2019 3rd international conference on education and e-learning*. https://doi.org/10.1109/ICEEL.2019.8840425.

Camilleri, V. (2023, October). Designing GBL for higher education: Pitfalls & recommendations. In T. Spil, G. Bruinsma, & L. Collou (Eds.), *Proceedings of the 17th European Conference on Games Based Learning* (Vol. 17, No. 1, pp. 869–875). Academic Conferences International. https://doi.org/10.34190/ecgbl.17.1.1900.

Campillo-Ferrer, J. M., Miralles-Martínez, P., & Sánchez-Ibáñez, R. (2020). Gamification in higher education: Impact on student motivation and the acquisition of social and civic key competencies. *Sustainability, 12*(12), 4822. https://doi.org/10.3390/su12124822.

Caillois, R. (1961). The classification of games. In K. Salen & E. Zimmerman (Eds.), *The game design reader: A Rules of Play anthology* (pp. 210–213). MIT Press. (Reprinted from Man, Play and Games, 1961).

Castillo-Parra, B., Hidalgo-Cajo, B. G., Vásconez-Barrera, M., & Oleas-López, J. (2022). Gamification in higher education: A review of the literature. *World Journal on Educational Technology: Current Issues, 14*(3), 797–816. https://doi.org/10.18844/wjet.v14i3.7341.

Chamberlin, B., Trespalacios, J., & Gallagher, R. (2018). Bridging research and game development: A learning games design model for multi-game projects. In V. C. Wang (Ed.), *Gamification in education: Breakthroughs in research and practice* (pp. 66–88). IGI Global. https://doi.org/10.4018/978-1-5225-5198-0.ch005.

Chamberlin, K., Yasué, M., & Chiang, I. C. A. (2023). The impact of grades on student motivation. *Active Learning in Higher Education, 24*(2), 109–24. https://doi.org/10.1177/14697874221127222.

CharacterGPT. (2024). *AI-based framework for character consistency and development.* arXiv. https://arxiv.org/abs/2405.19778.

Cheng, M. T., Rosenheck, L., Lin, C.-Y., & Klopfer, E. (2017). Analyzing gameplay data to inform feedback loops in The Radix Endeavor. *Computers and Education, 111*, 60–73. https://doi.org/10.1016/j.compedu.2017.03.015.

Chowdhury, P. N., Vaish, A., Puri, B., & Vaishya, R. (2024). Medical education technology: Past, present and future. *Apollo Medicine, 0*(0). https://doi.org/10.1177/09760016241256202.

Chui, H. L., Liu, Y., & Mak, B. C. N. (2016). Code-switching for newcomers and veterans: A mutually-constructed discourse strategy for workplace socialization and identification. *International Journal of Applied Linguistics, 26*(1), 25–51. https://doi.org/10.1111/ijal.12077.

Cordero-Gutiérrez, R., & Lahuerta-Otero, E. (2020). Social media advertising efficiency on higher education programs. *Spanish Journal of Marketing-ESIC, 24*(2), 247–62. https://doi.org/10.1108/SJME-06-2019-0045.

Costello, R. (Ed.). (2017). *Gaming innovations in higher education: Emerging research and opportunities* (1st ed.). IGI Global Publishing.

Christopoulos, A., & Mystakidis, S. (2023). Gamification in Education. *Encyclopedia, 3*(4), 1223–43. https://doi.org/10.3390/encyclopedia3040089.

Croxton, R. A. (2014). The role of interactivity in student satisfaction and persistence in online learning. *Journal of Online Learning and Teaching, 10*(2), 314.

Cullinan, M., & Genova, J. (2023). Gaming the systems: A component analysis framework for the classroom use of RPGs. *International Journal of Role-Playing*, (13), 7–17.

Daniau, S. (2016). The transformative potential of role-playing games: From play skills to human skills. *Simulation & Gaming, 47*(4), 423–44. https://doi.org/10.1177/1046878116650765.

DataReportal. (2024, October). Global social media statistics. *DataReportal*. https://datareportal.com/social-media-users.

Datsenko, T., Vyhovska, O., & Sinko, A. (2020). Social media and higher education institutions: Using social networks to recruit students. *The Modern Higher Education Review, 2020*(5), 86–97. https://doi.org/10.28925/2518-7635.2020.5.9.

Daul, S. (2014). *Game design for learning*. Association for Talent Development.

DeGloria, A., Bellotti, F., & Berta, R. (2014). Serious Games for education and training. *International Journal of Serious Games, 1*(1). https://doi.org/10.17083/ijsg.v1i1.11.

Danaei, K. J. (2019). Literature review of adjunct faculty. *Educational Research: Theory and Practice, 30*(2), 17–33.

Dinh, J. V., Reyes, D. L., Kayga, L., Lindgren, C., Feitosa, J., & Salas, E. (2021). *Developing team trust*. Organizational Dynamics, 50(1), 100846. https://doi.org/10.1016/j.orgdyn.2021.100846.

Dixson, M. D. (2015). Measuring student engagement in the online course: The online student engagement scale (OSE). *Online Learning, 19*(4). https://doi.org/10.24059/olj.v19i4.561.

Donovan, T. (2017). *It's all a game: The history of board games from Monopoly to Settlers of Catan*. Macmillan.

Dorożyński, P., & Dorożyńska, K. (2022). The role-playing game to increase students' activity and engagement in the teaching process—A pilot study of research & development campaign. *Currents in Pharmacy Teaching and Learning, 14*(8), 1046–52. https://doi.org/10.1016/j.cptl.2022.07.015.

Dotson, K. B. (2020). *The value of games: Putting play back into practice for children*. Rowman & Littlefield.

Dowling-Hetherington, L., & Glowatz, M. (2017). The usefulness of digital badges in higher education: Exploring the students' perspectives. *Irish Journal of Academic Practice, 6*(1), 1. https://doi.org/10.21427/D7Z13C.

Dyer, T., Aroz, J., & Larson, E. (2018). Proximity in the online classroom: Engagement, relationships, and personalization. *Journal of Instructional Research, 7*(1), 108–18. https://doi.org/10.9743/jir.2018.10.

Dymek, M., & Zackariasson, P. (2016). *The business of gamification: A critical analysis*. Routledge.

Elkind, D. (2007). *The power of play: Learning what comes naturally*. Da Capo Lifelong Books.

Fallahi, M. (2019). Making instruction work for adult learners. In *Outcome-based strategies for adult learning* (pp. 1–11). IGI Global. https://doi.org/10.4018/978-1-5225-5712-8.ch001.

Featherstone, M. (2016). Using gamification to enhance self-directed, open learning in higher education. In *10th European conference on games based learning*, University of the West of Scotland, Paisley, Scotland, 6-7 October 2016.

Fisher, S. G., Hunter, T. A., & Macrosson, W. D. K. (1998). The structure of Belbin's team roles. *Journal of Occupational and Organizational Psychology, 71*(3), 283–8. https://doi.org/10.1111/j.2044-8325.1998.tb00677.x.

Fisher, S. G., Wd, K., & Semple, J. H. (2001). Control and Belbin's team roles. *Personnel Review, 30*(5), 578–88. https://doi.org/10.1108/EUM0000000005940.

Foster, A., & Shah, M. (2020). Principles for advancing game-based learning in teacher education. *Journal of Digital Learning in Teacher Education, 36*(2), 84–95. https://doi.org/10.1080/21532974.2019.1695553.

Fraguas-Sánchez, A. I., Serrano, D. R., & González-Burgos, E. (2022). Gamification tools in higher education: Creation and implementation of an escape room methodology in the pharmacy classroom. *Education Sciences, 12*(11), 833. https://doi.org/10.3390/educsci12110833.

Franco, P. F., & DeLuca, D. A. (2019). Learning through action: Creating and implementing a strategy game to foster innovative thinking in higher education. *Simulation & Gaming, 50*(1), 23–43. https://doi.org/10.1177/1046878118819865.

Frank, D. (2011). *A tale of two games: An intertwining history of mainstream and educational video games*. (Doctoral dissertation). University of Wisconsin, Eau Claire.

French, F., Levi, D., Maczo, C., Simonaityte, A., Triantafyllidis, S., & Varga, G. (2023). Creative use of OpenAI in education: Case studies from game development. *Multimodal Technologies and Interaction, 7*(8), 81. https://doi.org/10.3390/mti7080081.

Gallardo, K. (2020). Competency-based assessment and the use of performance-based evaluation rubrics in higher education: Challenges towards the next decade. *Problems of Education in the 21st Century, 78*(1), 61–79. https://doi.org/10.33225/pec/20.78.61.

Gatzidis, C. (2012). Learning with digital games: A practical guide to engaging students in higher education. *International Journal of Games Based Learning, 2*(1), 43–57. https://doi.org/10.4018/ijgbl.2012010106.

GENEVA. (2023). *GENErating and visualizing branching narratives using LLMs*. arXiv. https://arxiv.org/abs/2311.09213.

Giousmpasoglou, C., Marinakou, E., & Zopiatis, A. (2021). Hospitality managers in turbulent times: The COVID-19 crisis. *International Journal of Contemporary Hospitality Management, 33*(4), 1297–318. https://doi.org/10.1108/IJCHM-07-2020-0741.

Ginder, S. A., Kelly-Reid, J. E., & Mann, F. B. (2018). Enrollment and employees in postsecondary institutions, Fall 2017; and Financial statistics and academic libraries, fiscal year 2017: First Look (Provisional Data) (NCES 2019- 021rev). U.S. Department of Education. Washington, DC: National Center for Education Statistics. http://nces.ed.gov/pubsearch.

Grande-de-Prado, M., Baelo, R., García-Martín, S., & Abella-García, V. (2020). Mapping role-playing games in Ibero-America: An educational review. *Sustainability, 12*(16), 6298. https://doi.org/10.3390/su12166298.

Grissom, J. A., & Condon, L. (2021). Leading schools and districts in times of crisis. *Educational Researcher, 50*(5), 315–24. https://doi.org/10.3102/0013189X211023112.

Halabieh, H., Hawkins, S., Bernstein, A. E., Lewkowict, S., Unaldi Kamel, B., Fleming, L., & Levitin, D. (2022). The future of higher education: Identifying current educational problems and proposed solutions. *Education Sciences, 12*(12), 888. https://doi.org/10.3390/educsci12120888.

Hammer, J., Beltrán, W., Walton, J., & Turkington, M. (2018a). Power and control in role-playing games. In J. P. Zagal & S. Deterding (Eds.), *Role-playing game studies* (pp. 448–67). Routledge.

Hammer, J., To, A., Schrier, K., Bowman, S. L., & Kaufman, G. (2018b). Learning and role-playing games. In J. P. Zagal & S. Deterding (Eds.), *Role-playing game studies* (pp. 283–99). Routledge.

Hartt, M., Hosseini, H., & Mostafapour, M. (2020). Game on: Exploring the effectiveness of game-based learning. *Planning Practice & Research, 35*(5), 589–604. https://doi.org/10.1080/02697459.2020.1778724.

Helmefalk, M., Lundqvist, S., & Marcusson, L. (2023). The role of mechanics in gamification: An interdisciplinary perspective. In Information Resources Management Association (Ed.), *Research anthology on game design, development,*

Hoque, N., Uddin, M., Ahmad, A., Mamun, A., Uddin, M. N., Chowdhury, R. A., & Noman Alam, A. H. M. (2023). The desired employability skills and work readiness of graduates: Evidence from the perspective of established and well-known employers of an emerging economy. *Industry and Higher Education, 37*(5), 716–30. https://doi.org/10.1177/09504222221149850.

Hossain, M. S., Kannan, S. N., & Raman Nair, S. K. K. (2021). Factors influencing sustainable competitive advantage in the hospitality industry. *Journal of Quality Assurance in Hospitality & Tourism, 22*(6), 679–710. https://doi.org/10.1108/JHTI-08-2020-0152.

Huang, Y. M., Silitonga, L. M., & Wu, T. T. (2022). Applying a business simulation game in flipped classroom to enhance engagement, learning achievement, and higher-order thinking skills. *Computers & Education, 183*, 104494. https://doi.org/10.1016/j.compedu.2022.104494.

Huberman, M. (1989). The professional life cycle of teachers. *Teachers College Record, 91*(1), 31–57. https://doi.org/10.1177/016146818909100107.

Hugaas, K. H. (2024). Bleed and Identity: A conceptual model of bleed and how bleed-out from role-playing games can affect a player's sense of self. *International Journal of Role-Playing, 15*, 9–35. https://doi.org/10.33063/ijrp.vi15.323.

Hung, A. C. Y. (2017). A critique and defense of gamification. *Journal of Interactive Online Learning, 15*(1), 57–72. https://www.ncolr.org/jiol/issues/pdf/15.1.4.pdf.

Ibisu, A. E. (2024). *Development of a gamification model for personalized e-learning.* arXiv preprint arXiv:2404.15301.

Ioannidis, M., & Kasapakis, V. (2022). Experience variations between immersive and non-immersive RPGs. *Proceedings of the 28th ACM Symposium on Virtual Reality Software and Technology* (pp. 1–2). https://doi.org/10.1145/3562939.3565654.

Irwanto, I., Wahyudiati, D., Saputro, A. D., & Laksana, S. D. (2023). Research trends and applications of gamification in higher education: A bibliometric analysis spanning 2013–2022. *International Journal of Emerging Technologies in Learning (iJET), 18*(5), 19–41. https://doi.org/10.3991/ijet.v18i05.39120.

Janssen, A., Robinson, T., Brunner, M., Harnett, P., Museth, K. E., & Shaw, T. (2018). Multidisciplinary teams and ICT: A qualitative study exploring the use of technology and its impact on multidisciplinary team meetings. *BMC Health Services Research, 18*, 444. https://doi.org/10.1186/s12913-018-3242-3.

Jaramillo-Mediavilla, L., Basantes-Andrade, A., Cabezas-González, M., & Casillas-Martín, S. (2024). Impact of gamification on motivation and academic performance: A systematic review. *Education Sciences, 14*(6), 639. https://doi.org/10.3390/educsci14060639.

Jennings, C. L. (2021). Best practices for motivating and supporting learning for adult and non-traditional learners. In *Ensuring adult and non-traditional learners' success with technology, design, and structure* (pp. 128–41). IGI Global. https://doi.org/10.4018/978-1-7998-6762-3.ch008.

Johnson, C. W., & Voelkel, R. H. (2021). Developing increased leader capacity to support effective professional learning community teams. *International Journal of Leadership in Education, 24*(3), 313–32. https://doi.org/10.1080/13603124.2019.1600039.

Johnson, W., Bauer, L., Li, X., Armenian, P., McCue, J., Storkan, M., Haight, S., Dhillon, S., Hitchner, L., Werner, J., Pettigrew, C., Rege, R., & Mateo, C. (2023). Expanding DEI curricula in emergency medicine graduate medical education: A pilot innovation project. *Western Journal of Emergency Medicine: Integrating Emergency Care with Population Health, 24*(3.1). https://doi.org/10.5811/westjem.61008.

Khan, N., Sarwar, A., Chen, T. B., & Khan, S. (2022). Connecting digital literacy in higher education to the 21st-century workforce. *Knowledge Management & E-Learning, 14*(1), 46–61. https://doi.org/10.34105/j.kmel.2022.14.004.

Kapp, K. M. (2012). *The gamification of learning and instruction: Game-based methods and strategies for training and education*. John Wiley & Sons.

Kelly, J. T. (2020). *Level up: Using gamification to improve student evaluation and motivation*. APSA Preprints. https://doi.org/10.33774/apsa-2020-0cxhs.

Khair, M. (2022). How RPG (Role Play Games) impact players' English ability. *La Parole: Journal of Language Teaching and Pedagogy, 5*(2), 51–67. https://doi.org/10.31850/laparole.v5i2.2617.

Kim, J., & Maloney, E. J. (2020). *Learning innovation and the future of higher education*. Johns Hopkins University Press.

Knowles, M. S., Holton III, E. F., & Swanson, R. A. (2020). *The adult learner: The definitive classic in adult education and human resource development* (8th ed.). Routledge. ISBN 9780367417659.

Komljenovic, J. (2018). Big data and new social relations in higher education: Academia.edu, Google Scholar, and ResearchGate. In B. William & D. Hartong (Eds.), *World yearbook of education 2019* (pp. 148–64). Routledge.

Kuo, Y. C., Walker, A. E., Schroder, K. E., & Belland, B. R. (2014). Interaction, internet self-efficacy, and self-regulated learning as predictors of student satisfaction in online education courses. *The Internet and Higher Education, 14*(20), 35–50. https://doi.org/10.1016/j.iheduc.2013.10.001.

Kaushal, V., & Ali, N. (2020). University reputation, brand attachment and brand personality as antecedents of student loyalty: A study in higher education context. *Corporate Reputation Review, 23*(4), 254–66. https://doi.org/10.1057/s41299-019-00084-y.

Laine, T. H., & Lindberg, R. S. (2020). Designing engaging games for education: A systematic literature review on game motivators and design principles. *IEEE Transactions on Learning Technologies, 13*(4), 804–21. https://doi.org/10.1109/TLT.2020.2992527.

Lameras, P., Arnab, S., Dunwell, I., Stewart, C., Clarke, S., & Petridis, P. (2017). Essential features of serious games design in higher education: Linking learning attributes to game mechanics. *British Journal of Educational Technology, 48*(4), 972–94. https://doi.org/10.1111/bjet.12467.

Leaning, M. (2015). A study of the use of games and gamification to enhance student engagement, experience and achievement on a theory-based course of an undergraduate media degree. *Journal of Media Practice, 16*(2), 155–70. https://doi.org/10.1080/14682753.2015.1041807.

Lee, M. R. (2021). *Leading virtual project teams: Adapting leadership theories and communications techniques to 21st century organizations*. Auerbach Publications.

Leow, M. C., Wang, L. Y. K., Lau, S. H., & Tan, C. K. (2016). Usability of RPG-based learning framework. *International Journal of Human-Computer Interaction, 32*(8), 643–53. https://doi.org/10.1080/10447318.2016.1156884.

Li, M. C., & Tsai, C. C. (2013). Game-based learning in science education: A review of relevant research. *Journal of Science Education and Technology, 22*, 877–98. https://doi.org/10.1007/s10956-013-9436-x.

Liberona, D., Ahn, S., Lohinlva, M., Garate, P., & Rojas, C. (2021). Serious games usage in higher education, experiences and guidelines. In S. Yu, T. Yu, & M. Khine (Eds.), *Learning technology for education challenges: 9th International Workshop, LTEC 2021*, Kaohsiung, Taiwan, July 20-22, 2021, Proceedings 9 (pp. 138–50). Springer International Publishing.

Lin, C.-Y., Hung, W., Fang, K., & Tu, C.-C. (2015). Understanding players' achievement values from MMORPGs: An exploratory study. *Internet Research, 25*(3), 315–34. https://doi.org/10.1108/IntR-04-2014-0110.

Liu, Y., Moretti, R., Bodenheimer, B., & Meiler, J. (2020). Foldit drug design game usability study: Comparison of citizen and expert scientists. *Motion, Interaction and Games*, 1–19. https://doi.org/10.1145/3424636.3426899.

Loup, G., Serna, A., Iksal, S., & George, S. (2016). Immersion and persistence: Improving learners' engagement in authentic learning situations. In *Adaptive and Adaptable Learning: 11th European Conference on Technology Enhanced Learning,*

*EC-TEL 2016*, Lyon, France, September 13-16, 2016, Proceedings 11 (pp. 410–15). Springer International Publishing. https://doi.org/10.1007/978-3-319-45153-4_35.

Mackh, B. M. (2018). *Higher education by design: Best practices for curricular planning and instruction*. Routledge.

Magie, E. (1903). The Landlord's Game [Board game]. United States Patent No. 748,626.

Majuri, J., Koivisto, J., & Hamari, J. (2018). Gamification of education and learning: A review of empirical literature. In *Proceedings of the 2nd international GamiFIN conference*, GamiFIN 2018. CEUR-WS. ISSN:1613-0073. http://ceur-ws.org/Vol-2186/paper2.pdf.

Mamgain, N., Sharma, A., & Goyal, P. (2014). Learner's perspective on video-viewing features offered by MOOC providers: Coursera and edX. 2014 *IEEE International Conference on MOOC, Innovation and Technology in Education (MITE)*, 331–6. https://doi.org/10.1109/MITE.2014.7020298.

Manzano-León, A., Camacho-Lazarraga, P., Guerrero, M. A., Guerrero-Puerta, L., Aguilar-Parra, J. M., Trigueros, R., & Alias, A. (2021). Between level up and game over: A systematic literature review of gamification in education. *Sustainability, 13*(4), 2247. https://doi.org/10.3390/su13042247.

Martin, F., & Bolliger, D. U. (2018). Engagement matters: Student perceptions on the importance of engagement strategies in the online learning environment. *Online Learning, 22*(1), 205–22. https://doi.org/10.24059/olj.v22i1.1092.

Martins, V. F., de Almeida Souza Concilio, I., & de Paiva Guimarães, M. (2018). Problem based learning associated with the development of games for programming teaching. *Computer Applications in Engineering Education, 26*(5), 1577–89. https://doi.org/10.1002/cae.21968.

McFarland, J. (2024). Cultural inclusivity and gamification. In *Pursuing practical change: Lesson designs that promote culturally responsive teaching* (pp. 151–91). Rowman & Littlefield.

McKeithan, G. K., Rivera, M. O., Mann, L. E., & Mann, L. B. (2021). Strategies to enhance student engagement in online settings. *International Journal of Education and Training Studies, 9*(4), 1–11. https://doi.org/10.11114/jets.v9i4.5135.

Merriam, S. B., & Baumgartner, L. M. (2020). *Learning in adulthood: A comprehensive guide*. John Wiley & Sons. SBN: 978-1-119-49049-4.

Miller, J. L., & Kocurek, C. A. (2017). Principles for educational game development for young children. *Journal of Children and Media, 11*(3), 314–29. https://doi.org/10.1080/17482798.2017.1308398.

Mirliss, D., May, G., & Zedeck, M. (2012). Bringing the classroom to life: Using virtual worlds to develop teacher candidate skills. In C. Wankel & P. Blessinger (Eds.), *Increasing student engagement and retention using immersive interfaces: Virtual worlds, gaming, and simulation* (Vol. 6, pp. 129–60). Emerald Group Publishing Limited.

Monsalves, D., Cornide-Reyes, H., & Riquelme, F. (2023). Relationships between social interactions and Belbin role types in collaborative agile teams. *IEEE Access, 11*, 17002–20. https://doi.org/10.1109/ACCESS.2023.3245325.

Mosquera, P., Paula, C., Albuquerque, W. N., & Picoto, W. N. (2022). Is online teaching challenging faculty well-being? *Administrative Sciences, 12*(147). https://doi.org/10.3390/admsci12040147.

Mujallid, A. T. (2024). Digital active learning strategies in blended environments to develop students' social and emotional learning skills and engagement in higher education. *European Journal of Education, 59*(4), e12748. https://doi.org/10.1111/ejed.12748.

Mrangu, L. (2022). Rubric as assessment tool for lecturers and students in higher education institution. *Acta Pedagogia Asiana, 1*(1), 26–33. https://doi.org/10.53623/apga.v1i1.98.

Nabie, M. J. (2015). Where cultural games count: The voices of primary classroom teachers. *International Journal of Education in Mathematics, Science and Technology, 3*(3), 219–29. https://doi.org/10.18404/ijemst.97065.

Narayanan, M., Shields, A. L., & Delhagen, T. J. (2023). Autonomy in the spaces: Teacher autonomy, scripted lessons, and the changing role of teachers. *Journal of Curriculum Studies, 56*(1), 17–34. https://doi.org/10.1080/00220272.2023.2297229.

Nawrin, T., & Sadek, A. (2022). Role of rubric in assessment of language learning in higher education. *Teacher's World: Journal of Education and Research, 48*(2), 112–29. https://doi.org/10.3329/twjer.v48i2.67555.

National Center for Education Statistics. (2023). *College enrollment rates*. U.S. Department of Education. https://nces.ed.gov/programs/coe/indicator/cpb/college-enrollment-rate.

Navo, M., & Williams, A. (2022). *Demystifying MTSS: A school and district framework for meeting students' academic and social-emotional needs (your essential guide for implementing a customizable framework for multitiered system of supports)*. Solution Tree Press.

Ninaus, M., Greipl, S., Kiili, K., Lindstedt, A., Huber, S., Klein, E., Karnath, H.-O., & Moeller, K. (2019). Increased emotional engagement in game-based learning – A machine learning approach on facial emotion detection data. *Computers and Education, 142*, 103641. https://doi.org/10.1016/j.compedu.2019.103641.

Nowak, L., Grabska-Gradzińska, I., Palacz, W., Grabska, E., & Guzik, M. (2023, September). Tool for game plot line visualization for designers, testers and players. In Y. Luo (Ed.), *International conference on cooperative design, visualization and engineering* (pp. 85–93). Springer Nature Switzerland.

O'donovan, R., & Mcauliffe, E. (2020). A systematic review of factors that enable psychological safety in healthcare teams. *International Journal for Quality in Health Care, 32*(4), 240–50. https://www.jstor.org/stable/10.2307/48626459.

Offenholley, K. H. (2012). Gaming your mathematics course: The theory and practice of games for learning. *Journal of Humanistic Mathematics, 2*(2), 79–92. https://doi.org/10.5642/jhummath.201202.07.

Park, J. S. (2017). Evaluating green IT initiatives using the sustainability balanced scorecard. *Journal of the Korea Safety Management & Science, 19*(3), 81–7. http://dx.doi.org/10.12812/ksms.2017.19.3.81.

Parshuram, A. R., & Ramesh, D. R. (2020). Gamification as a method of productivity increase. *Human Progress, 6*(1), 1. https://doi.org/10.34709/IM.161.1.

Plass, J. L., Mayer, R. E., & Homer, B. D. (Eds.). (2020). *Handbook of game-based learning*. Mit Press.

Prensky, M. (2002). The motivation of gameplay: The real twenty-first century learning revolution. *On the Horizon, 10*(1), 5–11. https://doi.org/10.1108/10748120210431349.

Prichard, J. S., & Stanton, N. A. (1999). Testing Belbin's team role theory of effective groups. *Journal of Management Development, 18*(8), 652–65. https://doi.org/10.1108/02621719910371164.

Pritchard, A., Jones, D., Bellomo, R., Hardidge, A., Harley, I., Tan, C. O., Nazareth, J., Guha, R., Ellard, L., Hu, R., Churilov, L., & Weinberg, L. (2021). Rapid response team activation after major hip surgery: Patient characteristics and outcomes (pp. 3–24) [Preprint]. Research Square. https://doi.org/10.21203/rs.3.rs-52563/v3.

Rahmani, F., Scott-Young, C., Tadayon, A., & van der Walt, J. D. (2022). Team composition in relational contracting (RC) in large infrastructure projects: A Belbin's team roles model approach. *Engineering, Construction and Architectural Management, 29*(5), 2027–46. https://doi.org/10.1108/ECAM-11-2020-0941.

Ramic-Brkic, B., & Balik, A. (2023). Reinventing progressive learning and teaching processes through gamification. In A. Hassan & M. A. Spector (Eds.), *Handbook of research on decision-making capabilities improvement with serious games* (pp. 266–93). IGI Global.

Rennie, F., & Morrison, T. (2013). *E-learning and social networking handbook: Resources for higher education*. Routledge.

Rivera, E. S., & Garden, C. L. P. (2021). Gamification for student engagement: A framework. *Journal of Further and Higher Education, 45*(7), 999–1012. https://doi.org/10.1080/0309877X.2021.1875201.

Roberts, R. E. (2020). *Teachers' self-efficacy, self-beliefs and self-perceptions of students' use of educational technology and applications before and after the Covid-19 lockdown in New Zealand*.

Romero, M., & Usart, M. (2013). Time factor in the curriculum integration of game-based learning. In P. Felicia (Ed.), *New pedagogical approaches in game enhanced learning: Curriculum integration* (pp. 248–66). IGI Global.

Roungas, B., Bekius, F., & Meijer, S. (2019). The game between game theory and gaming simulations: Design choices. *Simulation & Gaming, 50*(2), 180–201. https://doi.org/10.1177/1046878119982762.

Sabtu, M. A. S. (2023). Metaverse and soft skills development through video games. In A. Hassan & A. Hamdan (Eds.), *Metaverse applications for new business models and disruptive innovation* (pp. 120–32). IGI Global.

Saleem, A. N., Noori, N. M., & Ozdamli, F. (2022). Gamification applications in E-learning: A literature review. *Technology, Knowledge and Learning, 27*(1), 139–59. https://doi.org/10.1007/s10758-020-09487-x.

Salman, O., Khasawneh, Y., Alqudah, H., Alwaely, S., & Khasawneh, M. (2024). Tailoring gamification to individual learners: A study on personalization variables for skill enhancement. *International Journal of Data and Network Science, 8*(2), 789–96. https://doi.org/10.5267/j.ijdns.2023.12.001.

Sammel, A., Weir, K., & Klopper, C. (2014). The pedagogical implications of implementing new technologies to enhance student engagement and learning outcomes. *Creative Education, 5*(02), 104–13. https://doi.org/10.4236/ce.2014.52017.

Sams, D. E., Rickard, M. K., & Evans, K. K. (2023). Examining the effectiveness of marketing practices of a nonprofit institution of higher education: Internal service provider. *Atlantic Marketing Journal, 12*(1), 1–16. https://digitalcommons.kennesaw.edu/amj/vol12/iss1/12?utm_source=digitalcommons.kennesaw.edu%2Famj%2Fvol12%2Fiss1%2F12&utm_medium=PDF&utm_campaign=PDFCoverPages.

Sanchez, E., van Oostendorp, H., Fijnheer, J. D., & Lavoué, E. (2020). Gamification. In A. Tatnall (Ed.), *Encyclopedia of education and information technologies* (pp. 827–33). Springer International Publishing.

Sintani, L., Fransisca, Y., Anjarini, A. D., & Mulyapradana, A. (2021). Identification of the effectiveness of higher education marketing strategies using social media. *International Research Journal of Management, IT and Social Sciences, 9*(1), 1–9. https://doi.org/10.21744/irjmis.v9n1.1994.

Sari, R. P., Fadillah, I. Y., Al Hariri, R. B., Habibi, M. I., & Mega, R. U. (2021). Educational game development based on role play games for students with special needs. *Jurnal Teknologi Informasi dan Pendidikan, 14*(2), 178–84. https://doi.org/10.24036/tip.v14i2.464.

Saxena, M., & Mishra, D. K. (2021). Gamification and Gen Z in higher education: A systematic review of literature. *International Journal of Information and Communication Technology Education (IJICTE), 17*(4), 1–22. https://doi.org/10.4018/IJICTE.2021100101.

Schabas, A. (2023). Game-based science learning: What are the problems with teachers practicing it in class?. *Assyfa Learning Journal, 1*(2), 89–103. https://doi.org/10.61650/alj.v1i2.128.

Scherer, L., Stephens, A., & Floden, R. (Eds.). (2020). *Changing expectations for the K-12 teacher workforce: Policies, preservice education, professional development, and the workplace*. National Academies Press.

Sheldon, L. (2020). *The multiplayer classroom: Designing coursework as a game*. CRC Press.

Shoenberger, M. (2024). Tertiary learning usage of tabletop roleplaying games: Affordances and challenges. In T. Bowell, N. Pepperell, A. Richardson, & M.-T. Corino (Eds.), *Revitalising higher education: Insights from Te Puna Aurei LearnFest 2022* (pp. 80–6). Cardiff University Press.

Smith, P. G., & Merritt, G. M. (2020). *Proactive risk management: Controlling uncertainty in product development*. Productivity Press.

Smith, P. K. (1982). Does play matter? Functional and evolutionary aspects of animal and human play. *Behavioral and Brain Sciences, 5*(1), 139–55. https://doi.org/10.1017/S0140525X0001092X.

Smith, T. E., & Knapp, C. E. (2011). *Sourcebook of experiential education: Key thinkers and their contributions*. Routledge.

Soffer, T., & Cohen, A. (2019). Students' engagement characteristics predict success and completion of online courses. *Journal of Computer Assisted Learning, 35*(3), 378–89. https://doi.org/10.1111/jcal.12340.

Sousa-Vieira, M. E., Ferrero-Castro, D., & López-Ardao, J. C. (2021). Design, development, and use of a digital badges system in higher education. *Applied Sciences, 12*(1), 220. https://doi.org/10.3390/app120100220.

Spante, M., Hashemi, S. S., Lundin, M., & Algers, A. (2018). Digital competence and digital literacy in higher education research: Systematic review of concept use. *Cogent Education, 5*(1), 1519143. https://doi.org/10.1080/2331186X.2018.1519143.

Squire, K. (2011). *Video games and learning: Teaching and participatory culture in the digital age. technology, education--connections* (the TEC Series). Teachers College Press.

Stampfl, R., Geyer, B., Deissl-O'Meara, M., & Ivkić, I. (2024). Revolutionising role-playing games with ChatGPT. *Advances in Artificial Intelligence and Machine Learning: Research, 4*(2), 2244–57. https://doi.org/10.48550/arXiv.2407.02048.

Staudt Willet, K. B. (2024). Early career teachers' expansion of professional learning networks with social media. *Professional Development in Education, 50*(2), 386–402. https://doi.org/10.1080/19415257.2023.2178481.

Stornaiuolo, A., Higgs, J., Jawale, O., & Martin, R. M. (2024). Digital writing with AI platforms: The role of fun with/in generative AI. *English Teaching: Practice & Critique, 23*(1), 83–103. https://doi.org/10.1108/ETPC-08-2023-0103.

Strada, F., Lopez, M. X., Fabricatore, C., dos Santos, A. D., Gyaurov, D., Battegazzorre, E., & Bottino, A. (2023). Leveraging a collaborative augmented reality serious game to promote sustainability awareness, commitment and adaptive problem-management. *International Journal of Human-Computer Studies, 172*, 102984. https://doi.org/10.1016/j.ijhcs.2022.102984.

Tharpe, G. E. (2022). Career and technical education: Developing a well-equipped workforce (Order No. 30243423). Available from ProQuest Dissertations & Theses Global. (2758131425). https://proxying.lib.ncsu.edu/index.php/login?url=https://www.proquest.com/dissertations-theses/career-technical-education-developing-well/docview/2758131425/se-2.

Thorpe, A. S., & Roper, S. (2019). The ethics of gamification in a marketing context. *Journal of Business Ethics, 155*(3), 597–609. https://doi.org/10.1007/s10551-017-3514-1.

Tobias, S. E., & Fletcher, J. D. (2011). *Computer games and instruction*. IAP Information Age Publishing.

Toda, A., Cristea, A. I., & Isotani, S. (2023). *Gamification design for educational contexts: Theoretical and practical contributions*. Springer International Publishing.

Toda, A. M., Klock, A. C., Oliveira, W., Palomino, P. T., Rodrigues, L., Shi, L., & Cristea, A. I. (2019). Analysing gamification elements in educational environments using an existing gamification taxonomy. *Smart Learning Environments, 6*(1), 1–14. https://doi.org/10.1186/s40561-019-0106-4.

Thomas, K. W. (1992). Conflict and conflict management: Reflections and updates. *Journal of Organizational Behavior, 13*(3), 265–74. https://doi.org/10.1002/job.4030130307.

Topîrceanu, A. (2017). Gamified learning: A role-playing approach to increase student in-class motivation. *Procedia Computer Science, 112*, 41–50. https://doi.org/10.1016/j.procs.2017.08.017.

Torres-Toukoumidis, A., Carrera, P., Balcazar, I., & Balcazar, G. (2021). Descriptive study of motivation in gamification experiences from higher education: Systematic review of scientific literature. *Universal Journal of Educational Research, 9*(4), 755–63. https://doi.org/10.13189/ujer.2021.090403.

Tran, D., & O'Connor, B. R. (2024). Teacher curriculum competence: How teachers act in curriculum making. *Journal of Curriculum Studies, 56*(1), 1–16. https://doi.org/10.1080/00220272.2023.2237975.

U.S. Department of Education. (1974). *Family Educational Rights and Privacy Act* (FERPA), 20 U.S.C. § 1232g; 34 CFR Part 99. https://www2.ed.gov/policy/gen/guid/fpco/ferpa/index.html.

Ulfa, U., & Inayati, I. (2022). The use of educational games to enhance the English skills of children with special needs. *Premise: Journal of English Education and Applied Linguistics, 11*(20), 114–25.

Utoyo, A. W. (2018). Video games as tools for education. *Journal of Games, Game Art, and Gamification, 3*(2), 56–60.

van Gaalen, A. E., Brouwer, J., Schönrock-Adema, J., Bouwkamp-Timmer, T., Jaarsma, A. D. C., & Georgiadis, J. R. (2021). Gamification of health professions education: A systematic review. *Advances in Health Sciences Education, 26*(2), 683–711. https://doi.org/10.1007/s10459-020-10000-3.

Weymouth, & Atuah, R. (2022). Review of video games & simulation in computer science education. *2022 International Conference on Computational Science and Computational Intelligence (CSCI)*, 2091–2096. https://doi.org/10.1109/CSCI58124.2022.00376.

Yang, D., Kleinman, E., & Harteveld, C. (2024). GPT for games: An updated scoping review (2020–2024). *arXiv* preprint arXiv:2411.00308. https://arxiv.org/abs/2411.00308.

Zeng, J., Parks, S., & Shang, J. (2020). To learn scientifically, effectively, and enjoyably: A review of educational games. *Human Behavior and Emerging Technologies, 2*(2), 186–95.

Zhan, Z., Tong, Y., Lan, X., & Zhong, B. (2024). A systematic literature review of game-based learning in artificial intelligence education. *Interactive Learning Environments, 32*(3), 1137–58. https://doi.org/10.1080/10494820.2022.2115077.

Zhang, B., Shi, H., & Wang, X. (2024). An auxiliary development framework for lightweight RPG games based on Unity3D. *Computer Animation and Virtual Worlds, 35*(1), 1–13. https://doi.org/10.1002/cav.2206

Zhang, Z. (2024). *Realistic simulations in game design*. ProQuest Dissertations & Theses.

Zirawaga, V. S., Olusanya, A. I., & Maduku, T. (2017). Gaming in education: Using games as a support tool to teach history. *Journal of Education and Practice, 8*(15), 55–64. https://eric.ed.gov/?id=EJ1143830.

# Appendix A
# Examples of Detailed Avatar Bios Linked to Belbin's Roles

| Coordinator |
| --- |
| **Alex Michaels** is a 29-year-old Puerto Rican who grew up in a lower income urban neighborhood. Alex has a degree in Nonprofit Management from a public university and works as a community organizer helping disadvantaged children. Alex is a strategic thinker who has very good organization, communication, and people skills and is often able to successfully work with others, delegate tasks effectively to help the team resolve conflicts and keep teammates focused on their common goals. Alex can task analyze project needs and appropriately delegate work among the team. Helping the team stay motivated and focused on their objectives and managing conflicts are additional strengths. Alex sometimes has difficulty balancing empathy with leadership demands and others may think Alex is controlling and bossy. Alex is a single parent with one young child who is a toddler, and finding daycare has been a challenge. Alex has a very full schedule and often finds it easy to over commit to new tasks which can potentially lead to missed deadlines or collaboration opportunities if important details are overlooked which result in missed productivity opportunities. |
| **Completer-Finisher** |
| **Casey Jones** is a 35-year-old African American from a working-class background in a rural community, where resourcefulness and reliability were essential for managing day-to-day tasks. Casy can be depended on to get things done well and on time. Casey pays attention to details, finds and addresses potential concerns, and helps the team maintain high professional standards. Casey has a background in engineering, tends to focus too much on details, and is sometimes considered a rigid thinker by coworkers. Casey has difficulty assigning others to help with tasks because Casey wants to make sure things are done correctly and according to specific standards. Casey has difficulty accepting constructive feedback and is seen as critical by other members of the team. Casey is the primary caregiver for elderly parents, and managing those responsibilities can be a challenge. Casey is a diligent worker and effective problem solver. Unfortunately, Casey's pragmatic and conservative ideas can be perceived as rigid and unapproachable by other members of the team. Casey also may struggle when put in positions to make fast, unexpected changes and managing unexpected challenges. |

*(Continued)*

| Implementer |
|---|
| **Drew Logan** is a 40-year-old Irish American from a middle-class suburban background, has an MBA from a prestigious business school and works as a teacher in a public high school. Logan is married and has two children less than five years old. Drew is a volunteer coach after school and works long hours on the weekends to prepare lessons for students. Drew is commonly asked to assist the team by converting abstract ideas and suggestions into practical, action plans with very specific procedures. Drew often has a disciplined approach to problem-solving and may have difficulty considering other perspectives or deviating from the way Drew thinks things should be done. Drew is usually resistant to new or creative ideas as Drew is more interested in getting things done efficiently, and solving problems using established procedures is a logical path for Drew. Drew's biases might include a tendency to resist change and focus too much on process while potentially overlooking small details. |
| **Monitor Evaluator** |
| **Ellis Akecheta** is a 43-year-old Native-American with a PhD in Digital Marketing Science and Data Analysis. Ellis has a background in marketing and interpreting data in a way that is useful to the team. Ellis tends to be objective, analytical and able to help others make informed decisions according to their shared goals. Raised in an urban setting, Ellis works as a market analyst at Google Analytics. Growing up in a rural setting, Ellis is very conservative and motivated by data-driven decision-making. Balancing work demands with personal time can negatively impact team productivity between meetings and active involvement in team activities. Ellis may not respond well to enthusiastic and idealist comments not supported by facts and struggles when asked to make decisions without considering all the facts. Ellis is often described as being detached, unapproachable, and dismissive of ideas that are more creative or linked to subjective emotions. However, Ellis is a fair-minded person who sincerely desires to help the team make informed and balanced decisions needed to achieve their common goals. |
| **Plant** |
| **Jordan Harper** is a 26-year-old Caucasian American from a rural working-class background, has a bachelor's degree in Fine Arts, and works as a freelance photographer and writer. Jordan's background from a rural, working-class family brings a unique creative perspective to the team. Jordan is a creative idea generator for the team who is open to opportunities to help the team grow. Jordan believes everyone should strive to be better than they are and that collaboration of ideas will always result in better finished products. Jordan is a caregiver for younger siblings which sometimes leads to challenges in meeting deadlines for team projects. Jordan has a tendency to focus on abstract ideas and struggles with routine task completion needed to achieve team goals. Although Jordan has great ideas, they are not always practical solutions when organization, limited resources, and time constraints are a consideration. Jordan can get lost in the big picture and be resistant to alternative (more practical) suggestions. Jordan's teammates are often frustrated with the lack of follow-through. |

*(Continued)*

| |
|---|
| **Resource Investigator** |
| **Xaviera Chen** is a 46-year-old Chinese-American from an urban, middle-class background, excels at exploring new opportunities and building a large and potentially useful network of professional relationships and resources. Xaviera has a degree in Marketing and works as a business development manager. Xaviera, who is a caregiver for a younger sibling, has a progressive political outlook and focuses on building relationships and discovering new opportunities. Xaviera's enthusiasm for social interaction, connecting with people and discovering trends impacts decision-making. Xaviera is a charismatic person, strategic thinker and planner with a positive attitude that can be motivating for the team. Unfortunately, Xaviera may become easily distracted by new opportunities and social engagements which can result in neglecting ongoing tasks and failing to follow through with commitments. Xaveria struggles with organization, seeks external validation and tends to avoid undesired tasks. |
| **Shaper** |
| **Jordan Kennedy** is a 32-year-old Caucasian American with ADHD from an urban, middle-class background with a degree in Business Administration. Jordan is the Town Manager with a highly energetic and competitive nature that can be used to help the team meet their goals. Jordan can usually think and adapt to unexpected obstacles quickly. Jordan works well under pressure and can help teams find solutions and meet goals on time. Unfortunately, Jordan can be argumentative and impatient when ideas are questioned. The need to quickly resolve challenges (and check them off the list to move onto the next problem) can result in Jordan seeming dismissive of others' ideas and making decisions without considering potential consequences. |
| **Specialist** |
| **Sam Rivera**, a 38-year-old Mexican American with a physical impairment (needs a wheelchair) and an expert in Technology Applications. Sam has a graduate degree in Information Technology and works as a consultant for a tech company. Sam has exceptional problem-solving abilities and can help the team complete technology-related tasks by sharing useful insight analysis and innovative solutions to assist with achieving team goals. Sam is often described as a dependable team player who can provide accurate and well informed information. Sam is highly motivated and enjoys using specialized knowledge to help others. Unfortunately, Sam may struggle to see the situation from different perspectives. Sam tends to work independently and may not always be receptive to new ideas. |
| **Team Worker** |
| **Morgan Jackson** is a 28-year-old African American from an urban background, has a degree in social work and works in a community outreach program. Raised in a diverse environment, Morgan's background influences a deep appreciation for collaboration and understanding. Morgan is a caregiver for a sick parent which can sometimes limit availability for team projects and decisions. Morgan is very useful on teams and is often described as having insightful people skills, being an empathetic listener, and considering tasks and interactions from different perspectives. Unfortunately, Morgan may avoid confrontation and be too accommodating. Morgan is not comfortable in leadership roles because Morgan would prefer to avoid team members who are unproductive or unkind and they may ignore their own interests or needs to help others or avoid conflict. |

# Appendix B
# Belbin's Team Roles Strengths and Weaknesses for Avatars

| Coordinator | |
|---|---|
| **Powers (Strengths)** | **Vulnerabilities (Weaknesses)** |
| Delegates tasks | Can be perceived as manipulative |
| Facilitates decision-making | Might struggle with task-oriented issues |
| Clarifies team objectives | Can be seen as overly controlling |
| Ensures team alignment with goals | Might prioritize process over people |
| Motivates team | May face resistance from team members |
| Provides direction and guidance | May be perceived as insincere |
| Promotes collaboration | May favor some team members over others |
| Resolves conflicts | Might miss deadlines |
| Balances different viewpoints | May overlook minor details |
| Encourages communication | Can be seen as lacking empathy |
| **Implementer** | |
| **Powers (Strengths)** | **Vulnerabilities (Challenges)** |
| Turns ideas into actionable plans | Can be resistant to change |
| Organizes tasks systematically | Can be inflexible in adapting to new methods |
| Maintains high standards | Can be inflexible in adapting to new methods |
| Practical task applications | May be perceived as overly critical |

*(Continued)*

| | |
|---|---|
| Strong problem-solving skills | Slow to adapt to unexpected changes |
| Manages time effectively | May struggle with creative tasks |
| Maintains focus on objectives | May resist unconventional approaches |
| Demonstrates reliability in task completion | Might find it hard to inspire others |
| Provides structure and order | May overlook important details |
| Excellent at following procedures | May be reluctant to accept constructive feedback |
| **Monitor Evaluator** | |
| Identifying patterns in data | May overemphasize data over personal insights |
| Identifying both risks and opportunities | Can be seen as overly skeptical or dismissive |
| Creating objective assessment methods | Struggle with ambiguous or incomplete information |
| Comparing different options | Disengaged if they feel their insights are ignored |
| Providing constructive criticism | May focus too much on flaws rather than successes |
| Simplifying complex information | Might resist changes to established plans |
| Strategic planning | May appear negative or overly critical |
| Question assumptions and challenge ideas | Might over complicate or overanalyze issues |
| Identifying and evaluating metrics | Struggle with interpersonal conflicts |
| Creating thorough reports and analyses | May find it hard to be spontaneous |
| **Plant** | |
| Thinks outside the box | Can be seen as impractical or unrealistic |
| Provides creative approaches to problems | Might struggle with routine tasks |

(*Continued*)

| | |
|---|---|
| Motivates team members with new ideas | Can be perceived as aloof or detached |
| Capable of envisioning long-term goals | May become frustrated with rigid structures |
| Challenges conventional thinking | Can be easily distracted from primary objectives |
| May approach a problem from a unique perspective | Might struggle with detailed execution |
| Set ambitious goals | May have trouble with follow-through |
| Suggest original solutions | Can be resistant to feedback or criticism |
| **Resource Investigator** ||
| Quickly adapts to changing situations | May prioritize novelty over practicality |
| Identifies trends and opportunities | Might overlook important details |
| Builds rapport quickly | Can struggle with long-term focus |
| Finds and utilizes new resources | Might lack thoroughness in research |
| Promotes team's ideas effectively | Can be distracted by too many ideas |
| Excellent at networking and making connections | Can be seen as unreliable |
| Collaborates across functions | Can become overly reliant on others |
| Quickly identifies key contacts and stakeholders | Risk of over-promising and under-delivering |
| Provides fresh insights from external sources | Can have difficulty with routine tasks |
| Encourages team engagement with external networks | Can be seen as superficial in relationships |
| **Shaper** ||
| Excellent at setting challenging targets | Can be perceived as aggressive and demanding |
| Overcomes obstacles with determination | Might struggle with interpersonal relationships |

*(Continued)*

| | |
|---|---|
| Keeps the team focused on objectives | Can become frustrated with slower team members |
| Challenges complacency | May overlook others' contributions |
| Provides energy and enthusiasm | Can be seen as lacking empathy |
| Ensures tasks are completed efficiently | May have difficulty with detailed planning |
| Stimulates action and urgency | Can struggle with complex interpersonal issues |
| Effective at problem-solving under pressure | Might ignore minor details for the sake of speed |
| Promotes action and progress | Can be perceived as intense and inflexible |
| Provides clear direction in difficult situations | May have conflicts with passive team members |
| **Specialist** | |
| Provides in-depth knowledge in a specific area | Difficulty generalizing knowledge to other areas |
| Delivers high precision and accuracy | High confidence might be perceived as arrogance |
| Develops advanced solutions for complex problems | Reluctance to adopt new methods |
| Possesses thorough understanding of their field | Narrow focus can limit insight |
| Strong analytical skills | Struggles to trust others |
| Demonstrates strong problem-solving skills | Preference for solo work can lead to isolation |
| Excels in high-level technical skills | May hinder learning from others |
| Provides strategic insights based on expertise | May neglect overall project goals |
| Capable of detailed analysis and research | Rigid Thinking; Sticking to established methods |
| Excellent at mentoring and training in their area | May have Limited Collaboration Skills |

*(Continued)*

| Team Worker ||
|---|---|
| Understands team members' feelings and concerns | Tends to avoid conflicts |
| Offers help and encouragement to colleagues | May take on too much responsibility |
| Skilled at finding common ground | Struggles to set boundaries and decline requests |
| Strengthens team relationships and environment | Hesitant to make decisions to avoid upsetting others |
| Encourages Collaboration | Takes criticism personally, which can affect morale |
| Offers helpful feedback in a respectful manner | Can become emotionally overwhelmed |
| Ensures everyone feels valued and included | May avoid leadership roles to maintain harmony |
| Hopeful and encouraging demeanor | Focuses too much on interpersonal issues |
| Uses Conflict Resolution Skills | Finds it difficult to work in unstructured environments |
| Coordinates and plans team events and meetings | Seeks external validation for self-worth |

# Appendix C
# RPG Example—Positive Behavior Intervention Support Team Collaborative Classroom Management Solutions

| RPG Scenario PBIS TEAM |
|---|
| You are members of the Positive Behavior Support (PBIS) team at Riverview Elementary School. Your team is being asked to investigate and address reported classroom management concerns in Ms. Jones' third-grade classroom at Riverview Elementary. The classroom contains 24 students with very different academic and behavioral needs, including English Language Learners (ELLs) and students with attention difficulties. Disruptive behaviors reported by the teacher are transitions between tasks, peer conflicts, and students avoiding difficult tasks. The teacher also reports a lack of parent support and limited instructional supplies. Ms. Jones has tried several random but unsuccessful strategies such as awarding students with free time and candy when they follow directions. Now, your team must observe, research, and develop a realistic plan using evidence-based approaches to solve these problems. |
| Round 1 Introduction and Role Immersion |
| • **Task 1 Avatar Introductions**
• Each player introduces their avatar (e.g., school psychologist, behavior analyst, special education teacher), describing their background, expertise, and explain how their professional role can potentially contribute to identifying relevant information and helping the team to achieve their objective
• **Task 2 Classroom Problem Discussion**
• The team is asked to review a detailed description of the principal's observation of Ms. Jones' classroom that describes the instructional strategies and student responses to the strategies and activities during the lesson. The observation notes that students were consistently off task, out of their assigned areas, and engaging in inappropriate behavior. The teacher's efforts to redirect students were also noted in the observation. Each player is asked to take notes on the observation report, write down any questions they have and brainstorm potential challenges and suggestions for the team to consider and share those insights with the team when directed. |

*(Continued)*

- **Task 3 Collaborative Problem Identification and Prioritization**
- Using a guided facilitation process (moderated by the GM), the team references their notes and collectively identifies and prioritizes the most urgent concerns in the classroom. Each player proposes two possible data points they would collect (e.g., behavior logs, transition efficiency), and the team debates which ones will be most critical for diagnosing classroom problems.
- **Task 4 Planning for Data Collection**
- Each player will develop a list of questions for observations and stakeholder interviews (e.g., talking points for interviews with Ms. Jones, students, or parents). Players will work together to schedule which data will be collected by which team members. For example, the behavior analyst might focus on classroom behavioral patterns, while the school psychologist could observe student engagement during transitions.
- **Task 5 Wrap-Up and Task Assignment**
- By the end of this round, the team will agree on what data each team member will collect, assigning specific responsibilities for observations, interviews, and document reviews.
- **Before the Next Meeting**
- Each player will conduct observations or interviews and record data (e.g., observations in the form of video logs, interview transcripts). They should also review relevant course materials and notes and be able to connect what they have learned in the observations with what they have learned in the course. Players must return to the next meeting ready to present findings.

| Round 2 Strategic Quest Challenge I |
|---|

- **Task 1 Presentation of Collected Data**
- In this meeting the team leader will ask each player to share the made up information from observations and connect what they saw with the relevant course content. The data should include qualitative (e.g., student feedback, teacher impressions) and quantitative measures (e.g., frequency of disruptive behaviors, transition times).
- **Task 2 Team Discussion of Data Findings**
- After all the team members have shared their information, the team discusses the relevance of the data to the identified classroom issues, making connections to evidence-based practices from their coursework and avatar experiences. Players will work together to determine the primary cause of the classroom disruptions.
- **Short-Term Goal 2 (45 mins)**
- **Task 4 Data Collection Planning for Strategy Effectiveness**
- For each strategy, players will design specific methods to track effectiveness.
- **Wrap-Up**
- The team finalizes the strategy design and assigns players specific tasks for monitoring strategy implementation, ensuring all methods for collecting and analyzing data are ready.
- **Before the Next Meeting**
- Players should prepare to implement the strategies and gather baseline data for comparison once the strategies are in place.

*(Continued)*

## Round 3 Strategic Quest Challenge II

- **Task 1 Reviewing Collected Data Post-Implementation**
- Players present the data they've collected after implementing the interventions (e.g., updated behavior logs, transition checklists, engagement surveys). Each player highlights
- **Successes** Areas where data show clear improvement (e.g., fewer disruptions during certain times of the day)
- **Challenges** Areas where the interventions didn't perform as expected (e.g., students struggling with adherence to transition routines)
- **Task 2 Team Analysis of Data**
- The team discusses the trends and patterns in the collected data. Each player offers an analysis based on their avatar's expertise, and together they identify which interventions were the most and least effective.
- **Task 3 Refinement of Interventions**
- The team collaborates to decide which interventions should be refined, replaced, or expanded. Using evidence-based practices from coursework and professional experience, players suggest tweaks (e.g., increasing visual cues for transitions or modifying behavior tracking to focus on specific students).
- **Task 4 Action Plan for Refinement**
- Each player helps update the action plan for continued implementation, focusing on the next phase of interventions. Players will assign roles for monitoring progress and tracking effectiveness as interventions are refined.
- **Before the Next Meeting**
- Players prepare to implement the refined strategies and set new data collection goals for the next phase.

## Round 4 Debrief and Reflect

**Duration** 60 mins
- **Long-Term Goal 1 (60 mins)**
- **Task 1 Final Data Analysis and Strategy Effectiveness Review**
- Players will review final data collected over the course of the intervention and discuss the overall effectiveness of each strategy. The team will analyze
    - Long-term impacts on behavior
    - Improvements in transition times
    - Changes in student engagement
- **Task 2 Group Reflection on Collaboration and Learning**
- The team reflects on their collaborative processes, discussing how well they communicated, problem-solved, and adjusted strategies. Each player will share what they've learned about classroom management and the MTSS process.

# Appendix D
# School Leadership Team RPG Examples

### RPG Scenario #1 Building School and Community Relationships

Your goal in this RPG exercise as a member of the School Leadership Team at Smith Middle School is to improve school-community relationships and parental engagement to better support school activities and promote student achievement. Your team will work together to identify effective strategies and develop an implementation plan. You will begin by introducing your avatar roles on the team, sharing your relevant experiences and general ideas about what obstacles may be impacting community and family engagement at your school. You'll then work with your teammates to analyze current engagement practices, generate or use data (such as existing survey feedback from staff and families, meeting notes from the PTA and community involvement team) to identify more effective procedures to communicate with the students, faculty, staff, families, and community representatives to increase active parent involvement in your school community. Your team will collaborate to create a detailed action plan, including timelines, responsibilities, and ways to measure progress. You'll present your plan to mock stakeholders, such as community leaders and parent representatives. To complete this game, you must work together to solve the problems, overcome challenges, and successfully achieve your goals.

### Round 1 Introduction and Role Immersion

- **Task** Introduce yourselves and identify key objectives for improving school-community relationships and parental engagement.
- **Description** Each avatar member of the school leadership team should introduce themself to the team referencing relevant details from their avatar bios and motivations in relation to their team task. The designated team leader should share what the improvement plan will include and answer any questions the team may have. The team goal was designed by the school board (Increase parental participation in school events by 20% within the next school year). The team leader will share data collected for the team to review and analyze at the next meeting (parent, staff and student survey results, focus group reports, and summaries of interviews with parents, teachers, and students) to identify current barriers to involvement and develop an improvement plan. The team leader will guide the team as each avatar player shares their ideas in a brainstorming session (plus/delta chart) to identify what strategies have worked in the past along with the strategies that have not been successful.
- **Before the Next Meeting** Each team member should review data shared with the team, the required components of the improvement plan, relevant course materials and notes and come prepared to share their insights with the team.

*(Continued)*

| Round 2 Strategic Quest Challenge I |
|---|

- **Task** Analyze current community and parental engagement data and school practices.
- **Description** The team leader will guide the team as each avatar player shares their analysis of the data and shares potential (evidence-based) strategies the team might consider adding to their improvement plan related to the lack of parental involvement or insufficient community support. The plan should include strategies for enhancing communication, organizing community events, and creating more opportunities for parental engagement.
- **Before the Next Meeting** Each avatar player is assigned to a team to research successful community and parental engagement strategies (support with what you have learned are best practices in the course). Identify 2–3 potential strategies you will recommend to the team along with a detailed action plan of how those strategies could be realistically implemented—when, who will do it, what they need to do, potential barriers for success, and so on, suggestions on how to get it implemented and assess effectiveness. The team will share ideas and develop a plan using the plan template provided.

| Round 3 Strategic Quest Challenge II |
|---|

- **Task** Draft a detailed action plan for implementing 4 strategies during this school year which will likely improve parent and community involvement by 20%.
- **Description** Collaborate to create a detailed action plan that outlines specific steps, timelines, and responsibilities for implementing the proposed strategies with measurable goals, resources needed, and methods for evaluating the effectiveness of the new engagement practices. Share the plan with the school administration and key stakeholders.
- **Before the Next Meeting** To prepare for the final round, consider what you have learned about the practical applications of the course content. Think about your avatar background and experiences and how they differ from your own. Share your insights about this game experience and reflect on how your thinking has evolved throughout the course.

| Round 4 Debrief and Reflect |
|---|

- Your team leader will begin the discussion by answering the first question. After that response, the team leader will call on each player to share their thoughts on the same question. After all players have had the chance to respond, the team leader will answer the second question, and each player will share their ideas. The process will continue for any additional questions.
    - **Player Reflection**—Reflect on what you have learned about the application of your course content in this simulated real-world scenario. How did your avatar's perspectives and experiences differ from your own?
    - **Quest Insight**—What insights have you gained from this role-playing experience?
    - **Game Feedback**—What aspects of this game would you like to change or explore further?
    - **Mind Shift**—As you reflect on the game, your content learning and the importance of collaboration throughout the game, consider ways your thinking might have changed. Complete the following prompts. . . .
    - "I used to think. . ."
    - "But now, I think. . ."
- Follow each statement with an explanation

*(Continued)*

| RPG Scenario #2 School Safety |
|---|
| Your mission in this RPG scenario is to work as a member of the School Leadership Team at James Middle School. The goal of the team is to develop a plan for improving school security due to recent threats on social media. Your team will work together to analyze the recent security threats, review social media posts, evaluate the school's current security measures, and identify any potential vulnerabilities. Your team will propose immediate and long-term security improvements. Achieving your goal will require you to consider what you have learned about collaborative problem-solving in educational settings and educational leadership. You must work together will your team to develop a plan that is practical and effective. Your final plan will outline specific security recommendations, assign responsibilities, and determine timelines. |
| **Round 1 Introduction and Role Immersion** |
| - **Task** Introduce yourselves, review your team goals, and review expectations for the team moving forward.<br>- **Description** The team leader will invite each avatar member of the school leadership team to introduce themself to the team referencing relevant details from their avatar bios and motivations in relation to their team task. The team leader will share the information they have related to social media threats along with the school's current plan and the plans of five schools of similar size in the district.<br>- **Before the Next Meeting** Each member should review what they have learned about the importance of collaborative problem-solving and stakeholder support when developing effective improvement plans from the course so far. They should also review the data provided to the team at the first meeting related to social media threats, student discipline reports, information from the school resource officer, and plans from other schools of similar size. Individual avatars should consider the course content relevant to this scenario along with information provided to the team as well as their avatar's biography and motivations and write down ideas to improve the situation. Remember to approach and respond to the problem from the perspective of your avatar's experiences and motivations. |
| **Round 2 Strategic Quest Challenge I** |
| - **Task** Analyze recent security threats and propose improved security plan.<br>- **Description** The team shares ideas they have prepared (e.g., review of course content, social media data, school policies, student discipline data, results of the staff and family survey along with reports from various committees at the school related to the problem). Each avatar shares ideas as the team records the "plus/delta" of what we are doing right (and is going well) and how the security plans might be improved. The team proposes some suggested strategies for avatars to research, consider the practicality of the suggestion, and report back at the next meeting. The interaction is this round focus on the need for thorough analysis and creative solutions to achieve their common goal.<br>- **Before the Next Meeting** Research best practices for school security and crisis management. Avatars will work in teams to list draft proposals and share with the team at the next meeting potential ways to improve security, communication, and emergency response procedures. |

*(Continued)*

| **Round 3 Strategic Quest Challenge II** |
|---|

- **Task** Develop and draft a comprehensive security improvement plan.
- **Description** Collaborate to create a security improvement plan based on the proposals drafted by the avatars after Round 2. The plan should include specific action items, timelines for implementation, and assigned responsibilities. Each team member contributes their expertise to ensure the plan includes all required components and aligns with best practices for school safety.
- **Before the Next Meeting** To prepare for the final round, consider what you have learned about the practical applications of the course content. Think about your avatar background and experiences and how they differ from your own. Share your insights about this game experience and reflect on how your thinking has evolved throughout the course.

| **Round 4 Debrief and Reflect** |
|---|

- Your team leader will begin the discussion by answering the first question. After that response, the team leader will call on each player to share their thoughts on the same question. After all players have had the chance to respond, the team leader will answer the second question, and each player will share their ideas. The process will continue for any additional questions.
    - **Player Reflection**—Reflect on what you have learned about the application of your course content in this simulated real-world scenario. How did your avatar's perspectives and experiences differ from your own?
    - **Quest Insight**—What insights have you gained from this role-playing experience?
    - **Game Feedback**—What aspects of this game would you like to change or explore further?
    - **Mind Shift**—As you reflect on the game, your content learning and the importance of collaboration throughout the game, consider ways your thinking might have changed. Complete the following prompts . . . .
    - "I used to think. . ."
    - "But now, I think. . ."
- Follow each statement with an explanation

# Appendix E
# Individualized Education Program Team RPG Examples

| RPG Scenario #1 IEP Review |
|---|
| You are a member of an Individualized Education Program (IEP) team tasked with evaluating and improving quality of instruction and interventions provided for a highschool student with disabilities. The goal is ensuring services alignment with IEP goals and compliance with IDEA and FAPE laws. The student Abby Smith is due for her annual IEP. Your goal is to assess her progress and determine continued eligibility and service needs. If she qualifies, develop revised goals for her new IEP. She is currently receiving services for core academics (i.e., English and math) and executive functioning skill support (i.e., study skills). Teachers report Abby is struggling with attention difficulties, disruptive behaviors, and emotional outbursts, factors that are beginning to impact her academic performance. This team is being asked to evaluate and improve her current goals and interventions being used to better support her progress. Using all information, your team will develop specific recommendations for improvement, including goals, actionable steps, timelines, and responsibilities. You will draft a detailed plan to address any gaps identified during the evaluation process. Finally, you will present your recommendations to the IEP team, gather feedback, and refine your plan to ensure it is effective and meets all requirements. Your success depends on your ability to collaborate, think critically, and create a plan that truly addresses the student's educational needs. |
| **Round 1 Introduction and Role Immersion** |
| • **Task** Introduce yourselves and outline your roles and objective for IEP review and re-evaluation assessment.<br>• **Description** Each member of the IEP team introduces themself to the team sharing their expertise. This includes referencing relevant details from the bios of their avatars and motivations in relation to their team task. The designated team leader (i.e., principal) should share the agenda and meet expectations. During the meeting, each member discusses the role of their speciality in relation to the student and their approach to information gathering (i.e., plan to ensure the student is receiving quality instruction and evidence-based interventions in accordance with IEP and FAPE IDEA laws). The team collaboratively formulates a mission statement and sets clear objectives for assessing the current educational practices and interventions.<br>• **Before the Next Meeting** Each team member should prepare a brief introduction about their role including specific examples of previous experiences with Abby including any instructional assessment and intervention evaluations given. Reflect on what they hope to achieve in evaluating the student's current educational experience and progress or opportunity areas. Reflect on how to ensure compliance with IEP and FAPE IDEA requirements. |

*(Continued)*

| |
|---|
| **Round 2 Strategic Quest Challenge** |

- **Task** Evaluate Abby's current educational experiences and intervention/assessments to date.
- **Description** Review Abby's IEP and educational records to assess whether the instruction and interventions provided in general education classes align with the IEP goals and FAPE IDEA laws. The team should gather and analyze data from classroom observations, teacher reports, and student assessments to identify strengths and areas for improvement.
- **Before the Next Meeting** Each team member should summarize the IEP in their area of expertise and anticipate questions or concerns from other members. Be prepared to adapt team plans based on the feedback received in the meeting. Team members should draft potential goals for Abby's new IEP, if applicable.

| |
|---|
| **Round 3 Strategic Quest Challenge II** |

- **Task** Develop recommended strategies and goals for Abby's IEP Draft.
- **Description** Based on IEP team members analysis and data findings, develop specific recommendations addressing current goal areas. Draft a detailed action plan that includes steps, timelines, and responsibilities for implementing the recommended changes. Ensure the plan addresses any identified gaps and aligns with IEP goals and FAPE IDEA laws.
- **Before the Next Meeting** To prepare for the last game round, think about what you learned about the practical applications of the course content. Think about your avatar's background and experiences and how they differ from your own. Write down some of the important insights and lessons you learned, and how your thinking has changed.

| |
|---|
| **Round 4 Debrief & Reflect** |

- Your assigned team leader will begin the discussion by answering the first question. After that response, the team leader will call on team members individually to share their thoughts on the same question. Once everyone has had the opportunity to respond, the team leader will introduce the second question and ask each player to share their ideas. This process will continue for any additional questions.
- Player Reflection—Think about what you learned about the application of your course content in this game. How did your avatar's perspectives and experiences differ from your own?
- Quest Insight—What insights have you gained?
- Game Feedback—What aspects of this game would you like to change or explore further?
- Mind Shift—As you reflect on the game, the class content, and the importance of collaboration, share how and why your thinking has changed. Share your thoughts by completing the following prompts.

- "I used to think..."
- "But now, I think..."
- Follow each statement with an explanation

# Appendix F
# Marketing Teams RPG Example

| |
|---|
| **RPG Scenario # Increase University Enrollment** |
| Your goal in this RPG exercise is to work as a member of the Marketing Team at Riverview University to develop a marketing plan to increase student enrollment. You will collaborate with members of the team to identify current marketing challenges (website problems, mixed messaging, ineffective outreach), then develop a marketing plan. You will analyze the university's existing marketing efforts and then work together to develop a marketing plan that targets specific demographics (e.g., high school seniors, transfer students, international students). You will create tailored messaging and select the best channels for outreach. |
| **Round 1 Introduction and Role Immersion** |
| <ul><li>**Task** Introduce team roles and consider the enrollment data and marketing efforts</li><li>**Description** Each avatar member of the marketing team should introduce themselves to the team referencing relevant details from their avatar bios and motivations in relation to their team task. The designated team leader should share what the Marketing plan they have with the template of the plan they must develop and answer any questions the team may have. The team leader will share data collected for the team to review and analyze at the next meeting (current plan, new plan template, current student demographic information, keyword indicators from the previous marketing team, website data related to how people access the site and where it comes up in organic vs paid searches, financial constraints, timelines, etc.) The team leader will guide the team as each avatar player shares their ideas in a brainstorming session (plus/delta chart) to identify what strategies have worked in the past along with the strategies that have not been successful.</li><li>**Game Mechanics**<ul><li>**RECOGNITION** Players document contributions on a digital recognition board (e.g., Padlet).</li><li>**STATUS ACHIEVEMENTS** Players earn initial status achievements based on introductions and effectively linking assigned avatar bios with relevant team duties.</li></ul></li><li>**Steps for the Game Master**<ul><li>Facilitate introductions and ensure everyone has the opportunity to speak.</li><li>Distribute initial **SKILL BADGES** based on players' introductions (e.g., "Social Media Expert," "SEO Expert").</li></ul></li></ul> |

*(Continued)*

| **Round 2 Strategic Quest Challenge I** |
|---|
| - **Task** Conduct analysis of existing marketing strategies and identify areas for improvement.
- **Description** Players will work in groups to apply what they are learning in class as they review the current website content, faculty expertise, website mechanics, and identify important keywords to develop two customer personas and keywords that would effectively meet their target population.
- **Game Mechanics**
  - **OPPORTUNITIES FOR ADVANCED LEARNING** Conduct a mini workshop on marketing analytics before the group analysis.
  - **VITAL REWARDS** Provide additional resources for the players with insightful analysis.
- **Specific Steps for the Game Master**
  - Monitor discussions and encourage collaboration among players.
  - Share resources reviewing effective marketing analytics before the analysis. |
| **Round 3 Strategic Quest Challenge II** |
| - **Task** Develop an effective marketing strategy
- **Description** Players will work in groups to address the three target personas (high school seniors, transfer students, adult learners). They will use the key words they identified and customer behaviors to develop specific messaging to potentially attract those learners and decide on the best way to advertise to that group such as Instagram for high school students and LinkedIn for adult learners. They will use the AI marketing apps they learned about in class to generate an advertisement for each group on social media. The team will also review the main webpage and make suggestions for improving search engine ranking for each group.
- **Game Mechanics**
  - **ACCESS TO CONTENT** Provide curated resources on current marketing trends to assist players in their planning.
  - **SKILLS BADGES** Introduce titles for achievements based on contributions during this round (e.g., "Best Campaign Designer").
  - **OPPORTUNITIES FOR ADVANCED LEARNING** Share best practices for digital marketing strategies and engagement.
- **Specific Steps for the Game Master**
  - Monitor discussions to ensure players stay within budget constraints and adjust resource allocation.
  - Introduce titles for achievements based on contributions during this round.
  - Distribute initial SKILL BADGES based on players' introductions.
- **Before the Next Meeting** To prepare for the final round, consider what you have learned about the practical applications of the course content. Think about your avatar background and experiences and how they differ from your own. Share your insights about this game experience and reflect on how your thinking has evolved throughout the course. |

*(Continued)*

| **Round 4 Debrief and Reflect** |
|---|

- Your team leader will begin the discussion by answering the first question. After that response, the team leader will call on each player to share their thoughts on the same question. After all players have had the chance to respond, the team leader will answer the second question, and each player will share their ideas. The process will continue with any additional questions.
- **Player Reflection**—Think about what you have learned from the application of your course content in this real-world scenario. How did your avatar's perspectives and experiences differ from your own?
- **Quest Insight**—What insights have you gained from this role-playing experience?
- **Game Feedback**—What aspects of this game would you like to change or explore further?
- **Mind Shift**—As you reflect on the game, your content learning and the importance of collaboration throughout the game, consider ways your thinking might have changed. Complete the following prompts . . . .
- "I used to think. . ."
- "But now, I think. . ."
- Follow each statement with an explanation
- **Game Mechanics**
  - **RECOGNITION** Recognize individual contributions during the final presentations.
  - **SKILLS BADGES** Award skill badges for successful presentations and notable contributions (e.g., "Outstanding Presenter").
  - **STATUS ACHIEVEMENTS** Highlight innovative ideas and teamwork during the debrief.

# Appendix G
# Marketing Team RPG Example

| |
|---|
| **RPG Scenario Develop Marketing Plan for New Business** |
| Your goal in this RPG exercise is to work as a marketing team to develop a marketing plan for a new Carter's Bakery. You will start by introducing yourselves, describing your marketing roles, and sharing your expertise. Together, you will develop a marketing plan for this new customer that includes some market research (consumer persona, customer behavior, competitor information, etc.). You will use this information to create a marketing strategy that includes effective messaging, brand elements, promotional activities, and social media marketing plans. Your marketing plan which outlines specific action steps, timelines, budget considerations, and assigned responsibilities. You will gather feedback from the customer, address questions/concerns and refine your plan to enhance its effectiveness and alignment with the bakery's goals. Success depends on your ability to work as a team, develop creative marketing strategies, and create a plan that effectively positions the bakery in the local market. |
| **Round 1 Introduction and Role Immersion** |
| • **Task Introduce** yourselves and develop a collaborative mission statement for the bakery's launch campaign.<br>• **Description** Each avatar member of the marketing team should introduce themself to the team referencing relevant details from their avatar bios and motivations in relation to their team task. The designated team leader should share what the Marketing plan they have with the template of the plan they must develop and answer any questions the team may have. The team leader will share data collected for the team to review and analyze at the next meeting (ideas for current plan from new customer, new plan template, current geographical population data, keyword indicators from new website and proposed customer base, financial constraints, timelines, etc.). The team leader will guide the team as each avatar player shares their ideas in a brainstorming session (plus/delta chart) to identify what strategies have worked in the past along with the strategies that have not been successful.<br>• **Before the Next Meeting** Each team member should review data shared with the team, the required components of the new marketing plan, relevant course materials, draft notes about their findings, and come prepared to share their insights with the team. |

*(Continued)*

| Round 2 Strategic Quest Challenge I |
|---|
| - **Task Analyze** market research data and create a marketing plan for the current year.
- **Description** Review the market research data provided, which includes consumer behavior insights, competitor analysis, and target market demographics. Work collaboratively to develop a detailed marketing strategy, including positioning, messaging, and tactical plans. This includes deciding on branding elements, promotional activities, and digital marketing approaches.
- **Before the Next Meeting** Research successful marketing strategies for new businesses, particularly in the bakery sector. Prepare initial strategy ideas and be ready to discuss how to apply the research data to the bakery's launch. |

| Round 3 Strategic Quest Challenge II |
|---|
| - **Task** Draft and present a detailed marketing plan for the bakery's launch.
- **Description Collaborate** to create a detailed marketing plan that outlines the implementation of the strategies developed in Round 2. Include specific action items, timelines, budget considerations, and assigned responsibilities. Ensure the plan covers all aspects of the launch, from pre-launch teasers to post-launch follow-ups.
- **Before the Next Meeting** To prepare for the final round, consider what you have learned about the practical applications of the course content. Think about your avatar background and experiences and how they differ from your own. Share your insights about this game experience and reflect on how your thinking has evolved throughout the course. |

| Round 4 Debrief and Reflect |
|---|
| - Your team leader will begin the discussion by answering the first question. After that response, the team leader will call on each player to share their thoughts on the same question. After all players have had the chance to respond, the team leader will answer the second question, and each player will share their ideas. The process will continue with any additional questions.
- **Player Reflection**—Reflect on what you have learned about the application of your course content in this simulated real-world scenario. How did your avatar's perspectives and experiences differ from your own?
- **Quest Insight**—What insights have you gained from this role-playing experience?
- **Game Feedback**—What aspects of this game would you like to change or explore further?
- **Mind Shift**—As you reflect on the game, your content learning and the importance of collaboration throughout the game, consider ways your thinking might have changed. Complete the following prompts . . . .
- "I used to think. . ."
- "But now, I think. . ."
- Follow each statement with an explanation |

# Appendix H
## Medical Team RPG Example

| |
|---|
| **RPG Scenario #2 Medical Team** |
| Your goal in this RPG exercise is to be part of a multidisciplinary medical treatment team (e.g., neurologist, primary care physician, nurse, social worker, speech-language pathologist, physical therapist, etc.) in a local hospital managing treatment for a medically complex patient. An elderly man was recently admitted with symptoms of a stroke showing signs of limited mobility and mental confusion. Holistic care for this patient is expected. Your team will provide their expertise and gather all the necessary information, treatment strategies, and data to make well-rounded decisions. They will collaborate and develop a thorough medical plan to best support the patient's multiple needs. Your goal is to integrate your expertise across disciplines working with the team to propose and finalize a well-rounded and effective program. This plan will outline specific actions, steps, timelines, and assigned responsibilities covering all kinds of care in all modalities. It will also include a plan for patient follow-up appointments, patient and caregiver education and any other recommended resources. |
| **Round 1 Introduction and Role Immersion** |
| • **Task** Introduce yourselves and identify and prioritize key team objectives for managing a complex patient case.<br>• **Description** Each avatar member of the medical treatment team introduces themselves to the team identifying as their roles while referring to relevant details from their avatar bios and motivations. Team members share their expertise discussing their preferred methods for patient treatment. Each team member also shares their primary concerns and priorities for the patient. Lastly, the team develops objectives together and a group plan is created on how to proceed with medical care.<br>• **Before the Next Meeting** Each team member should prepare a short summary of previous medical experiences, and their recommended approach to patient care. Think about and be ready to share specific goals for the team based on your expertise and on how to address the patient's complex needs |
| **Round 2 Strategic Quest Challenge 2** |
| • **Task** Team members analyze the details and specific needs of the patient's case. Additionally the team develops a coordinated treatment plan.<br>• **Description** Each team member should review the patient's case study. This will include the patient's detailed medical history, current symptoms, and previous treatments. The team discusses the physical, emotional and social needs of the patient in respect to his medical conditions. They work together to develop a treatment plan that reflects their individual expertise. This plan includes diagnostic testing, treatment options, and patient support strategies before and after his hospitalization.<br>• **Before the Next Meeting** Team members should research best practices supportive to this case. Each member should be ready to discuss their specific plan benefits the patient's plan for optimal recovery. |

*(Continued)*

| **Round 3 Strategic Quest Challenge 2** |
|---|
| - **Task** Team members create a comprehensive treatment plan for the patient.<br>- **Description** Team members work together to finalize the group's detailed treatment plan. This plan prioritizes specific action items, timelines, and assigned responsibilities and covers all aspects of the patient's medical care, including follow-up appointments, patient education, and coordination between different care providers.<br>- **Before the Next Meeting** To prepare for the last game round, think about what you learned about the practical applications of the course content. Think about your avatar's background and experiences and how they differ from your own. How has it changed your thinking? |
| **Round 4 Debrief and Reflect** |
| - Your team leader will begin and answer the first question. After that, the team leader will call on each team member to share their thoughts on the same question. Once everyone has had the opportunity to respond, the team leader will introduce the second question and ask each player to share their ideas. This process will continue for any additional questions.<br>- Player Reflection—Think about what you learned about the application of your course content in this game. How did your avatar's perspectives and experiences differ from your own?<br>- Quest Insight—What insights have you gained?<br>- Game Feedback—What aspects of this game would you like to change or explore further?<br>- Mind Shift—As you reflect on the game, the class content and the importance of collaboration, share how and why your thinking has changed. Share your thoughts by completing the following prompts.<br>- "I used to think..."<br>- "But now, I think..."<br>- Follow each statement with an explanation |

# Index

Note: Page numbers in *italics* refer to figures and tables.

achievements   101, *102*, 103
Arcweave   *168*, 169–70
Artbreeder   167, 171, *171*
artificial intelligence (AI)   17, 43, 147–75
　accessibility, feedback, and multilingual support, tools *172*
　Dungeon   *168*
　help with RPG game development   165–7
　narrative generation and collaboration, tools   *168*
　novice game designers   165–7
　visual and audio design, tools *171*
assignments   48, 56, 82, 111
augmented reality (AR)   14
avatars
　biography   112
　bios, Belbin's roles   203–5
　characters   47
　completer-finisher   33
　coordinator   34
　implementer   33
　integrating opportunities for   80
　multidisciplinary care team, bios for   *44*
　people-oriented   34
　plant   36
　player   58–9
　resource investigator   35
　short-term goals   49
　specialist   37
　team worker   35

backward chaining method   55–7
Belbin, M.   33
　model   43
　theory   32
Belbin's team roles   38, *39–41*, 43, 51, 54
　avatars weakness   206–10
　enhance collaborations   31–2
beta test   90–1, 164–5
bleed   130, 131
Blooms Taxonomy   158
Bradley, Milton   9
brainstorming protocols   71
brand loyalty   159
business education   29

Canva   *171*
challenges, game masters   122–4
character-based RPGs   117
CharacterGPT   *168*, 170
chatbot   167
ChatGPT   165, *168*, 170
childhood games   9
classroom style learning approach   123–4
code-switching   154
cognitive overload   130
collaborative classroom management solutions   211–13
collaborative decision-making   129
collaborative digital platforms   165
collaborative RPGs   117
collaborative tasks   122
competition   127, 129, 131, 153

completer-finishers
    avatar   33
    impact quality control   33
constructive feedback   120
contemporary educators   162
contemporary instructors   155
content-relevant communication skills   154–6
coordinator avatars   34
course instructor   26
Covid-19 pandemic   13, 17
critical decision round   86
critical thinking   158
cross mechanics RPGs   118, *119*

DALL-E   *171*
data
    collection   149
    protection   149
    tracking   135, *136*, 137, *138–40*
debrief and reflect round   87
decision fatigue   130
decision-making   70, 122, 123, 147
design
    flaws   48, 109, 110
    a game   160–3
designing simpler tasks   80
Diffit   *172*
digital communication   154
digital literacy
    platforms   157
    skills   154
digital miscommunications   157
digital professionalism   157
Discord   *161*

effective game design   104–5
engagement, maximizing   121–46
ethical concerns, RPGs   *150–1*
ethical considerations, RPGs   148–9
experience
    game designers   7
    students   163–6
experienced-intermediate game designers   8–12, 17–18, 31–3, 81–3, 94–8
    online courses, RPGs   149–52
    overgamification   172–4

player motivation   142–4
policies, changing   152–4
role conflicts   124–30
social media integration   156–60
workforce demands   152–4
experiential learning activities   18
extrinsic motivation   142, 145

Facebook   *161*
Family Educational Rights and Privacy Act (FERPA)   149, 158, 160
feedback
    constructive   120
    loops   99, 129, 132, 135, *136*, 137, *138–40*
    player   118–20
Financial Discrepancy Simulation   29
first game round   83–5
flexibility   128, 133

game
    assignments   91
    collapse   109
    designing   160
    development, stages   164
    elements   94–5, 112
    frame   51–5
    log   2–3, 22–3, 145–6, 174–5
    manual   115
    play   8
    rRestart   133
    tasks   50–1, 117, 131, 152, 169
game-based learning (GBL)   6–8, 48, 116
    address digital literacy needs   14–17
    address higher education challenges   12–14
    Ampe   9
    in biology and chemistry   19
    Body Interact   19
    The Checkered Game of Life   9
    in communication and marketing programs   19
    Diabolo   9
    evolved   9–12
    experiences linked to human development   8
    Hide and Seek   9

in human resources   12
instructional formats   19
keep my teaching relevant   18
Kho Kho   9
The Landlord's Game   9
on learning success   20
Math Bingo   10
Math Blaster!   10
in medical programs   19
My Marriott Hotel   12
Pat-a-Cake   9
Pokemon Go   11
prepare students for real challenges   17–18
Prodigy   11
Reading Eggs   11
Recyclebank   12
in social sciences   12
in technology and computer science   19
used in any program   18–20
Word Bingo   10
game design
 common mistakes in   105–11
 effective   104–5
game designers   6–7, 26, 27, 121
 experienced-intermediate   8–12, 17–18
 novice   7–8, 12–17
game masters   26–7, 59, 66, 67, 90, 91, 112
 guide teams, experienced-intermediate game designers   130–5
 preparation basics   106–7
 prologue   121
Game Master's Prelude   147–8
game mechanics   93–120
 assess individual student learning   98–100
 cross mechanics   118, *119*
 and elements important   94–7
 immersive   118, *119*
 influence learning outcomes   98
 levels   96
 non-immersive   118, *119*
 quests   96
Game Restart Option   133

game rounds   91
 enhance learning   86–90
 first   *72–5*, 83–5
 fourth   *89*
 second   85–6
 third   86
game theory   30
 RPGs   30
 shape team interactions   30–1
gamification   1
 definitions of   7
 strategy   98
GENEVA   170
Goblin tools   167, *172*
Google Translate   *172*
GPTs   169–71
grade rubrics   *136*, 137, 141
Graduate Teaching Assistants   112–13
group-based RPG game rounds   124

healthcare virtual patient simulations   17
higher education   162
 adult learners, shifting expectations of   *15*
 challenges, GBL address   12–14
 course instructor in   26
 Covid-19 pandemic impacts   17
 game log   22–3
 game master's prelude   5–8
 gamification in   5–23
 GBL in   7–8
 RPGs, future   147–75
 technology in   14

immediate feedback   58, 59
immersive game mechanics   118, *119*
implementer   33
incentives   143
 play   81–3
individualized education program (IEP)   25, 47
 team, RPG examples   218–19
in-game support system   111
in-person sessions   84
Instagram   *161*
Institutions of Higher Education (IHE)   12–14, 16–18
instructional design   27

Index   229

instructors 67, 91, 162
interactive computer games 11
intermediate/experienced sections 2
internal audit challenge 29
intrinsic motivation 142, 144, 145
introduction and role immersion (Round 1) 83, 84
Investment Management Team 55
InVideo *171*

knowledge
 application 111–15
 students, novice game designers 163–5

law course 58
leaderboards 99
learning
 goals 121
 measure 135–42
learning management systems (LMS) 67
leveling up 99–101
levels 2, 96, 100–4
Lewin, Kurt 31
 Change Theory 31
LinkedIn *162*
long-term game goals 49–50, 54
long-term milestones 76

Magie, Elizabeth 9
marketing
 funnel 159
 teams, RPG example 220–4
mastery/skill-building motivation 142
medical team, RPG example 225–6
meeting agendas 71
Microsoft teams 16, 155
milestones 71–2, 75, *77–80*, 103
 long-term 76
 short-term 75–6
mind-mapping tools 165
mission 103
monitor evaluators 36

non-immersive game mechanics 118, *119*
nonverbal games 9

novice game designers 7–8, 12–17, 21–2, 26–31, 48–81
 artificial intelligence (AI) 165–7
 design a game 160–3
 ethical considerations, RPGs 148–9
 experience, students 163–5
 learning, measure 135–42
novice sections 2

observation logs 87
online
 communication 126
 courses, RPGs 149–52
 learning 16, 152
 polling tools 66
open communication 122
opportunities for advanced learning 100
outcome mapping 137, *137, 138–40*
overgamification 172–4

Pelling, Nick 10
people-oriented avatars 34
persuasive communicator 125
plant avatars 36
player
 dynamics 132
 feedback 118–20
 motivation 142, 143
 success 135, 137
PlayHT *171*
point system 98–9
policies, changing 152–4
positive behavior intervention support team 211–13
post-round debriefing sessions 131
power imbalances 129
problem-based learning RPGs 117
problems, minimizing 121–46
professional decision-making 130

quests 96, 103

real-time team activities 70
recognition 100
reflection round 86–90
resource investigator avatar 35
Rewardful 167

role
  authority, RPGs   128
  conflicts   124–30
  immersion   125
  theory   25–45
role-playing
  activity   1
  experiences   157
role-playing games (RPGs)   21–2, 26, 27
  accommodate my adult
      learners   70–1
  accounting programs   29
  achievement badges for   *102–3*
  add into my existing course   55–9
  assessment methods   *136–7*
  assess student skills effectively   67–9
  Belbin's team role considerations
      for   *39–41*
  beta test   90–1
  challenging and achievable   76–81
  character-based   117
  collaborative   117
  completer-finishers in   33
  complex tasks   76
  coordinator avatars   34
  create engaging avatars for   38
  for criminal justice students   31
  decision-making model   70
  designing   *52–3*
  developing   91
  effective game design   104–5
  elements   99–100
  formats   113–14, 117–18
  gender-neutral names and character
      traits for   *42*
  grading methods   99
  guide to designing educational   *60–2*
  healthcare administration   55
  implementers   33
  implementing game-based
      learning   *63–5*
  incentives play   81–3
  law course   58
  learning experience   122
  level-up examples for   *104*
  long-term game goals   49–50
  mechanics   118
  milestones   71–2, 75, *77–80*

monitor evaluators   36
"open-ended scenario" learning   124
opportunities for advanced
    learning   100
people-oriented roles   34
plan an effective first game
    round   83–5
planning   76
plant avatars on   36
point system in   98–9
problem-based learning   117
scenarios   59
self-assessment rubric for   *68–9*
short-term goals (SGT)   49, 50, 54
simulation   117
specialist   37
structured frameworks   70
TGEEE   *108–9*
Round-Robin brainstorming   71
RPG examples   211–13
    individualized education program
        team   218–19
    marketing teams   220–4
    medical team   225–6
    school leadership team   214–17
rubrics
    assess player and team progress,
        RPGs   *143*
    potential advantages   *143*

scenario-based RPGs   117
scheduling   133, 135
schisms   130
school leadership team   58–9, 157
    game   88
    RPG examples   214–17
screen sharing   66
scripted teaching   162
second game round   85–6
self-assessment   141
serious games   10
shapers   32–3
short-term goals (SGT)   49, 50, 54
short-term milestones   75–6
shout-outs   100
simulation RPGs   117
skill development   111–15
social/collaborative motivation   142

social learning   154
social media   147–75
   campaigns   157
   integration   156–60
   platforms   159
   tools   *161–2*
soft skills   144
specialist avatars   37
special roles   100
speech-language pathologist (SLP)   93
speech-to-text applications   165
status achievements   101
strategic quest challenge   85
structured frameworks   70
SurveyMonkey AI   167, *172*
SWOT Analysis model   71
synchronous online classes   16

task analysis   50
Taxonomy of Gamification Elements for Educational Environments (TGEEE)   *108–9*, 115–16
Tax Preparation and Planning Scenario   29–30
teacher-student and peer interactions   20
team
   cohesion   126
   engagement   25–45
   norms   128
   schisms   126
   worker   35
team-based problem-solving   126
team theory   30, 31
   principles   31
third game round   86
thought-oriented roles   36
traditional methods   142
traditional teaching methods   135
transactional distance   153
transferable skills   17–18
Tuckman, Bruce   31
   stages of group development   31
Twine   167
Twitter   *162*

Unity   170

verbal games   9
virtual reality (VR)   14
VITAL   105
vital rewards   100

workforce demands   152–4

Zoom   16, 133, 135, 155

# About the Authors

**Glennda McKeithan, PhD, NBCT,** is an associate teaching professor in the Department of Special Education at the University of Kansas. With over twenty years of experience in K–12 and higher education as a teacher, administrator, teacher mentor, and instructional coaching. She holds advanced certification in Curriculum Design and has additional expertise in autism, gamification, and digital marketing. She has researched and presented on the advantages of game-based learning at state and national conferences. Glennda lives in Zebulon, North Carolina, with her husband Michael and their three dachshunds—Oscar, Odell, and Spencer. She enjoys living just down the road from her kids Michael and Cindy, grandson Ryan, Bruno her grand dog, and her three grand cats. In her free time, she loves playing cards, chatting with her sister, and collaborating with former students on creative projects (like this book).

**Ann Marshall, SLPD-CCC,** is a practicing speech-language pathologist, researcher, and educator with over fourteen years of experience working with K–12 students in public schools. She earned her doctorate in speech-language pathology from the University of Kansas, where her research focuses on social skills curricula for autistic students. Ann is passionate about inclusive education and supporting neurodiverse learners through evidence-based communication strategies and interdisciplinary collaboration. Her work reflects a strong commitment to helping educators and students thrive in real-world school settings.

In addition to her research, Dr. Marshall brings creativity and fun to higher education through the use of gamified and immersive learning experiences. She has co-developed and facilitated role-playing learning modules in graduate courses and often serves as a "game master," guiding students through interactive, story-based instruction. Outside of academia, Ann is a yoga enthusiast, nature lover, and big believer in the power of connection—whether that's in a classroom, on a long walk, or over coffee with friends. She lives in Overland Park, Kansas, with her husband, Larry, three cats, and one very patient dog. She is the proud mom of Konrad, Adam, and Kelli—three incredible young adults, one of whom is currently in college. Ann also appreciates the love and steady encouragement of her close family friends, the Teagues and Baileys, who have always been in her corner. She enjoys the quieter moments, the louder game nights, and anything that blends purpose with play.